SEVEN DAY LOAN

This book is to be returned on
or before the date stamped below

1. 11. 4

1 0 DEC 2003

1 2 FEB 2004

- 2 APR 2004

1 5 APR 2004

3 0 SEP 2004

13/10

19/10

26/10

Explorations in Sociology

British Sociological Association conference volume series

Sami Zubaida (*editor*)	1 *Race and Racism*
Richard Brown (*editor*)	2 *Knowledge, Education and Cultural Exchange*
Paul Rock and Mary McIntosh (*editor*)	3 *Deviance and Social Control*
Emmanuel de Kadt and Gavin Williams (*editors*)	4 *Sociology and Development*
Frank Parkin (*editor*)	5 *The Social Analysis of Class Structure*
Diana Leonard Barker and Sheila Allen (*editors*)	6 *Sexual Divisions and Society*
Diana Leonard Barker and Sheila Allen (*editors*)	7 *Dependence and Exploitation in Work and Marriage*
Richard Scase (*editors*)	8 *Industrial Society*
Robert Dingwall, Christian Heath, Margaret Reid and Margaret Stacey (*editors*)	9 *Health Care and Health Knowledge*
Robert Dingwall, Christian Heath, Margaret Reid and Margaret Stacey (*editors*)	10 *Health and the Division of Labour*
Gary Littlejohn, Barry Smart, John Wakeford and Nira Yuval-Davis (*editors*)	11 *Power and the State*
Michèle Barrett, Philip Corrigan, Annette Kuhn and Janet Wolff (*editors*)	12 *Ideology and Cultural Production*
Bob Fryer, Allan Hunt, Doreen MacBarnet and Bert Moorhouse (*editors*)	13 *Law, State and Society*
Philip Abrams, Rosemary Deem, Janet Finch and Paul Rock (*editors*)	14 *Practice and Progress*
Graham Day, Lesley Caldwell, Karen Jones, David Robbins and Hilary Rose (*editors*)	15 *Diversity and Decomposition in the Labour Market*
David Robbins, Lesley Caldwell, Graham Day, Karen Jones and Hilary Rose (*editors*)	16 *Rethinking Social Inequality*
Eva Gamarnikow, David Morgan, June Purvis and Daphne Taylorson (*editors*)	17 *The Public and the Private*
Eva Gamarnikow, David Morgan, June Purvis and Daphne Taylorson (*editors*)	18 *Gender, Class and Work*
Gareth Rees, Janet Bujra, Paul Littlewood, Howard Newby and Teresa L. Rees (*editors*)	19 *Political Action and Social Identity*
Howard Newby, Janet Bujra, Paul Littlewood, Gareth Rees and Teresa L. Rees (*editors*)	20 *Restructuring Capital*
Sheila Allen, Kate Purcell, Alan Waton and Stephen Wood (*editors*)	21 *The Experience of Unemployment*
Kate Purcell, Stephen Wood, Alan Waton and Sheila Allen (*editors*)	22 *The Changing Experience of Employment*
Jalna Hanmer and Mary Maynard (*editors*)	23 *Women, Violence and Social Control*
Colin Creighton and Martin Shaw (*editors*)	24 *Sociology of War and Peace*
Alan Bryman, Bill Bytheway, Patricia Allatt and Teresa Keil (*editors*)	25 *Rethinking the Life Cycle*
Patricia Allatt, Teresa Keil, Alan Bryman and Bill Bytheway (*editors*)	26 *Women and the Life Cycle*

Social Relations and the Life Course

Edited by

Graham Allan and Gill Jones
School of Social Relations
Keele University

First published 2003 by
PALGRAVE MACMILLAN
Houndmills, Basingstoke, Hampshire RG21 6XS and
175 Fifth Avenue, New York, N.Y. 10010
Companies and representatives throughout the world

PALGRAVE MACMILLAN is the global academic imprint of the Palgrave
Macmillan division of St. Martin's Press, LLC and of Palgrave Macmillan Ltd.
Macmillan® is a registered trademark in the United States, United Kingdom
and other countries. Palgrave is a registered trademark in the European
Union and other countries.

ISBN 0–333–98497–8 √

This book is printed on paper suitable for recycling and made from fully
managed and sustained forest sources.

A catalogue record for this book is available from the British Library.

Library of Congress Cataloging-in-Publication Data
Social relations and the life course / edited by Graham Allan and Gill Jones.
    p. cm.
Includes bibliographical references and index.
ISBN 0–333–98497–8
    1. Social networks. 2. Interpersonal relations. 3. Family. 4. Life cycle, Human.
I. Allan, Graham, 1948– II. Jones, Gill, 1942–
HM741 .S64 2002
302.4–dc21   2002074805

10   9   8   7   6   5   4   3   2   1
12 11 10 09 08 07 06 05 04 03

Printed and bound in Great Britain by
Antony Rowe Ltd, Chippenham and Eastbourne

Contents

Part III   Re-formulations

List of Tables

List of Figures

Notes on the Contributors

Graham Allan is Professor of Social Relations at Keele University. His main research interests focus on the sociology of informal relations, including the sociology of friendship, the sociology of the family and community sociology.

Michael Anderson is Professor of Economic History at the University of Edinburgh. His interests include demographic and family change in nineteenth-, twentieth- and twenty-first-century society.

Sara Arber is Professor of Sociology and Co-Director of the Centre for Research on Ageing and Gender (CRAG) at the University of Surrey. Her research focuses on inequalities in health, ageing and later life. She was President of the British Sociological Association, 1999–2001.

Frank Bechhofer is Professor and University Fellow, Research Centre for Social Sciences at the University of Edinburgh, where he worked for many years on class and on social stratification, and his current research interests are in national identity, and also people's strategic behaviour.

Nadia Joanne Britton is Lecturer in Sociology at the University of Sheffield. Her research interests include ethnicity, identity and the criminal justice system.

Ruth Butler is Lecturer in Applied Social Research at the University of Hull. Recent publications include 'A break from the norm: exploring the experiences of queer crip's', in K. Backett-Milburn and L. McKie (eds) *Constructing Gendered Bodies* (2001).

Sarah Cheesbrough completed her PhD at the University of Southampton. Her research involved an exploration of the outcomes of family disruption using the 1970 Birth Cohort Study. She now works at the Social Exclusion Unit at the Office of the Deputy Prime Minister.

Fiona Devine is Professor of Sociology at the University of Manchester. She has written widely on aspects of class inequality, labour markets and political sociology.

Jean Duncombe is Senior Lecturer in the School of Social Studies at University College Chichester. Her research is concerned with family life and intimate relationships.

Eileen Fairhurst is Senior Lecturer at Manchester Metropolitan University. She has published a number of papers on ageing and the life course.

Val Gillies is Research Fellow in the Social Sciences Research Centre at South Bank University. She has been involved in a number of research projects involving family life and parenting.

Peter Halfpenny is Professor of Sociology and Director of the Centre for Applied Social Research at the University of Manchester. His research interests are wide-ranging and include social research methods, the philosophy of science, science policy and the voluntary sector.

Sheila Henderson conducts freelance research and consultancy and is a Visiting Fellow at the Social Science Research Centre at South Bank University. Her main research interests include: youth, identity and social change.

Janet Holland is Professor of Social Research and Director of the Social Science Research Centre at South Bank University. Her research interests focus on youth, gender, sexuality and family life. She is also interested in feminist theory and methodology.

Lynn Jamieson is Co-Director of the Centre for Research on Families and Relationships (CRFR) and a Reader in Sociology at the University of Edinburgh. Her research interests include family life, personal relationships and social change, the life course and identity.

Gill Jones is Professor of Sociology at Keele University. She has conducted extensive research on the changing shape of young people's transitions to adulthood, and inequalities in youth.

Elizabeth Kenyon is Senior Research Officer at the National Foundation for Educational Research. Her research interests include young people and housing.

Yaojun Li is Research Fellow at the Centre for Census and Survey Research, Manchester University. His research interests include social mobility, social and cultural capital, cross-national comparative studies, and statistical analysis of large-scale and complex datasets.

Catherine Maclean is Lecturer in Sociology in the School of Social and Political Studies at the University of Edinburgh. Her principal interests are the sociology of community, childhood, work–family balance, migration and qualitative research methods.

Dennis Marsden was, until recently, Professor of Sociology at the University of Essex. He is now a Visiting Professor in the School of Social Studies at University College Chichester. He has researched lone mothers, family violence, daughters caring for mothers and intimate relationships.

David McCrone is Co-Director of the Governance of Scotland Forum and Professor of Sociology at the University of Edinburgh. His interests include the sociology of Scotland, national identity and the comparative sociology of nationalism.

Sheena McGrellis is Senior Research Fellow in the Social Science Research Centre of South Bank University, based at the University of Ulster. Her research interests include young people, health, political identities and values.

Sara McNamee is Research Assistant on the ESRC funded 'Constructing Children's Welfare' project at the University of Bradford. Her main research interests lie in the area of childhood, youth, gender, sexuality and children's use of the media and communications technologies.

Rosemary Mellor was Senior Lecturer in Sociology at the University of Manchester until her death in 2001. Her research interests were in urban studies and urban regeneration.

David Morgan is Emeritus Professor at the University of Manchester and is a Visiting Professor of Sociology at Keele University. He has a part-time 'Professor 2' appointment at NTNU, Trondheim. He has written widely on aspects of family sociology, close relationships and masculinities.

Jane Ribbens McCarthy is Lecturer in Qualitative Research at the Open University. Her research encompasses many areas of family life, particularly parent-child relationships, and theorising of public and private.

Sue Sharpe is currently Research Fellow at the Social Science Research Unit, Institute of Education, University of London. She is also part of the team working on a Youth Transitions to Adulthood Project at the Social Science Research Centre at South Bank University. Her main interests include young people and gender, family life and relationships, and social aspects of men's health.

Tracey Skelton is a Lecturer in Human Geography at Loughborough University. She is the co-editor with Gill Valentine of *Cool Places: Geographies of Youth Cultures* (1997) and has published work relating to young women and methodologies of working with young people.

Robert Stewart is a consultant with MVA, Edinburgh.

Rachel Thomson is Senior Research Fellow in the Social Science Research Centre at South Bank University. Her main research interests include youth, sexuality and social change.

Gill Valentine is Professor of Geography at the University of Sheffield, where she teaches social and cultural geography and philosophy and research methods. She is (co-)author/editor of several books and has published widely on topics including: children and young people, geographies of consumption and gender and sexuality.

1
Introduction

Graham Allan and Gill Jones

Dances to the music of time

In the course of our lives, we follow, in Anthony Powell's phrase, a continuous 'dance to the music of time'. The steps and the music may change as we proceed, and sometimes we dance with a partner, sometimes in a group, and sometimes alone. Yet, the dancing continues. In a sense, this volume of essays is concerned with the choreography of family, household and generational dances in contemporary Britain. Each of the eleven essays focuses on different aspects of the steps and movements within these familial and household relationships – how they currently develop and change as time passes and circumstances alter. Through the chapters we can follow the individual's life course as it merges with others and diverges from them again, as family relationships alter with age and over time.

The papers were all originally given at the British Sociological Association's Annual Conference in April 2000. The over-arching theme of this conference was *Making Time/Marking Time* – appropriate for the Millennium Year. From the variety of papers given at the conference, we have selected for this volume ones which focus on the dynamic patterning of informal relationships that people sustain over diachronic time, that is, at different points in their life course. Its companion volume (Crow and Heath 2002) draws together papers which focus mainly on the synchronic organization of time.

It is easy to see that different relationships do have their own dynamic; over time, they develop, flourish, mature and eventually end. However they do not always do so in an orderly fashion, nor within a predetermined time-scale. Certainly at times, those involved may not see any clear pattern or rhythm in the relational dances they are performing; indeed they may at times feel that they are being swept along to music they no longer understand. From the outside though, it might be recognized that a new dance, with new rhythms and new steps, is emerging from the ashes of the old.

While the essays included in this volume fit into the broad realm of family sociology, they are not concerned exclusively with family ties. Some focus on relationships based on solidarities other than kinship, in particular household membership and community involvement. Like community studies, family sociology has long been concerned with time and change, even though it has not always been explicitly expressed in this way. Thus, much family sociology is, for example, concerned with intergenerational aspects of family relationships. Similarly, it is recognized that people have different family responsibilities and obligations at different times in their life course; that the nature and range of their family solidarities are liable to change over time; and that family behaviour alters across generations. Equally, some of the most seminal family studies in the UK have been concerned with the ways family systems as a whole have altered under the impact of external social and economic transformations. Consider, for example, the many debates there have been about the changing structure of family solidarity and household demographics as industrialization developed.

As this suggests, time affects family relationships at a number of levels. In particular, it is important to distinguish age, cohort and period effects. It is easy to conflate these, as empirically they frequently merge with one another. Put simply, in seeking to understand the changes that are occurring in patterns of family behaviour and domestic organization, it is necessary to distinguish between changes which result from people's changing life course positions; those consequent on the specific and peculiar experiences which people born in different cohorts have; and those which result from systemic change in the wider social and economic formation. Within family sociology, Tamara Hareven's (1982) writing has been particularly influential in signalling these different temporal influences on family relationships.

Historical change

To begin with, there are large-scale historical shifts in the ways in which family life is patterned. The emergence of new divisions of labour within households and families as industrialization developed provides a classic example of this level of change. Encouraged by shifts in material well-being, in gender ideology, in employment structure, in understandings of childhood needs, and in new constructions of domesticity, the establishment of married women as full-time housewives represented a significant change in the balance of marital and domestic dependencies. The complexities of such historical transformations in family patterns have long been debated within sociology, sometimes with subtlety, sometimes not. (See for example, Harris 1983; Cheal 1991; Gillis 1997.) The key point, though, is that family organization is not historically constant, either in its structure or content. In Medick's (1976) terms, as relationships of production, consumption and reproduction alter within the wider social and economic formation, so the organization of domestic, family and community life is in turn re-patterned, sometimes quite profoundly. While culturally such change is regularly portrayed as pathological – involving the decline in family and community life – the reality is generally quite different, though the transformations involved are not experienced uniformly by different groups or across family solidarities.

Cohort change

A second type of change occurs at the cohort level. Here the focus is on the temporal specificities which shape the experiences of those who are born in a particular period, or what Ryder (1965) terms the relationship between chronological time and physical age. (We use the term 'cohort' in preference to 'generation', reserving this latter for use in a kinship context.) Each age cohort is to some degree embedded in sets of social, political and economic relationships which are different from those of previous cohorts and which mark it off as distinct. Obvious, though extreme, examples are the ways in which major historical events, such as a war or an economic recession, influence the expectations and social relationships of the cohort directly involved in them, but not the cohort before, and less directly the one after. Nevertheless time-specific conditions will affect different sections of a cohort to differing degrees. Not everyone, for example, is affected by prolonged periods of high unemployment to the same extent; those with fewest qualifications living in areas of most rapid economic decline will experience unemployment differently from those with scarce skills living in more buoyant localities. Importantly too, historical change may initially be observed as a cohort effect. For example, rural out-migration may be a short-term consequence of cyclical rural depression and thus a reversible cohort-level change, or it may be the start of a longer-term historical process of urbanization. So too, while the radical demographic shifts which have been evident in Britain and other western countries over the last 30 years provide a clear example of a cohort change, some theorists argue that they also mark a longer-term historical transformation in nature of partnership commitment (see below).

Life course change

The third level of change, the individual life course level, refers to the ways family relationships alter as individuals construct their personal biographies over their lives. In part, this is simply a consequence of people having different levels of dependence, responsibility and freedom, in different family and household situations, at different ages – the child becomes an adult, the grandparent a widow, the lover a cohabitee. So too, other individual changes, such as geographical mobility or retirement, will pattern the forms family relationships take, as will the various ways people 'negotiate' different family solidarities and commitments (Finch and Mason 1993). Yet while life course changes focus on each individual's decisions and experiences, they are nonetheless structured by historical and cohort circumstances. For example, among many other factors, the development of new employment patterns, the extension and expansion of post-school education, developments in IT and communications, the vagaries of the housing market, and changing modes of consumption all impact on the individual life course and thus on the character of people's family lives. In particular, as well as reflecting changed behaviour, shifts in the demographic ordering of family relationships over the last 30 years have led to fresh understandings of 'normal' family development, with continuing consequences for the ways in which family ties are constructed over the life course.

The changing choreography

The chapters in this book are concerned with all three of these levels of change: historical, cohort and life course, but especially the latter two. More specifically, most are concerned with understanding the ways in which 'family practices' (Morgan 1996) have been altering. To draw on the same analogy as before, they seek to map out how the movements and rhythms of family, household and community 'dances' have changed. The demographic shifts referred to above provide a clear indication of the changes that have been occurring. Included among the more important changes are: higher levels of cohabitation; increased mean ages at first marriage and first child-bearing; lower marriage rates; higher rates of divorce; increased births outside marriage; more lone-parent households; an increased number of stepfamilies; and more non-familial households (Allan and Crow 2001; McRae 1999). These changes reflect the substantially different family and household experiences of current age cohorts compared with previous ones. Family and domestic relationships are not ordered as they once were; what Cheal (1991, 3) termed the 'standard theory of the family', with its neat and uniform demographic progressions, no longer applies. Overall, contemporary life courses have become far more varied and heterogeneous than was the case for most of the twentieth century.

These demographic changes are not the only type of change affecting family and household behaviour. Indeed in some regards the demographic changes are themselves just reflections of broader processes which are shaping contemporary domestic and relational organization. In particular, it can be argued that the growth of life course diversity and heterogeneity is linked to the growth of individualism within western cultures and the greater freedoms there are in all aspects of personal life. Individuals are now far freer than they were in previous generations to make life-style choices that in some sense reflect their own desires and wishes rather than following a pre-set conventional or normative order (Giddens 1991). The first indications could be seen in the growing acceptance of divorce as a solution to marital disharmony in the 1960s, along with increased pre-marital sexual freedom. However, since then the growth in lone parent-hood, births outside marriage and cohabitation, including, importantly, gay and lesbian cohabitation, all highlight the increased freedom individu-als now have to exercise choice over the ordering of their personal lives. This is not to say that these matters are now wholly individual, with exter-nal control totally absent. As some of the following chapters suggest, issues of parental control, peer pressure and social stigma are still of consequence. The point, though, is that there is now far greater acceptance of hetero-geneity, and more scope for alternative modes of life course ordering, than in even the relatively recent past.

Indeed, to a degree, freedom, diversity and change are themselves becoming institutionalized within the normal framing of life course trajec-tories. This can be illustrated by considering three issues, all integral to family and household organization. First, there is the heterogeneity now evident in the routes by which young people become independent of their parents. While social class and gender have long influenced this, in the past most young people became independent through leaving home to marry. This pattern has been changing, and the extension of education and loss of the youth labour market have, among many other factors, greatly affected young people's achievement of independence and definitions of adulthood (Jones 2002). Leaving home and forming households have become more complex processes. Many of those who leave the parental home return later, for example when they have finished their higher education or when, for whatever reason, a cohabitation ends (Jones 1995). The result of these changes is far more diversity and less predictability about the processes through which young people achieve independence and, indeed, about what 'adult independence' actually entails.

Second, there has been a very significant shift in the relationship between sex, marriage and child-bearing, a point highlighted by Kiernan, Land and Lewis (1998). As they argue, until the last part of the twentieth century sex, marriage and child-bearing were normatively tightly bound together in popular consciousness. Sexual activity outside marriage was not encouraged to any degree; in turn pregnancy and childbirth outside mar-riage were highly stigmatized. Allowing for ethnic and religious variation, this is no longer the case to anything like the same extent. Not only is sexual activity outside marriage now viewed as normal rather than morally questionable, but marriage itself no longer carries the moral force it once did. To quite a large degree, it now represents a life-style choice as much as the only proper way to organize sexual and domestic commitment. Consonant with these changes, childbirth outside marriage is now socially accepted far more than it was even a generation ago. It too has become a life-style issue rather than one of moral culpability. There are however exceptions to this argument, as the moral panics which overlie genuine concerns surrounding teenage pregnancy still testify.

And third, there are the changes occurring in partnership behaviour. In particular, understandings of 'commitment' have undoubtedly altered over the last 30 years with significant consequences for the patterning of life course trajectories. Obviously, the rise in divorce is one indication of this. No longer is it seen as reasonable for people to remain bound together simply because of a promise made, albeit in good faith, in an earlier phase of life. What takes priority is the quality of the relationship and the happiness it generates. The rise of cohabitation can also be understood as a prioritizing of relationship quality over formal commitment. Whether an alternative or a precursor to marriage, as a form of personal intimacy and domestic and sexual organization, cohabitation does not represent a 'once-and-for-all' contract as much as a contingent commitment premised on the continuing emotional, sexual and domestic satisfactions derived. As Giddens (1992) amongst others has suggested, these changes represent new modes of organizing sexual and emotional intimacy, modes which permit 'serial commitment' to a degree unacceptable in previous generations. Although as Jamieson (1999) argues, there is a danger of underestimating the strength of the 'ties which bind' couples in longer-term relationships, whether formalized through marriage or not, the overall outcome of these changing conceptions of commitment is a far greater diversity in people's household and family experiences over the life course.

At one level, and for some people, these matters can be recognized as life-style choices which are shaping individual life courses. However, it is now clear that they are more than this: they represent overall change at a cohort level as well as at a life course one. Moreover, as mentioned above, these changes are becoming institutionalized. They are being accepted as routine and 'normal', indeed often as appropriate and proper. In particular, at an individual level, change in partnership commitment and consequently in household constitution has become an accepted pattern, even though some of the consequences are seen as unfortunate especially for any dependent children involved. Collectively there is now a degree of heterogeneity and diversity within individual life courses quite distinct to the dominant patterns of previous eras. It seems feasible that these types of change will continue into the future, eventually becoming understood as a historical transformation in family and household patterns. Certainly some theorists, especially Giddens (1992) and Beck (Beck and Beck-Gernsheim 1995), have been arguing this, linking diversity in family formation and dissolution with wider socio-economic changes affecting gender dependency. While it is perhaps too early to judge this, there can be no doubt that these aspects of family and household order have been altering radically over the last 30 years, with significant consequences for those involved.

Organization of the book

The overall theme of the book, social relationships over the life course, is focused on the constructions and reconstructions which occur in family life, often associated with major life course events such as leaving home, partnership formation and dissolution, migration, or retirement. In identifying the complexity underlying each, it seems we have moved a long way from taking a standardized 'life cycle' approach to individual and family biographies. While some of the chapters which follow focus on the meaning of time within different relational settings, most are concerned with the personal and social consequences of the changing ways in which relationships within the domestic and familial domain are being constructed. They address newly emergent life course and relational topics, consequent upon the different family and household 'dances' which are now being fashioned. Among the topics examined in the chapters are the ways in which biographies originate and are constructed in early family experience, young adults' constructions of partnership and home, and the reconstructions of social relationships which occur later in the life course. However, though the focus is on new patterns and evidence of overall change, the chapters do not lose sight of the possibility that for some people, individual choice remains an impossible dream, and that structural inequalities, or family background, or social pressure, still play a large part in framing what individuals do.

The first chapter in this volume is Sara Arber's Presidential Address to the BSA Conference 2000. In this, Arber illustrates how relationships across genders and generations have altered over time using pension provision as an exemplar. Given the increases in life expectancy, and the tendency towards earlier retirement, pension entitlement has become crucial for the quality of life of increasing proportions of the population. Yet people tend not to plan for their pensions, and by the time they come to recognize the need to do so, it is often too late, especially given the growing importance of occupational and private pensions for income adequacy in later life. Pension rights are built up over a working lifetime and reflect individuals' employment and investment experiences over this period.

Built into this are historical and generational changes in pension opportunities and legislation, but equally crucial are the differential opportunities different social groups have to contribute to pension schemes. As Arber points out, currently some women with high qualifications and well-paid posts receive comparatively good pensions, but the majority of women do not. Although women who will be retiring over the next 20 years have had quite different experiences to their mothers and grandmothers, they still tend to have substantially less occupational pension entitlement than men do. Because their employment career has often contained periods of part-time employment, and probably periods out of the labour force, these women have made reduced pension contributions and have therefore accrued fewer pension rights. Overall the chapter highlights the importance of the interplay of historical and generational time in shaping people's life course experiences.

The remaining chapters of the book divide into three sections, addressing in turn: the relationship between children and their parents, patterns of family/household formation, and finally family/household re-formulations. These three sections reflect individual and family life courses, from being a child in relationships with parents, to negotiation of independent living, to formation of new families or non-familial households, and to re-formulations of these as the life course progresses. Emerging from the chapters and linking them are sub-texts, such as the relationship between biography and memory, and the barriers presented by social inequality and prejudice to the capacity of individuals to construct their own biographies.

Three chapters focus on the experiences of family life of children and young people. In the first of these, Val Gillies, Janet Holland and Jane Ribbens McCarthy address the generational relationship between parents and children, discussing time and the meaning of change as children (in a generational sense) grow up, comparing the perspectives of young people and parents. The research on which the chapter is based deliberately set out to explore parent-child relationships in 'conventional' families, rather than 'problem' ones (Gillies *et al.* 2000). A central strand in their analysis is the social 'connectedness' of the young people in their study, to their parents in particular, but also to the others in their family and friendship networks. The young people were aware that the commitment and support derived through these social networks were important in enabling them to develop autonomy, individuality and independence. The authors also note that even though adolescents and their parents emphasized different strands of continuity and change in their accounts, nevertheless constructions of past, present and future time were produced collectively.

In the second chapter in this section on children and parents, Jean Duncombe and Dennis Marsden examine some of the unresolved issues that parental divorce can leave for children. At one level their analysis is quite straightforward. Despite the advice that is frequently given by professionals and in guidance books, parents often find it extremely difficult to explain to their children why they are separating. This is partly because the causes of marital break-up are normally complex, involving different levels of explanation. Moreover, the two parents usually construct distinct accounts which highlight different aspects of their marital relationship as the reasons for their separation. They often want to protect their children from the harsher realities of the separation as well as to protect their own reputation(s). The authors found that while affairs often play a part in marital separation, this is not always acknowledged – and sometimes deliberately hidden – in the accounts of the separation provided to their children by the parents. However one result of parents' account constructions is that their children are frequently left in a state of 'unknowing' – finding it difficult to make sense, in their own terms, of why this highly significant event in their lives has occurred. As Duncombe and Marsden argue, this 'unknowing' can continue for many years, making it difficult for some children to understand their own biographies. Over time, the children may be able to 'piece together' an explanation that satisfies them, but doing so is often a more complex and dynamic procedure than is commonly acknowledged.

The third chapter in the section is also concerned with processes of biographical construction. Authored by Rachel Thomson, Janet Holland, Sheila Henderson, Sheena McGrellis and Sue Sharpe, it looks explicitly at the role of memory and time in children's understandings of moral order. By obtaining children's accounts of incidents in their past behaviour which they now regard as morally good or bad, the authors show the roles of memory in maintaining the past as relevant to the present, and incorporating the present with the past into an understandable biography. As the chapter demonstrates, memories are shaped through social interaction, and moral biographies are not constructed alone. Parents and others play their part in the routine re-telling of some of the events that the children remember. In the process, they put their own gloss on the events and signify the moralities – good or bad – involved. Thus the paper highlights the role of memory, the passage of time and the reconstruction of significant actions in the child's life in the formation of their current social and moral identities. The chapter implicitly highlights the problems experienced by individuals such as 'looked after' children who are unable to develop a collective memory of their earlier lives.

The second section of the book, Family and household formation, is concerned with early adulthood, with an emphasis on transitional statuses, which may be ambiguous and problematic. Young people's patterns of transition to adult independence, including patterns of household and family formation, have undergone considerable change and are now dramatically different from those of their parents' generation. Partly as a result of these changes, the construction of adulthood has become more complex, with success and failure in these transitions being more difficult to define. Certainly there are different strands in transitions to adulthood, which, though connected, represent different aspects of the move to independence. The chapters in this section focus specifically on family and household formation: teenage parenthood, peer-shared households, gay and lesbian identities, and remaining single. Each presents a challenge to the concept of normative transitions, and reflects an important element of social change. Some chapters make us question the transitional nature of some of the statuses now associated with youth. For example, though peer-shared households and periods of 'singlehood' are traditionally perceived as just transitional phases, both are now coming to be understood as valued and viable alternatives to a partnership home.

In the first of these chapters, Sarah Cheesbrough tests evidence of the intergenerational transmission of young motherhood and examines whether family disruption is also a predictor of an early birth. While the trend generally is towards later childbirth, or even childlessness, it is of concern that rates of teenage pregnancy in the UK remain high. Given the association between teenage motherhood and social exclusion, it is important that the causes are understood. Cheesbrough's study is based on the 1970 Birth Cohort Study. The detail of family and household change collected in this study allows fuller analyses of the association between family disruption and young motherhood among the cohort than is the case with earlier British cohort studies. As previously observed, there is a clear tendency for young mothers to be born to women who were themselves young mothers, suggesting a form of intergenerational trans-mission of patterns. However, women who experienced parental separation in childhood are not found to be more likely to become young mothers than those whose parents stayed together. It is those born to single (never-married) mothers and those who experienced a number of family transi-tions, especially into a stepfamily with stepsiblings, who are somewhat more likely to become young mothers themselves. Cheesbrough's analysis emphasizes the diversity of types of transition and outcomes among the increasing numbers of children experiencing family disruption and raises significant issues concerning policy responses to parental separation and stepfamily formation in the UK today.

The second chapter in this section, written by Elizabeth Kenyon, focuses on an aspect of household formation which is becoming increas-ingly common – peer-shared households among young, unrelated adults. The small but significant growth of this type of non-familial household, alongside single-person households, is a correlation of other changes occurring in the process of 'becoming adult'. In previous generations, most people living in independent households would have been married and 'settled' into a family home. With many young adults now delaying family formation, and with more single young people leaving home, this form of shared housing is becoming increasingly popular as a means of achieving independence prior to living with a partner. This is the case especially in urban areas where housing costs are high and can best be borne if shared. Kenyon's chapter describes the first qualitative study to examine how households such as these are formed, how they organize their domestic economies and what pleasures and dissatisfactions they entail. Focusing on her respondents' constructions of these households as 'home', she points out that they are not described as 'short-term' or 'stop-gap' solutions to immediate housing problems. In tying her findings in with Beck's (1992) theories of individualization, she shows how they may represent a preferred form of housing for a particular, contemporarily emergent, life course phase.

Sara McNamee, Gill Valentine, Tracey Skelton and Ruth Butler's chapter examines the transition to adulthood of gay and lesbian young people. They highlight the dilemmas and difficulties many face as a consequence of their sexuality. In particular, many feel marginalized and stigmatized, at odds with their peers in school and frequently finding it difficult to discuss their emerging sexuality with their parents and other family members. They highlight how 'coming out' as gay or lesbian can be a complex process for the young people concerned, involving periods of experimenting with their sexuality and attempts to test how news of a gay/lesbian identity might be received by family and friends. The study helps to challenge the notion of 'standard' pathways to adulthood and illustrates some of the complexities which can arise in defining adult identity.

The final chapter of this section focuses on single people in their 20s. Written by Lynn Jamieson, Robert Stewart, Yaojun Li, Michael Anderson, Frank Bechhofer and David McCrone, it explores people's understandings of their current single status, and their aspirations for their future partnership behaviour. In Britain, as elsewhere in much of Northern Europe, we have observed a lengthening of the time period before 'settling down' in a partnership home. The study found that while this period of singlehood was not expected by participants in the research to be prolonged, it was nonetheless highly valued. As a stage in the life course which is relatively unencumbered by social responsibilities, it is seen by women especially as a time for experimentation, for personal growth, for career development and for enjoyment. In some regards, it is understood as a 'selfish' phase, literally a time for the self before family and other social commitments take over.

The chapters in last section of the book, Re–formulations, explore how relationships in adulthood continue to shift and be renegotiated as a result of life course changes. The first two chapters focus on the restructuring of personal relations with migration, examining the impact this has on social participation and belonging. The last two chapters are concerned with different aspects of 'endings'. The first of these focuses on retirement and the ending of paid work, while the second addresses the topic of relational endings, a subject which has received very little attention from sociologists.

In her chapter, Catherine Maclean analyzes migration to a parish in a remote rural area of Scotland, exploring the success people have in establishing their home in the parish. She is particularly concerned with the ways in which some migrants come to be accepted as part of the community and are able to develop a firm sense of belonging, while others remain at best marginal. Rather than relying on simple notions of 'insider' and 'outsider', Maclean highlights aspects of time and the life course in her analysis. In doing so, she develops the concept of 'belonging trajectories' to explore these differences and to explain why some people are more able to establish integrative bonds than others.

The question of socio-spatial dislocation is also considered in the chapter by Fiona Devine, Nadia Joanne Britton, Peter Halfpenny and Rosemary Mellor, which examines the family and community ties of the middle class. The study, which was based on research into young middle-class professionals in Manchester, examines the routes used for in- and out-migration. While recognizing the diversity of geographical mobility, the authors demonstrate the continuing significance of family and friends for the migration decisions their respondents made. Indicating a degree of convergence between middle- and working-class family patterns, the authors suggest that at certain times in the life course – in particular those associated with child-rearing – family and friends represent important resources which can act as significant 'pull' factors in the migration process.

Eileen Fairhurst's chapter focuses on a later life course transition – that from paid work into retirement. Like the earlier chapters on transitions in youth and young adulthood, it identifies retirement as a more complex process than is commonly assumed, frequently involving a range of linked transitions rather than a straightforward movement from 'work' to 'non-work'. In addition though, the chapter also explores the different ways in which people speak about and conceptualize time in discussing retirement. In the process, the chapter shows the extent to which the rhythm of work influences our social lives before retirement, and highlights our consequent search for a new rhythm (involving new or renewed social relationships) to structure our post-retirement lives. Like the two chapters on migration which precede it, this chapter shows how loss, and endings, can be mitigated by new beginnings, as part of a continual process of construction and reconstruction.

In the last of these chapters, David Morgan develops a highly original perspective on relational endings, using the example of marital affairs to illustrate his arguments. As he points out, sociologists have not only paid relatively little attention to affairs, but, with the exception of divorce, have also ignored the ending of close relationships. Yet, if theorists like Giddens (1992) are right in suggesting that new modes of intimacy are developing, then the endings of intimate partnerships are likely to become as significant as their beginnings. In his analysis, Morgan considers the ending of a fictional affair – that enacted between Celia Johnson and Trevor Howard in the classic film *Brief Encounter* – and in so doing constructs a fascinating account of the nature of relational time. He explores how time is used as a metaphor in the film, constantly infiltrating this temporally uncertain, though ultimately short-term, relationship. Though based on a fictional account, the chapter opens up possibilities for exploring how individuals employ time in structuring their relationships, and forms a fitting conclusion for our collection of 'dances to the music of time'.

2
Gender and Generation: Changing Pension Inequalities Over Time

Sara Arber

Introduction

Gender has been a fundamental concern of sociology for more than two decades and has transformed the sociological landscape. Within sociology less attention has been paid to inequalities between generations. This chapter considers the nature of inequalities between generations at both the macro societal level and the micro level of the family using pensions as an exemplar. A key concern is to identify the connections between gender inequalities and generational inequalities, and relate these to recent societal changes. Another thread is to examine change over time, emphasizing the need for a dynamic approach to both gender and generation, recognizing how each generation of women encounters new opportunities and challenges.

A dominant concern in the early years of feminist scholarship was to document gender differences, pointing out the disadvantaged position of women in multiple and interrelated areas, from earnings to the domestic division of labour and access to resources within the family. While this remains important, such goals are now complemented by a concern with diversity among women, in particular to what extent inequalities among women are similar to or greater than among men on comparable issues.

The early years of the twenty-first century may witness little gender inequality for the small elite of highly educated women who continue to maintain a full-time attachment to the labour market and reap the rewards that this entails. However, this may co-exist with greater inequality among women than among men, particularly associated with women parenting under disadvantaged material circumstances, such as for lone mothers who are dependent on meagre poverty level benefits, or increasingly forced into subsistence-level low-paid jobs with little support from the state.

Contemporary society contains enormous diversity between generations. People over the age of 80 grew up before the war, experienced the war in their formative years and are part of the generation in which women largely gave up work on marriage and subscribed to very traditional gender roles. This contrasts markedly with the current generation of women in their 50s, the so-called 'baby-boomers' – born after the war who were beneficiaries of the welfare state throughout their formative years, enjoyed the right to free secondary education following the 1944 Education Act, benefited from the expansion of higher education in the 1960s, and entered a buoyant labour market in the late 60s (Evandrou 1997). Women of this generation are in many senses unique, having benefited not only from enhanced career opportunities, but also from control of their own fertility following the introduction of the pill and liberalization of abortion during the 1960s.

Gender, age, cohort and generation

The nature of gender inequalities and inequalities among women differs over time and between societies in concert with the ways in which gender roles and relationships vary historically and cross-nationally (Arber and Ginn 1995). This chapter emphasizes the dynamic nature of inequalities by focusing on the case of pensions. Before this a number of conceptual issues relating to age, ageing and the meaning of generations will be discussed.

Differences between age groups should be distinguished from cohort differences. Cohort originates as a demographic term, referring to people born in the same year (or group of years) who spent their formative years living through a similar historical period of time, such as the Second World War, and thus will have been subject to the expectations, social changes and opportunities extant at that time. We might therefore expect differences in the nature of gender inequalities between different birth cohorts, who have experienced varying levels of prosperity within a society.

The term 'generation' is widely used, but there is diversity both in popular discourse and in social-scientific writing about its meaning. Attias-Donfut and Arber (2000) point out that the term has at least four meanings, although there is some fuzziness and interchangeability in these. First, generation may be used to distinguish birth cohorts, as outlined above. Second, in kinship studies, generation relates to the lineage between grandparent, parent and child (Pilcher 1995). It is helpful to use the term 'family generations' to denote the genealogical rung of the ladder within a family lineage – being a father/mother or a son/daughter. However, parenthood in contemporary society often lasts 50 years, and the same individual is often simultaneously a child and a parent (Grundy *et al.* 1999).

A third and popular meaning of 'generation' is as a measure of time, the number of years between the age of parents and their children. This concept of generation is found in most cultures and in biblical writing. However, it is a very imprecise measure, since the length of generations in this sense may be from 20–40 years, and the average generational length varies according to the average age of child-bearing.

Finally, Karl Mannheim (1952) adopted a sociological stance by linking the formation of generations to social change. His argument was that birth cohorts become 'historical or social generations' when they live through a period of rapid social change and thereby develop a separate 'historical-social conscience' or collective identity, which influences their attitudes and behaviour and distinguishes them from preceding and succeeding generations. Such generations are distinguished by the historical experiences they have shared, which have shaped their common vision of the world.

The mid- and late-1960s marked a major change in attitudes towards women's roles, partly enshrined in legislation, such as the 1967 Abortion Act and the 1970 Equal Pay Act. These societal changes had a profound impact, especially on women. The effect will have been greatest for those in their formative years at that time, but will have had some impact on all members of society. The depth of the mark such changes leave will depend on the extent to which each generation is exposed to their influence. Mannheim emphasized the feeling of belonging to a generation that links a particular moment in history through shared experience. This conceptualization of generations is common in popular discourse which for example refers to the '60s' generation. There is clearly a close relationship between birth cohorts and generations, but the former refer simply to a span of years while the latter relates to a grouping with a distinct social identity (Becker 2000).

Welfare generations and the life course

Another use of the term generation is in the designation of 'welfare generations', resulting from the institutionalization of society into distinct stages of education, work and retirement – three 'welfare generations' (Attias-Donfut and Arber 2000). Thus, generations can be distinguished by whether or not they participate in paid employment and the contributions they make to systems of social security and the benefits they receive. This formulation resembles Laslett's (1989) division of the life course into 'four ages', although Laslett adds a 'Fourth Age', of 'decline and decrepitude' at the end of life. His Third Age, beginning at the age of 50, is characterized as one of opportunity following retirement from paid employment and after child-rearing; the Second Age corresponds to working life and the First Age to the extended period of education.

There is clearly a similarity between distinguishing 'welfare generations' and subdividing into age groups. The former concept may be preferred because it reminds us of the continuity between generations and of their linkages. Gender inequalities among one generation may themselves influence and be predicated on gender inequalities in another generation. For example, the extent to which women forgo paid employment to raise children during their working life will lead to financial penalties both during working life and in retirement, because of lower pensions. In addition, use of the term generation emphasizes that membership of one welfare generation rather than another is not contingent on chronological age but on the individual's relationship to the labour market.

However, the idea of a generation as a distinct self-contained entity may also be questioned. The blurring of life stages, as employment in mid-life becomes increasingly insecure, challenges the generational labels of 'worker' or 'pensioner' (Phillipson 1996). Phillipson criticizes the more economic view of 'welfare generations', and argues that the sociological view of generations is more complex, recognizing that each generation is linked through family ties with individuals in other generations and that inequities by class, ethnicity and gender outweigh those between generations.

The life course provides an important orienting framework, emphasizing that it is only possible to understand the present circumstances of women and men by reference to their prior experiences. This is most vividly seen in later life, since older women's and men's financial circumstances depend on their accumulated pension contributions and are therefore intimately tied to their previous role in the labour market. For women in mid-life, their health and well-being is associated with their previous history of child-bearing and their role as mothers. Increasingly well-being for women as well as men of working age is structured according to position in the labour market, which itself is closely linked to earlier success in the educational sphere. Many studies have shown how educational attainment is influenced by the child's family background, emphasizing the transmission of advantage and disadvantage between generations. Thus, a life course framework encourages researchers to see lives as dynamic and interconnected between the generations.

Intergenerational transfers

Gender is fundamentally related to the provision of a range of different types of support between the generations. These interrelationships should be examined both at particular points in time and dynamically over time. The nature of support and other forms of transfers between generations is wide-ranging and tends to vary at different stages of the life course. Taking this focus expands the definition of families to include a much wider set of kin than those who are co-resident (Marsh and Arber 1992).

Three-quarters of people in Britain are part of a three-generational family, which includes children, parents and grandparents, while a fifth are part of a four-generational family, including great-grandparents (Grundy *et al.* 1999). There is therefore considerable potential for individuals to be affected by intergenerational transfers. The types of transfers between generations include:

- care for children and grandchildren;
- informal care for frail, sick or disabled relatives, including personal care, emotional support and practical help with domestic work, shopping, gardening, decorating, transport and organizing finances/paying bills;
- financial support in the form of gifts of money, housing or goods, and inheritance;
- co-residence – which may embrace some or all of the above.

Women are disproportionately involved in transfers of care to children and grandchildren, and provide a greater amount of informal care to the older generation (Arber and Ginn 1991). Feminist sociologists have emphasized the oppressive nature for many mid-life women of providing informal care for older parents and the ways in which caring constrains opportunities for employment and other activities (Finch and Groves 1983). In relation to the provision of informal care there is greater gender equality in the provision of informal care intragenerationally, especially between spouses and siblings, than in intergenerational care (Arber and Ginn 1991). Women's dominant role in intergenerational provision of care for children and the older generation can be seen as part of the 'gender contract' (Ginn and Arber 2000b), which will be discussed later.

Financial and material support between the generations is influenced by the level of pensions and includes gifts of money or goods, assistance with purchasing a house or with financing the costs of higher education. The financial and material resources of the parent and grandparent generation have a major impact on their ability to support the educational and housing costs of the adult and grandchild generation, thus increasing inequality among families. The latter costs have increased markedly in recent years and are becoming a major transfer from parents and grandparents to adult children and grandchildren. The growth of owner occupation and the wide variation in the market value of property means that inheritance is a major and increasing source of wealth, perpetuating inequality among families. Inheritance, gifts or other kinds of financial transfers between living generations, namely *inter vivos* transfers, predominate as downward flows from the parent or grandparent generation.

It is important to examine the balance of upward and downward flows of each type of resource at specific points in time, as well as over a period of years and over a life course. Key issues are, first, the implications of the gendered nature of intergenerational transfers of care for women's ability to accumulate their own pensions and thus ensure their own financial security in later life. Second, to what extent receipt of intergenerational transfers is becoming a major source of inequality among individuals, as the role of the state in providing welfare diminishes. Such trends increase the importance of having an extended family and the material resources and cultural capital of that wider family. The level of pension receipt plays a critical role in influencing the nature and extent of financial and material transfers.

Research in Norway (Gulbrandsen and Langsether 2000) and in France (Attias-Donfut and Wolff 2000) has shown that the balance of financial flows *from* the grandparent to the parent generation is greater than vice versa. The flows provide an essential and increasingly important part of family welfare. At the macro-social level, the prevalent ideology within Britain is that older people are a burden on their families and on society because of the *costs* of pensions, health and social care. A role of sociology is to critically assess such cultural constructions and carefully document the relative flows of resources and support between the generations, particularly how these relate to gender and the perpetuation (or reduction) of advantage and disadvantage.

Changes in income inequality – the case of pensions

Sociologists have long debated gender inequality in earnings, documenting the level of the gender gap in earnings by age, type of occupation, and so on. Although social class was the fundamental division within British sociology in the twentieth century, consumption patterns and income have attracted increasing attention as dimensions of inequality. Most sociological interest regarding income has focused on people of working age, largely neglecting older age groups. Income has an important influence on life chances, and is widely discussed in the media and by lay people – employees know their income and are concerned about the size of their next pay rise. This contrasts markedly with pensions, any mention of which usually elicits a 'yawn' and glazed eyes. Sociologists have paid scant attention to pensions and the general public have little knowledge of how their current contributions to a pension will translate into actual income in later life.

The purpose of the following section is to illustrate, through an analysis of pensions, how legislative and other societal changes lead to changes in the nature and bases of inequality, and to show the importance of a life course perspective in understanding the gendered nature of contemporary inequalities. A key concern is to what extent the changing role of women in society and the labour market will translate into greater gender equality of pension income in later life, and how this is associated with inter-generational caring.

Gender inequality in pensions as forms of occupational and fiscal welfare

There have been major cohort changes in the financial well-being of older people over the last century, resulting from changes in both social policy and occupational welfare. The state National Insurance (NI) pension was introduced in 1911 as a contributory pension system. By 1946 it was extended to all working people in Britain, with the result that virtually all men could retire at the age of 65 with a flat-rate state pension. The Beveridge compact in 1942 defined married women as dependent on their husband with married women eligible at 60 to receive 60 per cent of the value of their husband's state NI retirement pension (Ginn and Arber 1994). Therefore during the 1950s and 1960s there was greater financial equality among older people because of the almost universal coverage of the flat-rate NI basic pension.

Concerns were expressed about the low level of the flat-rate NI pension, which fluctuated around 20 per cent of national average earnings until 1979. At the same time, there was growth in the number of employers who provided occupational pensions, largely as an employment benefit to valued male employees. Occupational pensions have been described as 'golden chains' used by employers to retain their investment in the skills and expertise of certain groups of employees. Occupational pensions form a major dimension of 'occupational welfare', which Titmuss (1958) contrasted with 'state welfare' and 'fiscal welfare', as well as with 'family welfare'. Sociologists have paid much more attention to state welfare – education, the health service and social security – than occupational welfare. The latter comprises the largely hidden benefits financed by certain employers, such as occupational pensions, holiday entitlements, sickness benefit, access to preferential mortgages and finance, private health insurance, company cars and other direct material advantages. Occupational welfare is profoundly unequal, with the greatest benefits going to those in managerial and professional occupations, and men benefitting to a much greater extent than women.

Fiscal welfare has been the subject of even less sociological attention than occupational welfare. It is more hidden and its consequences are even more inegalitarian and gendered. Fiscal welfare refers to tax revenue forgone, through various forms of tax reliefs. These reflect government policy in the same way as any other aspect of welfare spending, but because they relate to tax revenues *not collected* they are usually omitted from public scrutiny and are hard to measure. A particularly important area of fiscal privilege relates to tax reliefs on private pensions. Sinfield (2000) states that in the United Kingdom in 1996–7, over £12 billion of taxpayers' money was directed by the government through tax reliefs to support occupational and personal pensions. He estimates that this tax subsidy to those paying into private pensions 'cost the tax payer some 40% more than all selective or means-tested social security assistance paid to the poorest old people in the same year' (141). He quotes Agulnik and Le Grand (1998) who show that the value of tax relief on pensions is highly regressive, that 'half the benefit of tax relief on pensions goes to ... the top 10% of tax payers, and a quarter to ... the top 2.5%' (410).

Tax relief on pensions derives from a number of sources: employees' contributions are deducted before determining taxable income; employers' contributions are not taxed as income of employees and are a deductible business expense; and lump sum payments on retirement or death are exempt from tax (Sinfield 2000). Tax reliefs on pensions represented 2.4 per cent of GDP in the UK in 1995 (Adema 1999, cited by Sinfield 2000), much higher than in other OECD countries. Sinfield (2000) estimates that the value of tax reliefs on pensions in 1999–2000 was equivalent to about a third of annual spending on the National Insurance old age pension.

An increasingly important issue in contemporary British society is not only whether an individual is a member of an occupational pension scheme, but the quality of that scheme in terms of likely future pension income. Occupational pensions vary in their resulting level of pension income for the employee according to five main dimensions:

1. The relative level of pension contributions paid by the employer and the employee, from very generous schemes in which the employer contributes (but not the employee) such as the civil service, to the university academics superannuation scheme (USS) where the employer contributes 14 per cent and the employee contributes 6 per cent, to schemes where the employer does not contribute anything but simply handles the employees' pension contributions.
2. The number of years of service required to receive the maximum final salary pension (and/or lump sum). This is usually 40 years, but is paid after 30 years service in the police and fire service.
3. The proportion of final salary paid as a pension to those with sufficient years membership for the maximum pension, eg. two-thirds of the employee's final annual salary in the civil service and the police, and half the final salary in USS.

4. Whether a lump sum is provided on retirement or death and the size of that lump sum. Typical lump sums are three times the annual pension (as in USS), and are received tax free.
5. To what extent pension payments are index-linked and the method of index-linking.

The segregated nature of the labour market means that the quality of occupational pension schemes, as a form of occupational welfare, is strongly related to class, gender and ethnicity. Better schemes are provided to occupational groups where men predominate, in larger organizations and where there have been strong trade unions, at least in the past. Thus, women tend to be disadvantaged because they are less likely to work in such privileged occupations. Similarly, minority ethnic groups and others who face discrimination in the labour market are less likely to be in generous occupational pension schemes.

Apart from inequalities in pension income associated with occupational segregation, the key criteria affecting amount of occupational pension income is the level of final salary and the number of years of full-time employment. Women are disadvantaged on both counts. Among full-time workers, women's weekly earnings in 1998 were still on average only 73 per cent of men's, but in the crucial final years of employment, the gender gap in salaries is much greater (Rake 2000). Women in their 50s working full-time earn only 66 per cent of men's weekly earnings (Ginn *et al.* 2001). Thus, their pension income will be proportionately lower. The current generation of older and mid-life women have rarely had a continuous full-time employment career. A critical discriminator is the number of years of full-time employment within a working career – women and other disadvantaged groups in the labour market are likely to have an interrupted and shorter employment history and thus a substantially lower pension income.

The Conservative government pension reforms enshrined in the 1986 Social Security Act, made it no longer mandatory for employees to join their employer's occupational pension scheme. Many people, especially nurses and teachers, were persuaded by financial advisers to opt out of their employer's occupational pension scheme into a personal pension. This was nearly always against the best interests of the employee, since personal pensions rarely include any contribution from the employer and are financed entirely from the employee's contributions. The other major difference is that they are money-purchase schemes with the final amount of the pension dependent on the performance of investments, rather than based on the individual's final salary and years of scheme membership. A major selling point for personal pensions was that the pension received 'could' ultimately be much larger than the equivalent final salary pension, but *only* if investments did extremely well and annuities were favourable.

The reality is that claims were inflated. Moreover, many low-paid workers opted out of SERPS into a personal pension, against their best interests (Ginn and Arber 2000a).

The last 30 years have seen a shift from a situation in which the basic NI pension was a powerful income leveller in later life but at a low (near poverty) level, with married women receiving 60 per cent of their husband's basic NI pension. Recent years have seen an expansion in receipt of occupational pensions, which are themselves very diverse in their quality and resulting pension income. These have been joined by personal and stakeholder pensions, which on average yield a lower income in retirement than occupational pensions, and are also much less predictable. At the same time the value of the state NI pension has fallen from 20 per cent of average earnings in 1980 to 15 per cent in 2000, dropping further below the means-tested poverty level (Ginn *et al.* 2001).

Thus, an increasingly important concern in contemporary British society is not only whether an individual contributes to a private pension scheme, but their years of contributions and the quality of that scheme in terms of the likely pension income in retirement. The next sections will examine the income of the current generation of older people in Britain and then assess the pension prospects for the next generation of older women. These analyses draw heavily on recent work by my colleague Jay Ginn.

Pension income in later life

For the majority of older women, pension income consists solely of the flat-rate National Insurance pension (Ginn and Arber 1999). The major source of income inequality among older people is private (occupational and personal) pensions. Other sources of income include earnings; income from savings and investments; income from the means-tested Minimum Income Guarantee (MIG); and other state benefits. Focusing on the current generation of older people (aged 65 and over), older men are twice as likely as women to be in receipt of a private pension. The proportion of men receiving any kind of private pension increased from 64 per cent to 67 per cent over the eight years between 1985/6 and 1993/4, and for women from 27 per cent to 35 per cent (*ibid.*). However, this diminished gender difference in private pension receipt does not translate into greater gender equality when the average amounts received are considered. Among those with income from private pensions, women's income from private pensions fell as a proportion of men's over the eight-year period, from 65 to 56 per cent. Thus, although the gender gap in *receipt* of pensions narrowed, gender inequality in the *amount* received widened. The result of growing inequality in private pension income was that the distribution of total personal gross income (from all sources) became more unequal both among men and among women and between the genders. Over the eight–year period the gender gap in total income widened, with older women's median income as a proportion of men's falling from 71 to 62 per cent (*ibid.*).

Never-married older women are much more likely to receive a private pension than married women, 61 per cent and 22 per cent respectively, with widowed women occupying an intermediate position, 44 per cent (mostly receiving a survivor's pension from their husband), and 30 per cent of divorced/separated women receiving a private pension (*ibid.*). These differences by marital status largely reflect the lifetime employment profile of the current cohort of older women. The majority of older never-married women have had a full-time employment profile throughout their working lives, while the majority of married and previously married women left paid employment at the birth of their first child, later returning to part-time employment (Ginn and Arber 1996). A critical issue is to what extent changes in women's employment over the last 30 years will alter the pattern of pension inequality among the next generation of women.

The next generation of women – pensions

Sociologists have documented major changes in women's participation in paid employment over the last 30 years, and extensively debated the significance of these shifts (Ginn *et al.* 1996; Hakim 1996). Although British women's employment participation by age is becoming increasingly similar to that of men, it is still the case that over a quarter of working-age women are not in paid work and a third work part-time (Ginn *et al.* 2001). However, cross-sectional analyses provide a misleading picture in terms of the consequences of women's pattern of employment for pension acquisition. To understand the impact of employment on women's likely future pension income it is necessary to examine women's work histories using retrospective life histories or panel (longitudinal) data. The Family and Working Lives Survey (FWLS) collected pension histories, and estimated that among those over the age of 60 who had ever contributed to an occupational pension, men had an average of 24 years of occupational pension contributions, and women had an average of 16 years (Walker *et al.* 2000).

The British Household Panel Survey (BHPS) provides a valuable resource for such analyses. Rake (2000) used projections of simulated earnings based on the BHPS to document the growing diversity among women relating to educational level and child-bearing. She estimates that the earnings loss due to two children over the lifetime is £267,000 for women with low education, £130,000 for women with a middle level of educational qualifications, and only £18,000 for women with a degree or higher qualifications. The latter is because of the assumption that women with high qualifications do not take any time out of the labour market when they have children, retaining continuity with their existing employer, and moving to part-time work on average for only a small number of years. This contrasts with women with low educational qualifications who have a high earnings loss because of leaving the labour market (estimated as an £82,000 loss through 'lost years'), lower earnings because of undertaking part-time work (£100,000 loss) and because of the financial penalty associated with working in a part-time job (£85,000 loss).

Other authors contest Rake's very optimistic assumption of almost continuous full-time employment among highly educated women. Ginn's analyses using the General Household Survey and the Family Resources Survey paint a different picture. These are larger surveys than the BHPS, therefore provide more reliable estimates of small subgroups such as highly educated women with children, but have the disadvantage of not collecting employment or pension histories. Ginn and Arber (2002) show that among women graduates who have had children, under half are in full-time employment, irrespective of the age of their children and their own age (or birth cohort).

Focusing on men and women in their 40s provides an indication of the likely gender differences in pension position for the next generation. This is an important age for pension accumulation, with pension membership peaks for both men and women. Pension contributions in mid-life years have a disproportionate influence on late-life income, indicating the likely pattern of private pension income for the next generation of pensioners. Figure 2.1 analyses cross-sectional data from the Family Resources Survey for 1994–6 showing pension membership for men and women from different minority ethnic groups (Ginn and Arber, 2001).

White men in their 40s are the most likely to have a pension, 71 per cent, followed by Indian men, 57 per cent. Black (Caribbean origin) men are more likely to have a pension than any group of women. There is little difference between the pension membership of white and black women in their 40s, around 42 per cent having a pension. The rates of pension membership for Pakistani and Bangladeshi men and women are extremely low, with under 20 per cent of Pakistani and Bangladeshi men and only 5 per cent of Pakistani and Bangladeshi women having a pension. The figure shows an interaction between ethnicity and gender. White men are the most privileged, with a large gender difference between white men and women, but the gender difference between black men and women is much smaller. Indian men and women are less likely to have a pension than whites but the gender difference is similar. The seriously disadvantaged position of the Pakistani and Bangladeshi community is very clear. Thus, the diversity of incomes in later life for the next generation of older people will be divided on gender and ethnic lines, as well as class. The ethnic inequalities in private pensions among the current generation of older people reported by Ginn and Arber (2000c) are unlikely to be moderated for the next generation.

Pension scheme membership among women is strongly associated with childlessness and with relative freedom from responsibility for childcare, see Figure 2.2. Among women aged 40–49, 44 per cent who had never had a child belonged to an occupational pension scheme and an additional 13 per cent had a personal or self-employed pension. Over 40 per cent of this age group of childless women had no private pension coverage. Occupational pension coverage was only 30 per cent among women in their 40s with children over 16, and fell to 22 per cent among women with at least one child under ten. There was less difference according to parental status in membership of personal pensions, although this was lower for women with younger children. Thus, among women in their 40s with children under 16, about two-thirds had no private pension coverage in the mid-1990s. Among women in their 50s, pension coverage was even lower, at under 35 per cent, irrespective of child-bearing history. It is therefore clear that the vast majority of the generation of women retiring in 15–20

Figure 2.1 Percentage contributing to a private pension, by ethnicity (men and women aged 40–49)

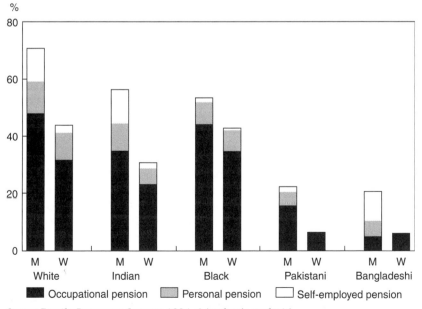

Source: Family Resources Surveys 1994–6 (author's analysis).

Figure 2.2   Percentage of women contributing to a private pension, by parental status and age group

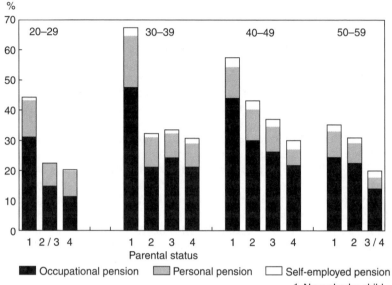

Occupational pension   Personal pension   Self-employed pension

Key   1 Never had a child
       2 All children aged 16+
       3 Youngest child 10–15
       4 Youngest child 0–9

Source: General Household Surveys 1994–6 (author's analysis).

years time will have little income from their own private pensions to support their old age. What is perhaps more surprising is the low levels of pension coverage among women in their 20s and 30s with children (under a third). The inescapable conclusion is that women's role in raising the next generation, despite the increase in women's employment participation, continues to incur a heavy cost in lost opportunities to accumulate an occupational pension.

Thus only an elite minority of highly qualified and well-paid women can avoid the adverse impact of motherhood on employment, earnings and pensions (Glover and Arber 1995; Jacobs 1997; Rake 2000). For the majority of British women, motherhood results in low income in later life.

The gender contract and the generational contract

This section will link issues associated with the gender contract at the micro-level of the co-resident and extended family – related to women providing care across the generations for children and older people, to arguments about the generational contract – at the societal level of payments for the cost of pensions. A recent concern has been with the implications of population ageing, combined with earlier exit from the labour market, which has fuelled alarmist predictions of inequitable welfare transfers between generations (Ginn and Arber 2000b). Some writers have argued that public pension levels can only be maintained by the working population paying more in some form or other, leading to intergenerational conflict over resources.

A key concern has been arguments about the relative merits of public Pay-As-You-Go (PAYG) pension schemes, such as the NI retirement pension, compared with private-funded pension schemes. In the former, contributions to a fund by employed people are used to pay pensions to the older population – a 'generational contract' in that each generation in retirement *relies on succeeding generations* continuing the arrangement. Whereas, in funded pension schemes (usually private and including both group [occupational] and individual or personal schemes), contributions are invested and the accumulated fund used *to pay the individual's own pension* at retirement.

The thesis that, in the context of an ageing population, welfare states create inequity between generations has been examined by economists using generational accounting techniques (Kotlikoff 1992; Becker 2000). These measure (or project) each cohort's financial inputs to the welfare state, in taxes and social insurance contributions, and receipts from it in terms of state welfare. Ginn and Arber (2000b) argue that such methods are flawed as measures of intergenerational equity for several reasons.

The idea of a generation as a distinct self-contained entity is questionable, as discussed earlier. The economic view of generations envisaged in generational accounting contrasts with the more complex sociological one, which recognizes that each generation is linked through family ties with individuals in other generations. Moreover, there is a blurring of life stages, as employment in mid-life becomes increasingly insecure, challenging the generational labels of 'worker' or 'pensioner' (Phillipson 1996). Generational accounting neglects all the family financial transfers which flow up and down between generations (Attias-Donfut and Arber 2000), discussed earlier. Perhaps most importantly no account is taken of the unpaid work performed by members of one generation (mainly women) for another. Physical reproduction and nurturing of the younger generation, as well as provision of informal care to the parent generation, are vital forms of transferred resources between generations and incur substantial costs for the carer; yet such care is socially constructed as non-work (Grace 1998) and finds no place in generational accounts.

Women have increasingly shouldered the *dual* tasks of raising the next generation while at the same time contributing to the formal economy, paying taxes and NI contributions. The total contribution of women to society is arguably increasing with each generation, relative to that of men. Yet, as shown in the previous sections, gender inequality in pensions remains stark. It is therefore important to examine the implications of women's unpaid work for intergenerational transfers of resources, in particular the ways in which the gender and generational contracts are intertwined.

The gender contract is a term which encompasses the norms concerning the division of paid and unpaid work between men and women. While the gender division of domestic and caring labour facilitates men's unfettered participation in paid employment, the employment participation of married and cohabiting women is constrained, especially if they have children, with adverse effects on their pensions as discussed earlier. Within contemporary British society, women who have children generally pursue a combination career, adjusting their employment to fit evolving family needs, with consequent interruptions to employment, periods of part-time employment and downward occupational mobility (Dex 1987; Ginn and Arber 1993, 1996; Jacobs 1997).

In assessing the value of women's contribution to society as mothers, it is pertinent to consider what happens when women withdraw from this fundamental aspect of the gender contract, either failing to care for their children or choosing childlessness, as an increasing proportion of women do (McAllister and Clarke 1998). Falling fertility rates can be seen throughout Europe due to childlessness, later child-bearing and smaller families (Eurostat 1995). Intergenerational transfers related to caring and supportive roles performed mainly by women facilitate bonds between generations, while adequate parenting promotes the physical health, emotional stability and creativity of each generation. We need to consider to what extent an individualistic, employment-dominated society threatens not only fertility but also the quality of life and well-being of relationships between the generations, and more generally within society (Rossi 1993).

Societal changes relating to the gender contract, in which women's paid work increases at the expense of unpaid, tend to inflate the GDP. As women's labour shifts across the private-public boundary, from unpaid to paid, the tax and social insurance base is broadened increasing the public resources available to pay pensions and health care costs. Yet how this money is spent, whether on rebates and tax reliefs for private pensions, or on better state pensions is a *political* choice. Women who conform most closely to the ideal-typical gender contract, by withdrawing from the labour market when they have children and having substantial periods of part-time work, tend to have the lowest personal income from pensions in later life, while those employed full-time and continuously for most of their working life have the highest.

The structure of a country's pension system influences the severity of the pension penalty of motherhood (Ginn *et al.* 2001). Whereas public pension schemes tend to be universal and to compensate in various ways for the effects of caring responsibilities, private pensions are selective in coverage and discriminate against those without full-time continuous employment. Thus the gender contract and the generational pensions contract are linked in several ways, while each is changing over time and varies between societies.

In the debates over intergenerational equity and privatization of pensions, little attention has been paid to existing gender inequality of pension income and to the likely impact of state welfare retrenchment on older women in the future. This omission is particularly serious since women constitute the majority of older people, especially among those aged over 75, and because older women are already more vulnerable to poverty than older men. There has also been scant attention to the likelihood of growing income inequality in later life associated with ethnicity and class.

The British pension reforms since the early 1980s have most adversely affected those women who have conformed to the gender contract, giving priority to their family roles (Ginn and Arber 2000b). The Labour government elected in 1997, despite having criticized the Conservatives' pension reforms, has not reversed them. Instead, new private-funded 'stakeholder pensions' (in effect, personal pensions with lower charges and more flexibility) introduced in April 2001 will do nothing to lessen the pension penalties suffered by women and others whose lifetime earnings are reduced by their caring responsibilities (Ginn and Arber 2000a).

In conclusion the contract between generations cannot be fully understood in isolation from the gender contract. The gender contract interacts with the generational contract in several ways. Women's role in physical reproduction maintains the numerical balance between generations, while nurturing and socializing children underpins the next generation's productivity, supporting the viability of pension provision. Changes over the last 20 years have tended to encourage individualism, opposing the logic of family life. Yet societies depend on the family to care for the next generation, as well as to provide care and support to frail and disabled members of the older generation. If women behave in accordance with economic rationality, maximizing their earnings and private pensions, the unintended effects on fertility, population structure, and quality of life may be too high a price for society to pay.

Acknowledgements

Many of the analyses presented in this chapter were conducted through joint research with Jay Ginn. I greatly appreciate her comments on an earlier version of this chapter and her continued collegial work. I am grateful to the Office of National Statistics for permission to use data from the General Household Survey, and to the Data Archive at the University of Essex for access to the data.

Part I
Children and Parents

3
Past/Present/Future: Time and the Meaning of Change in the 'Family'

Val Gillies, Janet Holland and Jane Ribbens McCarthy

Introduction

Flux is an essential characteristic of 'family' life. The inevitable passage of chronological time, characterized by constantly evolving circumstances and life experiences, mean that change and transition are major features of every individual's life. But such themes are most commonly associated with 'youth' as a particular phase of life and studied within the context of the move from childhood to adulthood. Studies tend to focus exclusively on the young person's experience of change, underestimating the significance of the embedded, relational nature of transitions to adulthood. Consideration of the young person's social context in the form of 'family' relationships is generally confined to a psychological analysis of variables influencing developmental outcomes (Gillies *et al.* 1999). Yet, such a one-dimensional focus on young people as the sole object of change risks obscuring the important turning points and continuities experienced by other 'family' members, concurrent with the process of 'growing up'.

Previous research has shown 'family' relationships to be of fundamental importance to the lives of young people (Gillies *et al.* 2000; Holland *et al.* 2000; Jones and Wallace 1992). In contrast to common individualized depictions of teenagers as progressively severing 'family' ties to reach independent adulthood, young people remain firmly connected to a social network of 'family' and friends (Holland *et al.* 1999). This social context represents more than a set of influencing variables, in that it can be viewed as constituting individual experiences of transition to adulthood. As Pilcher (1995, 2) notes 'full recognition of the role played by social and cultural factors in shaping the ways in which human beings grow up and grow old is a fairly recent development'. Additionally, not only are such transitions socially constructed, they are also jointly interpreted and experienced as significant change.

In this chapter we explore the process of becoming 'adult' as a connected 'family' experience. By drawing on in-depth interviews with 16 to 18 year olds, and with mothers and fathers of teenagers, we aim to highlight the way turning points, transitions and continuities are constructed and lived within a 'family' context. In attempting to provide a more integrated analysis of family experiences of youth transition to adulthood, we will focus on how change is understood and interpreted from the perspective of young people and their parents, exploring these experiences from these variable standpoints.[1] In order to provide a more holistic analysis of youth transition we will examine how these standpoints both concur and diverge to generate specific meanings and definitions of the past, present and future.

'Family' and the individual life course

In the past, sociological research on youth transitions has been mainly concerned with young people's passage from school to work. Youth was studied as a social category, with a particular focus on the structural factors determining the process of reaching 'adult independence'. The sociology of 'family' was conducted as a separate body of work, centring primarily on marital relations, wider kin or the parenting of younger children. While youth researchers perceived young people as moving beyond the influence of their parents, 'family' researchers seemingly overlooked adolescence as a significant 'family' issue. Until recently, there was very little sociological research in Britain incorporating the separate spheres of 'youth' and 'family' studies (Gillies *et al.* 1999). Studies attempting a more holistic analysis of transitions to adulthood began to bridge the gap by re-integrating the public and private worlds of young people. For example, Jones and Wallace (1992) explored the way young people's economic and social relationships with their parents change as they come to be recognized as independent citizens. As Jones and Wallace pointed out, the emergence of a 'life course' perspective within sociology has encouraged a theoretical reintegration of the study of young people's lives. A life course analysis attempts to describe individual pathways through an age-differentiated life-span, placing them in a social and historical context.

This focus on the way young people negotiate their route into adulthood has also characterized attempts to theorize the effects of recent economic and social changes. In particular many authors have utilized Beck's concept of the 'risk society' to explain young people's lives in an uncertain and constantly shifting world (Beck 1992; Furlong and Cartmel 1997; Roberts 1995; Storrie 1997). According to Beck's 'individualization' thesis, a new age of modernity is replacing the old established certainties of industrial society, bringing with it a new set of risks and opportunities. As the established structures of social reproduction fragment, people are portrayed as becoming increasingly 'emancipated' from the roles and constraints associated with traditional social ties. A consequence of this new freedom is ongoing exposure to risk, which has to be negotiated at every turn in the life course. This is thought to lead to individualized life-styles in which people are compelled to accept their agency by reflexively constructing their own biographies. Giddens (1991) presents a similar account of 'high modernity', emphasizing the reflexive process of creating the self through day-to-day decisions. According to Furlong and Cartmel, this intensi fication of individualism has led to an 'epistemological fallacy' in which the experience of self-determination and personal responsibility obscures the powerful constraining forces of existing social structures.

Theories advocated by Beck and Giddens have also been criticized on the grounds that they generate an over-individualized account of life transitions. As we have demonstrated elsewhere (Holland *et al.* 1999), growing up and becoming adult is shaped by the continuing relevance of 'family' relationships to the lives and experiences of young people. In sharp contrast to the assertions made by individualization theorists, that weakened social ties are the inevitable feature of late modernity, we have emphasized the relational, interconnected nature of young people's understandings.

According to Hareven (1978), the life course approach can enable an analysis of collective as well as individual development, shifting emphasis away from ages and stages, towards a focus on how individuals and families move through transitions. Elder (1978) also suggests that the life course perspective can be used to view 'family' as the interconnected life histories of its members. However, as Bernardes (1986) has argued the notion of a 'family life course' implies a particular objective definition of family. Instead Bernardes suggests that the idea of the 'family life course' be reconceptualized in terms of individual pathways coinciding upon 'multidimensional developmental pathways'. This alternative view of 'family transitions' allows for a more detailed exploration of individual experiences of change within diverse 'family' forms. Theorizing young people's transitions to adulthood within a life course perspective which incorporates a collective, 'family' understanding of change and development also guards against generating an over-individualized account of life experiences.

Assessing change and 'family' evolution

The analysis presented in this paper is based on a sample of 32 teenagers, 30 mothers and 31 fathers from mixed class and ethnic backgrounds. Some of these individuals come from 14 'family clusters' where three family members are related. Most of the remaining interviews were with individual, unrelated teenagers and parents, although some interviews were conducted with just two related members from the same 'family'. A variety of methods were used to obtain the sample, ranging from formal approaches through particular institutions and organizations, to more informal approaches through personal contacts.

The interviews were in-depth and open-ended, starting from participants' own understandings. More structured questions concerning parent-teenager relationships were asked towards the end of the interview. Participants were also invited to respond to a set of five vignettes detailing specific dilemmas involving teenagers and parents. Young people and parents were asked to reflect back on their lives and consider changes and developments in 'family' relationships, life-styles and individual personalities. Teenagers and parents were also encouraged to discuss their current lives and relationships, and to contemplate possible future change. Growing up and becoming independent was a major focus of these discussions, with 'family' members describing their experiences of continuity as well as significant change. Despite the centrality of the concept of independence in defining change there were discernible differences as well as commonalities in the way teenagers and parents conceptualized their past, present and future. (For a different approach to the way that time and change are understood by young people and their parents which has produced complementary findings, see Thomson *et al.*, Chapter 5 in this volume.)

Past: perceptions of change and transition

Teenagers gave little sense of their experience of moving from childhood to adulthood, athough they clearly constructed these stages as distinct and separate. For the young people in this sample being an adult was qualitatively different from being a child, particularly in terms of psychological and personal consciousness. 'Growing up' was described as a process of becoming agentic and personally responsible, and was predominantly referred to as a transition that had already occurred. In fact a number of young people were able to specify a particular event or occurrence that precipitated their growing up, such as making older friends, moving house, experiencing their parents' divorce or living independently.

In their descriptions the young people appeared to construct these experiences as catalysts that motivated them to become more mature and adult. Consequently, growing up was portrayed as less of a natural, passively endured development and more of an adaptive, agentic action. Several young people explained how they grew up in response to changes in their lives, emphasizing how they began to take control of their behaviour and decisions. For many, accepting personal responsibility, both for their own lives and for other people's, was a defining feature of having grown up.

From the parents' point of view, past change and transition were natural and inevitable features of their life as a 'family'. Most were able to identify a series of important changes that had occurred over the years and discuss their consequences for individual 'family' members. Overwhelmingly, these changes were represented positively, and linked to notions of natural development and progress. But while teenagers and parents both constructed change as a normal and welcome experience, young people were more likely to place themselves at the centre of their transitions, claiming agentic control over the pace and timing of becoming adult. For example, Neil explained how he reflected on his bad behaviour at school and made a conscious decision to 'grow up':

This teacher come in ... and said to us ... as you're getting older and going to go to the next school you're gonna build up a reputation for yourself and it's not gonna be good for you and it's gonna go on your record and everything. So that made me think, you know, well it's time I grew up now, stop being this kind of person. If I have to use violence or self-defence then I have to but there's no need to go around looking to use it against people for no reason.

Neil, African-Caribbean, middle-class young man

Parents' discussions of how their children had changed over the years differed noticeably from those of young people in terms of their overall interpretation of 'growing up'. The teenagers stressed their experience of becoming someone different, while parents rarely discussed the significance of a personal/psychological transition to adulthood. Instead parents were more likely to pinpoint physical change, noting how their children have grown taller, started shaving, begun periods etc. This focus on physical as opposed to psychological change was in complete contrast to the teenagers' assessments, which contained practically no descriptions of physiological development. Parents also placed greater emphasis on the continuity of their children's personalities through childhood and into adulthood. While teenagers were keen to highlight the difference between their responsible, agentic adult personae and their childhood selves, parents were far more inclined to identify consistencies.

Most of the young people expressed a strong sense that they had undergone some form of personal change over the years. Although some of these changes were linked to growing up and becoming more mature, others were constructed as part of an ongoing personal development. Again (like growing up) this development tended to be portrayed as conscious and self-propelled, with many teenagers describing their changed subjectivity as a particular achievement. One young woman described how she was in the process of making her self 'a certain sort of person', while another explained how she had consciously altered her life-style and her friends, having decided her recreational drug use was becoming dangerous. Others focused on the significant role particular events played in changing them as people. Both of the gay teenagers in our sample explained how their decision to come out to their parents and friends had impacted positively on their self-confidence, as this quote from Arun demonstrates:

> I think I've changed a lot, yeah, especially coming out. Before I used to have less confidence, I always used to shy away and hide – anything gay that came about, you know, especially at school and that I used to just pretend I didn't hear, just walk off, but now since coming out and meeting my friends and that, that made me more confident.
>
> Arun, Indian, working-class young man

The development of confidence was a very dominant feature of the young people's accounts of their changing selves. A large number described how they had been shy and quiet as children, but had gradually become more self-assured and assertive. In explaining this change several young people described how they had 'learnt' to become more confident and assertive by consciously altering the way they responded in social situations. For instance, Leonie explained how she learnt how to deal with racism and bullying at school:

> When I was small I was quite shy, like I didn't really em, go out with many people, especially in my first school because I had a lot of people like racism – because they didn't know any better, so but as I got a bit older I learned to just forget about them, or just carry on my own way. Because I used to let them control me. And not just think about what they're saying, let them put me down and believe what they were saying. But after like sitting down and thinking about it I thought to myself there's no point, I might as well just get on with my own life and things like that.
>
> Leonie, African-Caribbean, middle-class young woman

In contrast to the teenagers' experience of achieving self–confidence as part of a consciously planned objective to become someone different, parents focused on the significance of their children's increased freedom and autonomy. So whilst many parents also highlighted themes of confidence, assertiveness and sociability when prompted to evaluate their children's development over the years, these changes were generally interpreted as part of the process of growing up as they begin to interact in adult environments.

Parents and young people also differed in terms of the personal meanings they attached to past change. While the majority of young people experienced change as a positive development,[2] some parents were less overtly enthusiastic, discussing the losses as well as the gains associated with their children's transitions. Several gave poignant descriptions of the way their 'family' had become more atomized as children grew up, expressing a reluctant acceptance of this change as inevitable. For example, one father explained how the times of 'family' days out together had passed:

> Ehm, for me personally the change is less involvement I suppose. They're more independent. They go shopping on their own, get the bus, go into town, obviously before it would be we'd all muck in and get in the car and the dog would get in the back and we'd all go off on picnics and things like that. That obviously doesn't exist any more. But er, we've got lots of holiday photos of those sort of scenarios.
>
> Kevin, white, middle-class

None of the teenagers' accounts contained nostalgia for the past, and very few discussed change in terms of loss. Young people focused instead on changes, current circumstances and future plans. Thus, the past had a very different significance for parents compared to their children. For parents, the past provided a sense of continuity and forward development. For the teenagers the past, and more particularly their childhood, signified a period of passive dependence, bearing little relevance to their experience of themselves now as responsible, agentic individuals.

Present

In discussing their present circumstances and relationships, teenagers and parents both focused on the theme of independence as a marker to evaluate the past and the future. However, this concept held a different significance from each perspective, highlighting alternative meanings that young people and parents attributed to becoming independent. For the teenagers, acquiring a level of independence and self-determination was indicative of their accountability as young adults. While they generally welcomed their increasing autonomy as a new freedom, the process of becoming independent was understood in terms of the linked themes of responsibility and individualism. The majority of the young people we interviewed saw independence as signifying a new liberty to act as an individual, but also as obligating them to account for the consequences of these individual actions.

For parents, independence was predominantly an emancipatory concept associated with personal freedom and opportunity. Most parents[3] portrayed independence as a valuable liberty that teenagers should be able to enjoy. For example, Claire described the way in which her daughter's life had become less restrictive and more active as she had grown older:

> I mean she puts in a lot of overtime as well, and she has fun. She goes out pubbing, clubbing, she's got a boyfriend, you know, so she's never

really here. Days off she goes with him to London, you know, she's very free, 'cos she can come in and do what she likes. When she's home from work, you know, she'll put her stuff, whatever, change, have a bath, dinner and out. Very independent as well.

Claire, white, working-class mother

All of the parents identified their children's independence as an important and necessary gain, and most also valued the difference it had made to their own lives.[4] Many (fathers as well as mothers) described how they felt less obligated and restricted as a parent of a teenager, associating the increased freedom of their children with an increased freedom for themselves and using the word independence to describe this new-found ability pursue a life separate from their children. The knowledge that children are able to look after themselves appeared to relieve parents of much responsibility and worry and was presented as the source of considerable satisfaction and security. Some saw it as a specific parental duty to ensure that their offspring successfully make the transition from dependant children to independent adults. Others described the pride and pleasure they derived from watching their children become capable, self-determining adults.

Teenagers, on the other hand, appeared to construct independence as a personal resource that they themselves had built and developed over the years. For many young people, becoming more independent was a gradual process associated with adaptation and negotiation. They described how they actively manipulated opportunities and altered the status of their relationships in order to become more self-determining. Again, accepting responsibility was presented as the key to gaining greater respect and independence from parents. Young women in particular emphasized the role of trust in gaining greater independence. For example, Emma described her parents' confidence in her ability to make her own decisions: 'I think they do trust me, that's the most important thing they do trust me' (Emma, white, working-class young woman).

The gradual gaining of independence was a theme common to many of the teenagers' accounts, although in the main, discussion was confined to more subtle, less conscious changes. Several young people described how they had slowly pushed out the boundaries of their behaviour within their families. For instance, Toby explained how, without explicitly asking, he reached the point at which he was able to have his girlfriend stay over in his bedroom:

I mean she used to come round with her friends and stuff, I used to have a few friends over or something, and then, um, and so we'd just sort of be up in my room, most of the evening, and then they'd all leave in the morning, and then, uh, I don't know, eventually it was – she just used to come round.

Toby, white, middle-class young man

Toby's mother, Laura, gave a similar account of the way her son had subtly manipulated and stretched the boundaries of parental control:

> That was handled very cleverly I must say. He always had lots of friends who would stay the night, boys, when they were much younger and then, er, he had sort of em, any girls that were involved in the group. And then just incredibly casually, suddenly the friend of the girlfriend wasn't here and it was just Libby here one evening and Libby stayed the night.
>
> Laura, white, middle-class mother

For many parents, transition to independence was marked by specific milestones such as their child establishing a sexual relationship. Parents also attached particular importance to events such as reaching a certain age, gaining qualifications or a driving licence, achieving some financial independence, or leaving home. Interestingly, mothers and fathers appeared to be far more focused on the significance of their children gaining adult status than the teenagers themselves. Parents were more likely than the teenagers to discuss the implications of reaching 16 or 18, in terms of rights and opportunities that had been (or would be) accorded to their children. They were also more likely to highlight the importance of a first boyfriend/girlfriend, while in contrast few teenagers identified their personal relationships as indicative of their development. Notably though, both parents and teenagers portrayed earning money, passing exams and leaving home as particularly significant moves towards fully 'independent adulthood'.

Newly acquired independence for young people and their parents was often discussed in terms of 'family' life naturally evolving and changing over the years. For the young people, evolving relationships with parents was a major focus of their discussions, with most feeling they had now established a closer, more equal bond with their mother and father. In describing how relationships with parents had changed over the years, many young people emphasized a current ability to talk more easily with them. A large number explained how they valued being able to have 'adult' conversations with their parents, contrasting this experience with earlier relationships based around care and control. For example, Neil noted how the frequency and the substance of conversations with his father had changed:

> We're starting to talk more. It's not that we didn't talk before it's just that I didn't really think we had anything to talk about, so it'd be more like – hello, good morning, and asking questions if I can go somewhere and stuff. But now I'm getting older we started talking about the world cup.
>
> Neil, African-Caribbean, middle-class young man

Parents themselves also commented on the way communication with their teenagers had become more egalitarian and reciprocal. For many, this change derived from less involved, more separate 'family' relationships, precipitated by their children growing up and becoming individuals in their own right. Mothers and fathers described how this significant change in the basis of the parent–child relationship, led them to re-evaluate their teenagers as companions and confidantes as opposed to vulnerable dependants. Many mothers and fathers referred to their teenagers as 'friends' or 'mates', and many described how their relationship had improved in quality over the years. For example, Brian described how a new closeness had developed between himself and his son:

Em ... he, he spends a lot of time, more time with me now. You know, I go to football with him a lot, and we're planning to go off next week to the bike show at the NEC, the mountain bike show. And, it's good to go out, and he, he'll take me, and he'll tell me about this and that, where I can't tell him. And that's a different scenario. Well it's usually round the other way where Dad says – this is this, and this and this. And it's the opposite way around now. So that's a good feeling.

                                    Brian, white, middle-class father

For parents, this shift in the basis of relationships with their children, from care and responsibility to reciprocal friendship was generally appreciated, but was often seen as entailing difficult emotional adjustments. In order to maintain an emerging relationship with their children as 'young adults', parents explained how they felt obliged to show a new respect for their teenager's privacy and personal autonomy. Several parents (particularly mothers) described how they had deliberately contained their emotional investment in their children's lives, by avoiding over-involvement and managing their own worries and anxieties. For example, Susan acknowledged her daughter's need for privacy with her boyfriend, while describing her own desire to intervene in their arguments:

Sometimes if I've gone upstairs and – no I wouldn't say that I've eavesdropped but I've heard, on occasions she's been a bit upset and I think it's if he's had a drink and things come out and she gets a bit upset, and I mustn't get involved in that, it's between them, but I want to go in there and say you know, 'What's wrong? Can I help'? But I can't because that's – if she wants my help she's got to come and ask me. I can't say to her, 'Look I heard you crying upstairs now what's this all about?' Because she's not eight years old now. Em, if she was that upset at anytime I'd have to wait for an opening to sort of say, 'I've noticed this that or the other. Is anything wrong?'

                                    Susan, white, working-class mother

Although changed relationships were generally represented as a necessary and progressive part of transition to adulthood, parents and teenagers also discussed their appreciation of certain continuities. While young people constructed adult status in terms of independence and personal responsibility, the enduring significance of relationships with parents was also emphasized. In contrast to the academic literature emphasizing individuation as an essential developmental process, the majority of young people in our sample still valued and relied on a close relationship with their parents. The knowledge that parents are available to provide emotional and practical support when needed appeared to be particularly appreciated.

Parents themselves tended to be more specific in identifying important continuities in their relationships with their teenagers. While they found it reassuring to know that their children were becoming increasingly self-reliant, both mothers and fathers stressed their ability to maintain a close emotional relationship with them as teenagers. Parents described how they were still able to enjoy cuddling their children (daughters in the main), and how they expected to retain a strong emotional bond with them throughout their lives. For example, Christine explained how her relationship with her daughter had remained close:

We're close, there's a lot of physical contact, yes. She still will, um, she quite surprises me sometimes when we're out, and she will ... like when we go up to London, she'll quite often hold my hand when we're going, looking for, you know, going through the Underground, looking at all the maze of tunnels and where we should be, and she'll quite often hold my hand, still.

Christine, white, middle-class mother

Parents also tended to emphasize the continuing significance of their role in guiding and advising their children. While they largely portrayed their teenagers as on their way to self-reliance, parents still perceived themselves to be important givers (and increasingly receivers) of love, support and guidance.

Consequently, teenagers' and parents' discussions of their present circumstances centred around an evaluation of change and continuity. From both standpoints, the concept of independence was a key feature of their lived experience, allowing individuals within the 'family' greater self-determination and freedom, while also enabling a respect for and maintenance of enduring 'family' bonds. As one mother of a teenage son noted of her current 'family' life, 'it's got looser, more space, but not less close'.

Future: forward trajectories

In thinking ahead to the future, both teenagers' and parents' discussions became noticeably individualized, focusing around specific objectives and personal challenges. For the teenagers, consideration of the future was generally structured around immediate plans and ambitions, like passing exams or getting a job. Most of the young people perceived themselves as progressing through a practical series of steps to a future goal, and were able to locate themselves in this process by describing what they had already achieved and what they were expecting to achieve subsequently. Both concrete and more abstract speculation on what might lie ahead was articulated in a noticeably different style from the young people's descriptions of growing up and developing an adult persona. While past changes and accomplishments tended to be expressed in terms of psychological development, future goals appeared to be associated with instrumental decision-making. When asked to think ahead the young people largely focused on life-style and material factors as opposed to personal or psychological growth.

From the parents' perspectives, the future was a twofold concept incorporating both their children's prospective life chances and their own personal destiny. In discussing the future of their children parents were generally optimistic, with most conveying an assurance that their teenagers were progressively moving forward. Many parents admitted to worrying about the difficulties and the challenges facing teenagers as they take control of their own lives, but a large number also emphasized their trust and faith in their children's abilities to negotiate life-chances effectively. As one father explained, his fears centred not on his daughter's competence, but on the hostile environments she might encounter:

> We do worry about her in our way, and when she's out we don't sleep, but we, we don't worry about her getting in trouble, but it's what other people can cause trouble to them, you know? Cos it happened to her about six months ago. Some people started on her, not Emma personally but her friends as well. They was all walking down to watch the fireworks, they're a nice bunch of kids, and uh, this other lot who lived in Heather Green apparently started on all the boys, and Emma had the sense enough to run in a shop and uh, didn't get away with it, but she seen what happened, it scared her. Er, and they went to court last week and got eight months.
>
> George, white, working-class father

Young people also expressed a broadly optimistic view of the future, emphasizing their determination to achieve their objectives. Securing a good career was central to most young people's accounts of the future, and some of them were particularly clear about the sort of career they wanted to pursue and the necessary steps to get there. Money was another important factor highlighted by many young people, particularly working-class teenagers. For the most part, the young people were remarkably focused on the practicalities of achieving future aims. The vast majority were able to outline some sense of how they would like the future to be, however vague. Those who felt more uncertain about what lay ahead tended to perceive this as a problematic lack of direction. Several teenagers were concerned by their lack of clear aims and objectives, Toby, for example, said: 'I suppose you know, what I'm gonna do when I'm a bit older, it does worry me. It didn't used to, 'cos I thought I'd think of something, but I don't know what I wanna do' (Toby, white, middle-class young man). While some parents were also concerned about their children's lack of direction, most explained how they played an active role in ensuring their teenagers made appropriate choices and decisions. Although parents tended to express their faith in their children's abilities to build their own successful future, they also described how they felt they actively supported this forward trajectory.

In terms of the parents' considerations of their own future lives, there was less instrumental goal-setting. Nevertheless many parents, particularly mothers, did discuss specific aims, plans and intentions, like establishing a new career (or developing an existing one), travelling or taking up more social invitations. Some parents expressed a strong sense of entitlement to a 'life of their own', having committed much of their adult years to their children.

A striking quote came from Claire, who described the powerful subjective change she has undergone since her daughter has become more independent. From Claire's perspective, increased freedom from parental responsibility has allowed her to emerge from her 'cocoon' as a mother, with new confidence as an individual in her own right:

'cos all of a sudden I had this confidence from nowhere, it was as if I was a butterfly coming out of a cocoon or something, you know, I'd been stuck in this little drudgy mother role or whatever, then I was suddenly out. And even my friends said, 'I can't believe you've changed', and they've gone the other way now. Where they used to be the very loud ones out, and I used to sit there quietly, if anyone spoke to me I'd get up and go to the toilet instead of speaking to them. Whereas now I can walk into a pub on my own, or I'll go with friends and they're more quiet, and I'm loud, and I'll be chatting to anyone. I don't know why, it's just role reversal, it seems to be. I'm out of my cocoon now! (laughing).

Claire, white working-class mother

Although teenagers' and parents' accounts of the future were characterized by a relatively narrow focus on individual directions and personal goals, implicit references to enduring 'family' ties were identifiable in most accounts. Many of the young people's specific aims and objectives were underpinned by an expectation that parents would provide practical and emotional support. Similarly, while parents acknowledged and enjoyed their greater freedom, they were also assured of their continuing relevance to their children.

Conclusion

The themes of change and continuity were central to teenagers' and their parents' discussions of the past, the present and the future. Change, in terms of transition to independence, was recognized and welcomed as progressive, but continuity, in the form of enduring 'family' relationships, was also stressed as an important mainstay, connecting parents and their children together. While there was much commonality in the way transitions were discussed in terms of natural development and evolution, parents and teenagers clearly attached different meanings to the processes of growing up and growing older. These contrasting understandings of the significance and direction of change over the years, provides an important insight into the way individuals experience transitions at different points in their life course.

As we have shown, the young people's accounts of personal change and growing up were striking in terms of the emphasis placed on agency and responsibility. Becoming an adult was associated with abandoning the passivity of childhood and taking control as an autonomous subject. The inability of young people to remember and explore their experiences of being a child appears to underline this interpretation of growing up as developing an agentic self. It seems likely that childhood was a difficult subject for teenagers to discuss because it predates their definition of themselves as individuals in their own right. (For a related argument, see Holland *et al* 1999.) As far as the young people were concerned past, present and future change was interpreted in terms of conscious, considered development, although the ability to change and develop positively as an individual was closely associated with social context.

Two other related features emerged from this analysis of the young people's accounts of change and transition. First, in discussing growing up, most of the teenagers focused on psychological and emotional developments as opposed to physical or structural changes. For the majority of young people in our sample growing up was about achieving a mature outlook on life, while discussions about changes in appearance and status were notably minimal and confined to responses to direct questions. Second, accounts of growing up tended to be constructed around the active acceptance of responsibility as opposed to the procurement of rights. For a large number of young people, growing up was associated with a decision to become a responsible adult, rather than achieving greater freedom or personal autonomy.

These findings have important implications for theories which stress the individualized experience of growing up in late modernity. Our analysis broadly supports the claim that young people see themselves as personally responsible for negotiating transitions to adulthood. The emphasis placed on psychological development and individual agency also corresponds with Beck's claim that young people now 'conceive of and organise themselves as tinkerers of their own personalities' (Beck 1997, 164). Nevertheless, this individualism was clearly contained within a wider social context, characterized by interdependent 'family' relationships. Young people's status as connected individuals cushioned what Furlong and Cartmel (1997, 8) have described as a heightened sense of risk and insecurity deriving from 'the combined forces of individuality and accountability, on the one hand, and vulnerability and lack of control on the other'. Although young people did accept personal responsibility for their decisions and life chances, they also located themselves within a social network characterized by commitment and mutual support.

In contrast to the teenagers' focus on personal development, parents were more likely to evaluate change in terms of their children's physical development and age-related status. For them, psychological continuity in the form of their child's essentially stable personality was an important feature linking past, present and future. Holding onto constants within a process defined by flux and forward motion appeared to be a meaningful way for parents to retain a sense of conjunction with their children. Continuity also provided a reference point from which parents were able to assess the changes that had occurred over the years. Although most parents were clear that their children's transition to independence significantly altered their relationship, being a mother or father was still constructed as emotionally and practically meaningful. Changes in 'family' life and in parent–child relationships were discussed as necessary adaptations to accommodate an inevitable process, but stable attachment was presented as a vital continuity.

Paradoxically for Beck's thesis, it was parents who placed more emphasis on the concept of freedom in their discussions of past, present and future change. For many parents, growing up was characterized by increased personal autonomy for their children and greater citizenship rights to pursue individual desires. This focus on freedom and self-determination was also applied to their own lives, with a large number of parents interpreting transition as part of their personal life cycle, of moving from independent adult, to responsible parent and back to independent adulthood again. More general themes of responsibility and accountability were, however, noticeably muted in comparison to the teenagers' accounts. Although trust and reliability were emphasized as important features of parent–teenager relationships, parents rarely highlighted responsibility as a consequence of freedom.[5] Contemporary teenagers appear more aware of the costs of individual freedom, in terms of risk, uncertainty and personal accountability. For the young people in our sample, personal autonomy was often experienced as an individual liability that is buffered and mediated through interdependent 'family' relationships.

In conclusion, teenagers' and parents' discussions of past, present and future highlight the way in which constructions of time are jointly produced, but experienced from different standpoints. Instead of viewing 'family' as an external influence on individual transitions and turning points, we have focused on a set of concurring or meshed life courses in order to generate an integrated analysis of the meaning of growing up. We argue that this approach facilitates a more comprehensive understanding of the context in which young people become adults, while also providing an insight into the process of 'family' change.

Notes

1. For a more detailed discussion see Ribbens McCarthy, Holland and Gillies, (in press).
2. Although the majority of young people represented past change as positive, three teenagers did describe negative experiences associated with particular problems, including heroin addiction, depression and illness.
3. While most parents associated independence with freedom, two Asian mothers linked their definition of independence to a broader sense of responsibility, suggesting that becoming independent entails knowing right from wrong. From this perspective independence is interpreted less as autonomous self-sufficiency and more as a responsible conformity.
4. Parents may have been working with a more complex notion of movements in and out of dependence and independence over the life course (Ribbens McCarthy, Holland and Gillies 2000).
5. Alternative possible explanations of these generational differences could relate to either cohort or life course position (Ribbens McCarthy, Holland and Gillies 2000).

4

'The Never-ending Story': Children's Gaze and the Unresolved Narrative of Their Parents' Divorce

Jean Duncombe and Dennis Marsden

All sorrows can be borne if we can put them into a story.
Hannah Arendt 1958, 175

Does he know that he lies? ... That's what mamma says I'm to tell him – 'that he lies and he knows he lies'.
Henry James 1980, 21

This chapter will discuss how some young adults fail to come to terms with the 'never-ending story' of their parents' divorce, because inconsistencies in that story prevent them from satisfying their burning desire to discover 'the truth' about why their parents split up. The context of our discussion is the changes in demography and divorce legislation which have provoked controversy over whether the children of divorced parents should be viewed as victims – as 'damaged' adults-in-the-making – or whether some may grow emotionally through their experiences of 'family reordering'. In conventional terms, the 'never-ending story' of parental divorce might be viewed as a 'sleeper effect' that emerges belatedly to damage some young adults' lives. However, we want to argue that such 'stories' can also be seen as processes of narrative construction through which young people *actively* – although not always successfully – attempt to recreate their identities when faced with the trauma of parental divorce.

Because discussion of the impacts of divorce has become increasingly polarized and partisan, we need to locate this chapter in current debates. Many writers who initially welcomed divorce as personally liberating, have subsequently had to come to terms with evidence that *some* children may suffer *some* kinds of adverse effects from divorce. Unfortunately, this reassessment has coincided with crude claims from the politically and religiously inspired 'pro-marriage' movement in the US and UK, that *all* children suffer serious damage from divorce (Freely 2000). In the face of such bigotry, it is tempting to play down any adverse effects and emphasize opportunities for growth. However, we would argue that it remains necessary to acknowledge and understand any 'damage' from divorce to see how it may be reduced. Although only a minority of children of divorce will suffer the full frustrations of the 'never-ending story', we suggest below that the potentially damaging processes through which such 'stories' arise are widespread.

We will first comment briefly on the difficulties of researching the impacts of divorce and family reordering upon children. We will then outline some recommendations from research and counselling concerning how parents should behave and what it is suggested they should tell their children in order to minimize any emotional damage. Unfortunately, research suggests that – at least by these criteria – many parents 'behave badly', and we will describe how this behaviour may adversely affect some children.

Our own small-scale study[1] indicates that emotional damage may arise where children are frustrated in their search for 'the truth' of their parents' divorce. However, paradoxically, the intensity of the child's desire to know the truth – the child's 'gaze' – may itself contribute to the difficulty of finding one simple, unchanging and satisfying narrative.

Difficulties in researching divorce effects

Our interest in the longer-term effects of divorce is in line with changes in the conventional wisdom from research and counselling. Divorce used to be viewed as a discrete event whose potentially traumatic consequences were likely (by analogy with Kubler-Ross's [1970] model of death and grieving) to begin to be resolved within a year (Ferri 1976). Today, however, readjustment to divorce is viewed as a potentially lengthy social and psychological process whose consequences may continue into adulthood (Burghes 1994; Furstenberg and Cherlin 1991; Wallerstein and Kelly 1990).

It has been suggested that stigma from divorce may diminish as divorce rates rise (Burghes 1994) so that the focus of research might switch from damage to

> [the] opportunities in every crisis for people to rebuild what was destroyed or to create a reasonable substitute; to be able to grow emotionally, establish new competence and pride; and to strengthen intimate relationships far beyond earlier capacities.
>
> Wallerstein and Blakeslee 1989, 277; see also Stacey 1991

However, the evidence of any growth is sparse and equivocal (Neale and Wade 2000; Smart and Neale 1999; Wallerstein and Kelly 1990). Indeed, contrary influences from the rise of 'victim culture' and 'victim stories' (Plummer 1995) now increasingly encourage children to perceive them-selves as 'damaged' by their parents' divorce.

Our focus on the 'story' of divorce also runs counter to the trend for research to locate sources of damage remote from the divorce itself. In a wide-ranging review, Krantz (1991) traces the shift in research perspectives, from pessimism about the adverse effects of fathers' absence, to optimism that divorce might prove liberating for women; but subsequently back to pessimism about the continuing impacts of parental strife, and the further disruptions and economic privations of single-parent or stepfamily life, whose outcomes depend mainly on how well mothers cope (see also Cockett and Tripp 1994; Kiernan 1992; Rodger 1995). Krantz (1991, 254) concludes that: 'a detailed and clear-cut picture of the effect of divorce on children does not exist'.

Indeed, some large-scale surveys suggest that a majority of children show no adverse effects from divorce itself, although children may be damaged by conflict between their parents, whether married or divorced (Amato and Booth 1997; Cherlin *et al.* 1991; Elliott and Richards 1991). However, such findings are often based on relatively crude measures. So, for example, 'parental conflict' may be overt or concealed, continuous or spasmodic, poisonous or constructive, extreme but 'normalized'. Moreover, as Furstenberg and Cherlin (1991, 66) conclude: 'Even less is known about the long-term consequences of divorce than about the short-term.' (Also see Amato 1993; Burghes 1994.) Ideally, the exploration of more subtle phenomena requires in-depth follow-up studies, but even the best of these are relatively small scale, unrepresentative and lacking controls. In various comments on her ten-year follow-up study of divorcing couples, Wallerstein has summarized the shifting trauma – or 'damage' – suffered by some children in the following ways:

> Growing up is inevitably harder for children of divorce because they must deal with psychological issues that children from well-functioning intact families do not have to face ... The danger in every crisis is that people will remain in the same place, continuing through the years to react to the initial impact as if it had just struck.
> Wallerstein and Blakeslee 1989, 179, 198

> The enduring effects ... may not be visible immediately or in subsequent specific behaviours or symptoms but may forever shatter the individual's guiding conception of the world as relatively safe and reliable.
> Wallerstein *et al.* 1988, 197

Some children's failure to 'work through' and 'move on' from their parents' divorce appeared in a loss of confidence in their parents and worries that they might repeat their parents' mistakes: 'This identification with being a child of divorce may be one of the lasting sequelae of the experience of parental divorce during childhood' (*ibid*. 210).

Limiting the emotional 'damage' to children

The findings of research and counselling indicate that when children form their own perspective on their parents' divorce, this influences their emotional and behavioural reactions, which in turn affect events and other people (Krantz 1991). It therefore seems desirable to consider how parents may help children to form positive perspectives. Wallerstein and Kelly (1990) suggest that children's capacity to understand and cope with divorce depends on their level of maturity (at the time of divorce, and later when they see divorce differently) but also on whether the divorce 'makes good sense', appearing rational, amicable and moral. In short, children are seeking 'the truth' of their parents' divorce, but a truth they can understand and accept.

Various research and counselling literature points to recommendations about how divorcing parents should behave and what children want and need to know, if emotional damage is to be limited:

• Parents should avoid conflict in front of their children, because this may frighten them or make them feel insecure.
• Well before the divorce, both parents should explain to all the children what will happen (especially to them), if necessary tailoring the 'story' to individual children's level of understanding.
• The story should be agreed and simple, omitting what children need not know (sexual difficulties, affairs etc.): 'Mum and Dad don't love each other (don't get on) any more, so we're going to live apart. You mustn't feel it's your fault; if anybody's, it's ours. And we'll still be your Mum and Dad, and both love you just the same.'
• Children need encouragement to remain children, and discouragement from dwelling on the divorce or uncertainties about the future.
• Parents should behave civilly towards one another, and should co-parent by both showing an active interest in meeting their children's needs.

To assist co-parenting, divorce law has attempted to de-emphasize 'fault' and 'blame' and to move towards reconciliation and mediation. Also, children's rights legislation treats children's relationships with individual parents as if they are unaffected by parental quarrels (Smart and Neale 1999). Unfortunately, however, there is virtually no evidence that co-parenting works (Furstenberg and Cherlin 1991) and indeed these idealistic recommendations tend to be undermined by 'parents behaving badly'.

'Parents behaving badly'

Divorcing parents tend not to appreciate fully the potential conflicts between their own and their children's happiness, and how divorce may threaten children's sense of security. Even children who are aware of parental disharmony seldom expect or want their parents to divorce, and indeed children may be profoundly shocked by 'modern' divorces where a quiet loss of intimacy leads parents to seek fulfilment in new relationships (*ibid.*).

Divorce is also often acrimonious because it *appears* one-sided, initiated by one partner and resisted by the other, so despite legal attempts to de-emphasize 'fault', post-divorce relationships are often marred by recriminations over blame, especially where one partner has had an affair (Arendell 1994; Furstenberg and Cherlin 1991; Simpson 1998; Smart 1999; Wallerstein and Kelly 1990). Interestingly, sociologists have scarcely discussed the links between divorce and affairs (Lawson, 1989; Reibstein and Richards 1992) or how affairs may affect children – who often know more than parents realize (Cole 1999). In fact, the 'double standard' ensures that mothers who 'desert' their children for their lovers will be stigmatized, so most divorced mothers remain with their children, who inhibit her from forming new relationships. However, most divorced fathers start 'new' relationships relatively quickly (Smart 1999; Wallerstein and Kelly 1990), with a speed that suggests these are often affairs previously concealed from, or condoned by, their wives.

Parental conflict (and gendered parenting) means that mothers usually have to explain divorce to the children, often after fathers have left, but a few children are told nothing. Mothers may then become preoccupied with securing maintenance and independence from fathers who may initially attempt to sustain the marriage, but cease visits and payments once the marriage is clearly over (Smart and Neale 1999; Wallerstein and Kelly 1990). Sadly, mothers' preoccupation may seem to girls like rejection, while mothers' difficulties in controlling boys may deteriorate into barked orders and confrontations (Hetherington, 1979; Wallerstein and Kelly 1990). Later, however, resident mothers are more able and prepared to discuss emotional matters with their children, especially daughters.

In contrast, divorce often seriously interrupts fathers' relationships with their children (Smart and Neale 1999; Wallerstein and Kelly 1990), because many fathers have not been used to co-parenting even within marriage. Up to half lose contact within two years: 'Uncomfortable and unskilled at being an active parent, marginalised by infrequent contact, focused on building a new family life [often with a new, younger partner] many fathers fade from their children's lives' (Furstenberg and Cherlin 1991, 74, 195). Even fathers who retain contact experience difficulties in communicating emotionally, seeing their emotions as 'their own business', not to be shared with children (Duncombe and Marsden 1993). Instead, they *do* things, especially with sons, or express concern by lavish spending on gifts or outings (so-called 'Disneyland Fathers'), much to the anger of their impoverished wives (Bradshaw *et al.* 1999; Wallerstein and Kelly 1990).

Confusingly for children, parental relationships may fluctuate. Wrangles over money or access may increase hostility. Yet sometimes the parent who initiated divorce, or even both partners, may experience regret, particularly if neither has a new relationship (Smart 1999; Wallerstein and Kelly 1990). Indeed, some occasionally sleep together, or even remarry (Weiss, 1975). Christmas and other family occasions may bring a sense of *déjà vu* and nostalgia for happier times. Such memories, together with the sense that 'children need a father', may help mothers to do emotion work to sustain the fathers' image in their children's eyes, although children's continued contacts with fathers also encourage them to pay child support and give mothers free time (Bradshaw *et al.* 1999; Duncombe and Marsden 1993; 1998; Smart and Neale 1999). Sometimes, however, mothers may establish 'mischievous alliances' with their children to undermine the father (Wallerstein and Kelly 1990). Indeed, mothers may work 'counter-cyclically', building the father up ('he's a good man really') if children's hostility threatens the relationship, or highlighting his faults if children seem too uncritical. However, even neglectful fathers may retain a symbolic importance for children, to the annoyance of mothers whose home-making they take for granted (Marsden 1969).

'The never-ending story': secrets and lies

Research and counselling have suggested that children have a powerful desire to find 'the truth' of their parents' divorce – or at least *a* truth that they can understand and accept as satisfying. However, counselling practice and legislation on divorce and children's rights favour a model of co-parenting where parents behave amicably throughout, and children are given a simple, non-threatening explanation of the divorce but discouraged from dwelling on the detail. Unfortunately, research also shows that, judged against this ideal, parents often tend to 'behave badly' and some children do indeed suffer emotional damage, although any connection is complex.

In the remainder of this chapter we will draw on our own small-scale research to explore what happens when children's search for 'the truth' of their parents' divorce comes up against 'parents behaving badly'. And we will trace how, for some young people, this clash results in frustration – a story of their parents' divorce that seems 'never-ending'. (We refer to these young adults as 'children', to underline the key relationship.)

The children in our small study had learned about their parents' divorce in stages. Usually they had been told something at the time of divorce, often by their mothers, and later questioning had brought further versions of the story from one or both parents. Some children had gained information from relatives or family friends, or discovered things by accident or by more active searches; and their understanding of divorce had also changed as they matured.

However, they had become confused by a range of contradictory, changing and incomplete stories, so that some now suspected their parents of trying to keep divorce 'secrets' from them, by refusing to talk, evasions or 'lies'. The following quotes capture their frustration: 'I just want to know the truth. I don't see why I can't. I don't see why it's so bloody complicated!' (Rose, 19). 'I just came home and said to Mum one day: "I want to know the truth. Can we spend a few days ... I just want to know the truth" '(Rachel, 19):

> I need a truth I can live with. It doesn't have to be 'the truth', if you know what I mean ... I said to Mum, 'I want you to give me a story that I can *say* is the truth, and then I never want to speak about it again ... That's got to be it.'
>
> Caroline, 22

Some remembered the brief and cryptic story they had been given at the time of the divorce: 'Even at the time I wondered why. I couldn't see it, I thought they got on all right. I couldn't *ask* why, 'cos mum was always crying' (Rose, 19). 'Mum just says to me on the train one day, "We're leaving Dad" and when I says, "Why?" she says, "He drinks too much"' (Kerry, 23). However, some children were grateful that persistent questioning had eventually produced answers more suited to their maturity:

> I know it sounds funny, but I like to hear the story over again. When Mum and Dad split, Mum told us on the train to my Nan's, she just said, 'We're not really friends any more' ... I was about ten then, I didn't think much about it, I was ... in shock I suppose ... But when I was 16, I sort of thought of going to live with my Dad for a bit, but I ... had to clear it with Mum first ... And this time ... she's quite good my Mum, she sort of told me ... well everything ... said about sex and that, and he wasn't much good, and he worked away a lot ...
>
> Caroline, 22

But talking more, even mainly with one parent, did not necessarily bring a clearer story:

> It's very hard. Some days my Mum says Dad's a bastard ... that's usually when she hasn't got the money ... she says, 'He doesn't love us, he's had affairs, he drinks, he lies, he's a bully' ... all that stuff. Some days *I* hate him ... But then some days, she says to me, 'He's a good man, a kind

man ... He really loves you.' Sometimes she even says all the things in the *same* day, and I don't know *what* to think!

Rachel, 19

Lacking a clear explanation, some children turned to other sources, particularly close relatives – who might, however, be putting together *their* own stories from scraps of information shaped by prejudice. In this way some children learned of affairs that neither parent had been willing to divulge, although any new slant on the story depended on the side of the family to which the informant belonged:

> It was really confusing ... We used to go to my Gran's [father's mother] on Sundays with Dad, and she didn't like my Mum. She used to call my Mum 'common as muck'. My Gran said, 'Your mum's a whore.' I was really shocked ... I didn't like that ... I don't go there no more.
>
> Kerry, 23

Holly (18) had received a similar shock at the house of family friends, and even as she recounted the story, she seemed to gain new insights:

> Suddenly they said, 'Don't you mind about that woman?' I didn't know what they were on about. They said my Dad had been having an affair with her for years – since I was a baby, in fact! I couldn't believe it! I'd met her round his, but *he's* always told me he met her later ... Looking back I can see all sorts of things. Stupid really. I wonder if Mum knew ... Looking back she was always round our house, she was Mum's best friend, in fact ... Now I come to think about it, it was only a couple of days after they'd split ... I went round to see if Dad was all right ... and she was there then! Looking back, I suppose *that* was funny. Makes me question what it's all about ... makes me want to say to my Dad, 'Is *this* why you split, was it really *your* fault?' Mum says I shouldn't blame Dad, but other times she says it *is* his fault. Tell you the truth, I'm a bit fed up with Mum for putting up with it, if she knew ... and not telling me ... I don't see Dad any more now ... Mum thinks I'm wrong, I should still see him – she says I'll regret it. But I just don't wanna know. I'll always love him ... and actually I don't even mind the girl-friend ... It's 'cos of all the lies ... yes, the *lies*.

Where parents were unforthcoming, some children accidentally discovered 'clues' in the family home. Simon (19) recalled:

> When I was 14, I was searching around ... you know how kids do, not bad or anything ... and I found these photos – I can't hardly bear to speak about it even now – I found these photos of my Dad and *her* doing

... you know what ... and there was a date on the back and I couldn't *believe* it 'cos it's when I was only little! My Dad wouldn't usually talk, but once when he was angry he said they split 'cos Mum had an affair and he couldn't forgive her. But I looked at these... I feel *sick* to think about it ...

Other children became intensely curious and searched deliberately, although any 'evidence' only heightened their curiosity – particularly if it incriminated the parent they blamed for the divorce. Kerry (23) confessed:

I was a really nosy teenager, I was always looking in drawers and things since I was small ... secret presents ... condoms ... but, well ... since they're not living together (I know it's awful ... I wouldn't tell anybody)... but I still look ... and only recently I found these letters – *old* letters – written when I was small ... written by my Dad to ... 'the bitch' [laughs] ... that's what I've always called her. He lives with her now, 'the bitch' ...

The hostility of some daughters against their father's new girl-friend was sometimes heightened by his insistence on bringing her whenever he met his daughter: 'He's got no time for me. He only sees me now when he wants a baby-sitter. I don't tell him, but I can't bear it ... *her*, you know ... with him ... ' (Claire, 19).

Sometimes, stories from parents or other relatives, together with children's own discoveries might satisfy for a while, but there was always the risk that any new knowledge might reawaken old questions or provoke new ones:

I always thought I knew the truth ... Mum goes: Dad didn't talk to her, he drinks too much, and she was lonely ... and 'cos Dad didn't talk to *me* much either, well, I could understand how she got fed up and they split up. So I've always been on her side ... I love my Mum. But just last year I found out *she* had an affair ... I just can't believe it ... the *lies*.

Barbara, 21

When I was little I tried to talk to my Dad ... ask him why, sort of thing ... but he said, 'It's none of your business. That's between me and your mother' ... But when I was 16, I sort of needed to know ... *his* side... to know why ... I asked him again ... but he just shouted at me: 'None of your business!' So I asked his girl-friend (she lives with him ... I suppose she's a sort of a stepmum – God, I hope not!) ... She said, 'I suppose you're old enough to know,' and she told me it really was Dad that left, not Mum ... 'cos Mum was having an affair. But when I went back to Mum, she said, 'Dad's a liar, he *would* say that – that's because *he* was having an affair,' and she told me that he was jealous, he thought she was having an affair but she wasn't ... I don't know who to believe. I love my Mum *and* my Dad, and my Nan says to me, 'It doesn't really matter now, it's all a long time ago.' But I need to know ...

Simon, 19

I don't care ... I'm fed up with trying to find out what the truth is. First of all she says, 'This is the truth,' but then Dad says, 'This is the truth and *she's* a liar,' and Mum says *Dad's* a liar. They're *all* liars as far as I'm concerned and that's why I give up on it ...

Rose, 19

I find it's hard ... the truth ... At the time, Mum left home she'd been having an affair – horrible bloke, *years* younger than her – but later Mum said that she couldn't stand Dad's drinking ... He *did* drink a lot, when I think about it ... And now Dad says – when he's feeling 'understanding'! – she probably married too young, they'd both grown apart. But the really peculiar thing ... sometimes they seem to change and, kind of, regret getting divorced ... well, Mum said to me once ... We'd sometimes be round Mum's for Christmas and Dad used to pop in, it was just like old times – well, I don't know if the boys liked it so much! – and we thought – well, *I* hoped – perhaps they might ... you know ... be getting together again ... But then later, they'd be quarrelling again ... things could get quite nasty. Then Dad says, 'She always was a self-centred bitch. *She* had the affair, *I* didn't' ... Then one day Mum even said *he'd* had affairs. It would go on like that, years and years. We *hated* it – I used to get really upset, I'd say, 'For God's sake, act your age!' My brother says it's *all* a pack of lies on both sides, and he shuts off from it, he doesn't wanna know. But I *do* ... How can I ever get married and make it work ... or any sort of relationship really ... if I can't understand what's happened. Sometimes I think their divorce has ruined my life.

Isobel, 21

This comment illustrates how several children – particularly brothers and sisters – may get different information and may adopt different attitudes towards their parents. Indeed, some siblings had fallen out badly over blame for the divorce, and it may be brothers who commonly try to curtail such arguments.

As already indicated, the parents' mutually contradictory stories could lose them their children's respect:

I used to respect my Dad, but not now ... Not so sure about my Mum. I want to love my Mum *and* my Dad, but I'm finding it really difficult. I just don't trust them any more. I can't trust them to tell the truth.

Simon, 19

I don't *trust* my Dad. He's a pathological liar, he just can't help it. As the years go by, I've come to think he doesn't know he's lying, he's come to believe his own lies ... Like he says to me, 'I didn't meet her until after me and your mother split,' but I *know* now that's not true. But when I say to him, 'I *know* Dad,' he just won't have it, he goes mad! ... I used to respect him, but how can you respect someone who *lies* all the time ... I just want him to tell me the *truth* ... say he's *sorry* ... for how much he's hurt us ... *Mum* tells me the truth, but *he* won't. He's a coward, and I don't respect him for that. He's too scared to tell me the truth.

Kerry, 23

How I see it now ... I've got a mother, but I haven't got a father. There's a man involved in my birth, and he lives with that cow, but he's not my Dad.

Holly, 19

Sometimes, loss of trust and respect for the parents who had formerly represented stability could bring a more generalized insecurity:

I remember saying to my Dad, when I was about 17, I kind of realized, I said, 'I don't think I respect you any more, you and Mum. I used to do what you said, but from now on, if you tell me to do anything, I don't see why I should.' I don't trust any of them any more, and what's worse, I somehow don't trust myself either, in what I think I believe. Over the years they've told so many lies, both of them, or they *seem* like lies ... I'm never going to get married. How can I get married when I don't know the *rules* of marriage. Nobody tells you the rules of marriage.

Isobel, 21

How can *I* make a relationship work if they won't truthfully tell me what went wrong with *theirs*!

Rose, 19

How can it be? I want somebody to explain how my life is ruined for me ... I want to understand how it's happened. Don't I have a right to know.

Barbara, 21

Sadly, even after some parents had 'moved on' by agreeing to stop arguing about who broke up the marriage, their children still felt that before *they* could move on, they wanted a clear acknowledgement of who was to blame for putting them through so much pain and insecurity:

Mum's married now, and Dad's married, and Mum even seems like she's quite friends with Dad now, but I can't stand it! I can't *bear* it that they still do things together. After all it's *his* fault, and *her* fault, 'the bitch'. How can Mum forgive 'em, 'cos I can't forgive 'em 'cos them two have ruined my life.

Kerry, 23

In contrast, Simon (19) said he would no longer mind what the 'true' story was or who was 'to blame', as long as there was *a* story, but unfortunately (by his account) his parents, although prepared to behave amicably in public, would still not agree to share the blame equally:

How I'd like it to be is *nobody's* fault ... but my brother says, 'It's no good thinking that, because it is *somebody's* fault and we need to know whose fault it is,' and I agree with that. But I can't stand all the rows ... Mum says 'It's *Dad's* fault.' Dad says 'It's *her* fault,' and *I* don't care. I'd like them to be friends, and I really like it when they do things together, like they came to my school play ... What I'd like is if they could both have ... a kind of shared story ... one that didn't blame anybody. But when I said that to my Mum ... what I'd like, she said, 'That's not fair ... 'cos ... he left us, I didn't ask him to go. Why should *I* take half the blame just to make *you* feel better.' Mum said to me that Dad going off, *that's* the truth and I've got to learn to live with it.

In this section we have presented some comments from children to illustrate their difficulties in understanding and making sense of their parents' divorce. In various ways, these children express their bewilderment, frustration, anger, sadness, sense of loss, and broader disillusionment and insecurity. What they say illustrates how sometimes – and of course we make no claims as to how often – children's search for 'the truth' of their parents' divorce goes badly wrong, and becomes a 'story' that apparently 'never ends'.

Why the 'never-ending story' never ends

Finally, however, we will discuss why some children's desire to find an end to the 'never-ending story' of their parents' divorce may be fruitless. We will first look more generally at the processes of 'narrative construction', before focusing on some of the particular difficulties faced by children whose parents divorce.

In discussing divorce, Simpson (1998) stresses how narrative construction is bound up with individuals' subjectivity and sense of identity, so that the ability to construct a coherent narrative of past events is an important index of psychological well-being. He contrasts the putting together of 'chronicles' – events arranged in sequence – with the process of narrative construction, which is dynamic, interactive and imaginative, helping individuals to work through changes in their relationships with others or to plan change. Interestingly, Simpson suggests that divorced women tend to engage in the imaginative emotion work of reordering family relationships, while divorced men tend to resist their loss of marital power by clinging to self-justificatory chronicles of past 'wrongs'! Referring to Goffman (1981), Simpson describes how the processes of re-working or re-telling past events may involve 'mind talk', where individuals re-live or engage in imaginary conversations with absent others and plan future action.

Clearly, Simpson's analysis of divorce is relevant to our own small study. We have indicated how some children repeatedly go over the various explanations of divorce given to them by individual parents and by others. Seen in terms of narrative construction, these children appear to be looking for a narrative that will embody answers they can live with, concerning who their parents really are and hence, to some extent, who they themselves are. Ideally, they want parents they can continue to respect; parents who do not tell them 'lies' and who do not 'behave badly' towards them or one another. Presumably, through their questioning, many children do manage to construct a narrative that allows them to 'move on'. However, our small study has highlighted situations where children's attempts at narrative construction have failed, either because the various stories cannot be reconciled, or because the revelations about parents are somehow too shocking.

Paradoxically, a major obstacle to narrative construction lies in the way that the child's 'gaze' – under which the conduct of divorcing parents is scrutinized and evaluated – itself prompts the parents and others to distort the 'truths' that children are seeking. For example, we suspect that the recommendations from counselling that we outlined earlier may prompt parents and others to offer children answers that are below their levels of maturity, and at variance with what they may learn from others or from their own discoveries. Also, parents who have themselves moved on from the divorce, may limit their explanations in order to help their children to do likewise, despite the fact that for children the divorce may remain the 'present'.

Above all, parents may give distorted accounts because the child's gaze forces them to consider the issues of 'fault' and 'blame', which, despite divorce reform, are still very much present in everyday thinking. Although research suggests that children often love and want to be fair to both their parents, the children in our study were still, in what may seem an unsophisticated way, searching for something, or someone, to blame. However, under their children's gaze and indeed under the gaze of society, parents may become defensive or evasive, blaming one another, because there are some 'truths' or versions of events, particularly concerning sexual incompatibility and affairs, they would rather conceal. Mothers may keep quiet to avoid losing their credibility as carers, while fathers tend to view their sexual behaviour as 'their own business', even though a relationship with a new girl-friend often drastically changes their behaviour towards their children. Yet knowledge of their parents' sexual incompatibility, or a concealed affair, might be the key to the understanding that children are seeking.

However, there are deeper and more intractable obstacles to children's attempts at narrative construction. Some appeared to be seeking a narrative that contained an acceptable, unambiguous and permanent truth, yet narrative construction is essentially imaginative and *dynamic*. The level of sophistication of the child's gaze changes with growing maturity, so that answers to the question of why the parents divorced may grow less satisfactory with the passage of time. But also, in attempting to construct their narratives, children must inevitably gain information from various sources, including adults who are themselves engaged in constructing their own narratives of the divorce.

Parents and others may offer incomplete, individually slanted, conflicting and inconsistent or changing stories of 'what really happened'. But rather than being devious or evasive, these stories may represent the parents' own changing versions of divorce, inflected by their mood at that particular moment. Indeed – to adopt a relativist or postmodern stance – the child's quest for 'the truth' about divorce is doomed from the start, because often there is no single permanent version of what caused the divorce that is accepted by both parents and that is consistent with other accounts. Indeed, because both parents and others are engaged in constructing their own narratives, in seeking to find the fixed 'truth' of the divorce, the child is aiming at not one but two or more targets that change continually with the passage of time.

Note

1. Jean Duncombe first encountered the phenomenon of the 'never-ending story' when working for a while as a student counsellor. The case studies come from two focus groups of FE students (eight female; and six female and one male) and follow-ups, for an ESRC project (unfunded 1997) on divorce and stepfamilies, and also from follow-up discussions with volunteers (two male and six female) from family studies seminars (all age 17 to 23). (Both authors are also divorced parents!)

5
Researching Childhood: Time, Memory and Method

Rachel Thomson, Janet Holland, Sheila Henderson, Sheena McGrellis and Sue Sharpe

Introduction

The research from which this paper is drawn set out to document the moral landscapes of almost 2,000 young people aged 11–16 in five contrasting locations in the UK.[1] One aim of the study was to develop an understanding of how social and intergenerational changes have affected the legitimacy of sources of moral authority. We were interested in how young people experience social change and how social changes are manifest in their lives and moral landscapes. At the outset of our study we consulted young people about the aims and methods of the research, exploring the meanings that they attributed to the key terms of our investigation. A clear message emerging from this consultation was that we should ask them only about things they knew. So we needed to find ways of gaining access to what they knew about their own processes of moral development and their understanding of social change. No single method was likely to resolve the conceptual and practical difficulties involved in this, and we developed a number of different approaches. In this paper we describe two of these approaches, discuss the type of data generated, and reflect on their relative success.

The first of these methods concerns the relationship of the individual to the past through memory. We undertook our own memory work as a research team to place ourselves reflexively in the research, translating this into use with our participants by drawing on their early memories in individual interviews. The starting point of the second approach is that ideas of social change are collectively constructed and that an important way in which young people apprehend social change is through accounts offered to them by parents and other adults about *their* experiences in the past. We developed a research assignment for the young people to undertake. They were invited to interview a key adult, asking them to compare the experience they had of being young, with what they saw as the experience of young people today. Both these methods gained access to different dimensions of young people's experiences and knowledge of social change relating to values, but continuities emerged in the data generated by the different methods. (For a different but complementary approach and findings related to time and change in relation to young people, specifically in the family, see Gillies, Holland and Ribbens McCarthy in this volume.)

The exploration of memories: memory work in the research team

Memory work was first developed as a method of social research by the German feminist and scholar Frigga Haug (1987), who used it in the exploration of female sexuality. Haug developed this method of enquiry in conjunction with a theory of the development of the self that argues for the importance of memories of significant events and experiences in the social construction of self. In this way, memory work as a method of enquiry and analysis models the process of identity construction – the self is constructed through reflection on memories. Haug's method has been elaborated by a group of Australian feminist researchers for the purposes of studying emotion and gender. They recommend it as 'a method *par excellence* for exploring the process of the construction of the self ... It gives insight into the way people appropriate the social world and in so doing transform themselves and it' (Crawford *et al.* 1992, 41). Psychological literature supports the assumption that recollection is reconstructive, and strongly influenced by motivation (Target 1998).[2]

We were also interested in memory work as a resource for the study of childhood. The suggestion by James and Prout (1990, 228) that it can be 'hard to separate the location of childhood in time past from its referential position in time future' is endorsed by other commentators who have observed the problems associated with adults exploring a life stage or social category in which they themselves have a significant investment having been in it themselves, possibly recently (Alldred 1998). To some extent the social study of childhood can be seen as inevitably having autobiographical elements which can be productively made visible. As a research team we were concerned to develop a critical awareness of our own investment in the arena of the research, yet to locate these accounts socially and historically to avoid being drawn into a 'timeless culture of childhood' (James and Prout 1990, 228). We believed that by evoking our own memories of being the age of those we were researching we would develop insight into processes of social change and continuity, as well as facilitating a child-centred approach in the research.

Memories of childhood relate to a biographical narrative, yet they also fall into place in a wider historical narrative, a register of social and cultural change that provided the backdrop for all our memories. Although the age range of our research team was less than 30 years, behind our collective memories lay a social history spanning postwar treatment of tubercular children, shell-shocked men and 'fallen women', dramatic educational change, the impact of Americana, rock' n'roll and Elvis on the imaginations of young women, mods (the first and second time round), the atomic bomb, war, troops in and troops out of Northern Ireland, and children's TV culture. This social backdrop formed a cumulative history, pieced together from the traces that it left on the past in individual memories. Our memories were marked by the specificities of our childhood locations: rural, seaside, urban, suburban and nomadic. Each of these spaces had its own moral boundaries and meanings. For example those spaces controlled by adults and other authorities (the home, the school, the church) and those in which children create their own power relations (the playground, the street, the lane, the bedroom).

The young people's memories

The memory work we undertook as a team informed the qualitative methods that we employed in the study. Unsolicited memories and anecdotes of the past were a common characteristic of young people's moral discourse emerging in the research. As we developed an awareness of the way in which our own values were implicated in our developing selves, we became interested in exploring similar questions with the young people in the study, wanting them to reflect more systematically on their own past and on early memories. In the individual interviews (the final stage of the study) we asked young people to describe their earliest memory of something being wrong or bad, and something being right or good, and then to consider why it was that they remembered this particular event or experience. The discussion of the memory formed the basis of their subsequent reflections in the interview on the process of their own moral development.

Psychological research has identified *implicit* or procedural memory (non-conscious knowledge of how to do things, including how to relate to people, the quality or shape of experiences) and *explicit* memory (autobiographical memory which can be reproduced as narratives of events). This research further suggests that implicit memory may be encoded and retained from infancy in contrast to explicit memory which does not become durable until three or four years of age (Sandler and Fonagy 1997; Weiskrantz 1997). The majority of young people in our study, consistent with these findings, recalled memories between the ages of four and seven. Verification of age was established through key moments of transition such as starting school, the arrival of a new sibling or, for example, the presence of a birthday cake. In general young people found it more difficult to recall memories of something being right or good, and frequently needed prompting in this task. In contrast memories of something wrong or bad seemed more easily recalled. Here we draw primarily on the latter. We ask why things are remembered and find themes in what is remembered: power and powerlessness, transgressing boundaries and memories of identity.

Why remember?

Crawford *et al.* (1992), following Haug, suggest that 'what is remembered is remembered because it is in some way problematic or unfamiliar, in need of review. The actions and episodes remain because they were significant then and remain significant now' (38). We were hoping that in asking for early memories of right and wrong we would be able to tap similarly unresolved, significant episodes, and so gain a different perspective on the young people's childhoods from what might be expected in interviews. The accounts of some of our participants were also consistent with this interpretation. These young people reflected that they had unresolved feelings associated with their early memories of wrongdoing, which were most frequently expressed as guilt. A number of young people recalled memories of blaming others for their own misdemeanours, generally those with less power than themselves, most often younger siblings. For some, the unresolved nature of their transgression continues to weigh on them:

Judy:	I can think of one thing, it felt really wrong at the time but it seems a bit silly now. I remember going into this, my mum's friend owned a big sweet shop and there were all different kinds of um, elaborate sweets and things, and I bought, I hadn't bought, I was choosing some, and I had them in my bag and I put one in my mouth but it was disgusting and I didn't know what to do with it so I just took it out of my mouth and I put it back in the sweets (laughs) which I didn't mean to do but I was very young then, very young.
Interviewer:	How old do you think you were?
Judy :	Um – I must have been five probably. I always remember that, I don't know why, it was a pink egg, kind of, it looked like a mini egg but it had, I don't know, cinnamon or something on it and – uurrh – it was horrible.
Interviewer:	And was anyone else there?
Judy :	Nobody saw, I kept it quite secretive and I just like put it in the thing, and, I still bought all the other sweets, well, my dad did anyway.
Interviewer:	Did you tell anyone?
Judy:	No, (laugh) I didn't want to because also it was my mum's friend's shop and my mum was like chatting to her and so I couldn't exactly say, oh, mum, I just stuck a sweet in there by the way, but no, I never told anybody.

Interviewer:	But did you realize that it was wrong at the time, or later on?
Judy:	When I got home I felt really, really guilty and I wanted to say something but I thought if I said something I'd just get into so much trouble so.

yw,13/14, S7, ind. int.[3]

Other memories suggest a collective process of memory construction, with others such as parents and family sharing an investment in the memory. One young woman's first memory of doing something wrong is that of taking her feeding bottle into school, transgressing the line between the worlds of home and school, of babyhood and childhood:

Adele:	In P1 I took a wee bottle to school, just, you know, a teat bottle.
Interviewer:	And how old were you then?
Adele:	Four.
Interviewer:	Four years old. That's a really early memory.
Adele:	I remember that.
Interviewer:	How did you know what you had done was wrong?
Adele:	'Cos everyone keeps remembering me about it.

yw, 15/16, S4, ind. int.

The social and interactive processes of memory construction and their relationship to the construction of identity are neatly summed up in the phrase 'everyone keeps remembering me about it'. The attention and the meaning making that can attend the social transgressions of the young make it unsurprising that the moral lessons of the memories recalled by young people in our study were ambiguous or layered.

What is remembered?

There were definite themes that recurred in the memories that young people recounted.

Memories of power and powerlessness

For Crawford *et al.*, all memories are marked by emotion, but emotion was particularly charged in some young people's memories and relative positions of power and powerlessness were marked. In a couple of cases young people had memories of emotional and physical violence within the home, both between parents and from parents towards themselves or siblings. These kinds of memories make the vulnerability of children to the actions and feelings of adults painfully clear while also hinting at the damaging legacy of such relationships in the longer term. More common were memories of conflict between siblings. These conflicts could involve very strong, and often violent feelings.

In a couple of cases young people recalled memories where they got into trouble for being deliberately destructive. These examples are particularly interesting as they provide a picture of the child as powerful, enjoying their own ability to cause havoc and in the following case to cause conflict between parents:

> *Karen:*   Yeah. I remember my mum getting on with me for cutting the washing on the line – cutting my dad's shirts up and the towels and sheets and all. And I thought 'Oh, she wants me to, she thinks they're too big.'
> *Interviewer:* What age were you when you did that?
> *Karen:*   Three. (Laughs)
> *Interviewer:* Mmm.
> *Karen:*   I was a wile wee evil child ...
> *Interviewer:* So whenever you were doing it did you know it was wrong?
> *Karen:*   Yeah, I did.
>
> yw, 13/14, S2, ind. int.

Transgressing boundaries

Another recurrent theme concerns memories relating to space and learning the social meaning of the spatial boundaries of the child's world (Gordon *et al.* 2000). The example given earlier of taking a bottle to school vividly captures the intersection of a series of boundaries: home and school, the private and public, babyhood and childhood. Other memories concern spatial boundaries in a more literal way, going to places that are ruled 'out of bounds' by adults. In some cases these spaces were considered to be dangerous and so unsuitable for children at all. In others, they are spaces that are ruled out of bounds in certain circumstances and at certain times. The complexity of when and with whom it might be acceptable to go to the park, for example, gives some insight into the intense negotiations about freedom, supervision and consultation to which children are subject:

> *Cynthia:* ... I was about nine and I still wasn't allowed up the park on my own and I had to ask my mum if I could go with my friends and their dad and my mum says that would be all right but it turned out that their dad couldn't go. So, I was asking my friends if I could go back up to the house for a minute and tell my mum there was no adult going to be there. But they said it would be all right (all) just go on so I kept asking them and they convinced me not to, so I just went up the park and got into trouble later for it.
>
> yw, 12/13, S4, ind. int.

Questions of space and the transgression of space also arise in a more domestic context. In these cases children tell stories of the consequences of undertaking the wrong actions (usually play) in the wrong places (inside the house). So for example, vases fall from mantelpieces, bleach spills onto carpets, mud pies are brought into the house and playing with footballs results in windows being broken.

Perhaps the most common theme to characterize these recalled memories was that of stealing: stealing money from parents and other trusted adults, stealing food (often chocolate) from shops, or a combination in the form of spending the change on sweets when entrusted with money to go to the shops. Again, these acts can be understood as transgressions of boundaries, but this time the boundary between the world and belongings of the child and that of the adult. If one of the defining features of early childhood for young people in the West is economic dependence, then we could argue that in taking money or goods from adults, children are also taking or disrupting key elements of their authority. The lesson learned from episodes remembered as stealing by young people, is that while it is acceptable to be given to by an adult, it is not acceptable to take:

Shannon: I was really little whenever I stole something. I really wanted this little rose brooch that my mum wouldn't let me have it – in the shop. I didn't know right from wrong really so I just thought 'Put it in my pocket'. I didn't know what money meant really, and when I got home and showed it to my mum and she started screaming at me. I realized then I had done something wrong really wrong, and I never did it again, so

Interviewer: What age were you then?

Shannon: I must have been about three or four, probably about four I'd say. But I've never stolen, never again.

Interviewer: So you didn't actually know whenever you were doing it that it was wrong?

Shannon: No I didn't but I could tell, like – I was wondering why my mum wouldn't let me have it because I was used to getting my own way most of the times. When I got home I realized whenever she was shouting. In the end I got it, but I learned never to steal again.

yw, 13/14, S1, ind. int.

Memories and identity

All of the memories that we collected from young people in our study had significance for them in terms of their contemporary identities, even if this was simply in terms of the immediate impact of the recalling and retelling of that particular memory. Some young people had engaged more obviously in 'identity work' in relation to their memories than others. For example, the young woman who recalled herself as a 'wile evil child' was currently enjoying an identity as a wile evil teenager and her memory of chopping up the sheets was consistent with her current rejection of conventional femininity.

In a number of cases young people recounted memories for us that had great biographical significance for them, marking key moments, turning points or moments of understanding.[4] The memory recalled by the following young man, both concerns an early experience of punishment, but more profoundly also marks a critical moment for him in the recognition that the beating that his father gave to him and his sisters was itself wrong. Significantly he has no memory of what he did to warrant the punishment:

Devon:	Four is definitely my earliest memory – because I remember my birthday cake – and er – that was – well I don't know if it was when it started but that was when I first, when me and my sisters, when we first started erm, getting hit when we was naughty, sort of thing and erm, so yeah, I guess that really my first memory, something being wrong.
Interviewer:	Do you remember what you did that was wrong?
Devon:	No.
Interviewer:	Yeah. But you remember getting belted for it.
Devon:	Mm. That sort of stayed throughout most of life. I remember the hits, but I don't actually remember what I did.

ym, 19, ind. int.

While it is impossible to understand the state of mind or moral awareness of the four year old, this memory plays a crucial part in the biography of the 19 year old who has tried to come to terms with the experience of domestic violence.

In asking young people to remember how they first understood that something was wrong, we did not distinguish between observations of their own behaviour and their interpretations of the behaviour of others. As we have shown above, there is an enduring ambiguity in the notion that something is wrong. While you may get punished for doing it, you may also be rewarded indirectly, and while it may be wrong for you to do it this may be a conditional rather than absolute state of affairs. It is where young people's memories of something being wrong relate primarily to the behaviour of others, particularly the adults around them, that this ambiguity is most intense.

So, not only are memories of the past central to identities of the present, but it is the moral complexity of these memories and the difficulty in resolving the tensions and allegiances that they represent that make them so central. In that sense identities can be understood as an accumulation of unresolved memory.

Time in social relationships[5]

It was clear from both our own memory work and the memories cited by the young people that the construction of memory is more than an individual process, involving family members, and relived and restructured in the light of experience, changing identities and particular audiences. If we move from a focus on the memories of individuals to an exploration of shared memories or understandings of social change we find the collective dimension of the construction of memory more explicit.

Evidence for change

Conversations with older people clearly informed young people's views of change although some of these views were more grounded in evidence than others. In some cases young people drew on particular conversations that they had had with adult relatives in order to document change, in this case around the etiquette of fighting:

> *Kerry*: I mean, my mum says like when she was little she was always taught not to fight; now girls they just scrap and scrap and that's the end of it.
>
> yw, 13/14, S5, ffg

In other cases young people contrasted their own views with those of an older generation, this was particularly the case in areas such as racism and homophobia where young people tended to distinguish themselves from the prejudices of the past:

> *Sandy*: My Grandad is like old, and he calls them like chocolate drops and that and I tell him 'Don't call them that – like that. I don't, I just call them black – I wouldn't call them Paki or anything.'
>
> yw, 14/15, S7, mxfg

In the following example observation led to comments about the weakening of the marriage bond:

> *Lauire*: The grannies and grandas are all together still and nowadays there's loads of people who split up.
> *Stella*: I think they used to stay together for longer definitely. Now they're splitting up after a year or two years.
>
> yw, 13/14, S4, mxfg

Many discussions of change were less grounded in direct evidence drawing primarily on popular discourse. References to 'the olden days' commonly arose during discussions of change in sexual mores, and while change was generally assumed, the exact nature of this change and the extent to which past 'problems' had been resolved were far from clear. Young people tended to debate these points among themselves:

> *Lorraine:* There's more [sex] around now than what it used to be in the old days – they never used to think of it till they got married.
> *Lola:* Well, yes, they did 'cos look how like – many old people like they've got about 13 children. (Laughter and indistinct comments)
>
> yw, 14/15, S6, ffg

These examples show that it is difficult for young people to comment on abstract questions of social change since this is beyond their experience. Young people themselves suggested that what they did know about social change was shaped by accounts of the changing conditions of childhood from parents and other adults. We hoped that the 'research assignment' would be a method that would enable us to capture these conversations and young people's reactions to them. We asked young people to interview an adult about the changes and continuities between their own childhood and that of the young person, noting which of those changes were positive and which negative, using a simple interview schedule. The young people were also asked for their own opinions. The research assignments were voluntary for all those who participated in the questionnaire phase of the study, and a total of 274 assignments were returned.[6]

An analysis of the research assignments identified a range of themes that characterize the comments of adults and young people: education, family relationships, childhood and youth, 'the good life', and threaded throughout the themes were changes in the situation and experience of women. Not surprisingly, we found that there were strong continuities between the comments of the adults and those of the young people, but there were also important differences. Here we report on changes observed by adults and young people.

Education

The strongest themes to emerge related to education. Adults talked about how schooling had changed since their own childhood particularly in relation to punishment. Teachers today were regarded as less strict, commanding less authority and no longer able to administer corporal punishment using the strap and the cane. The overall consensus was that education had changed for the better and educational standards and opportunities had improved. Adults also considered that education is more important to young people today since in the past school was considered far less relevant than getting a job, and that many young people would have been expected to start earning and contributing to the family economy at an earlier age.

In line with the adult responses 18 per cent of the young people mentioned changes in corporal punishment in schools. The majority of these (75 per cent) felt that doing away with the cane was a good thing, and their responses reflected a principled rejection of violence and physical punishment which we found through other methods used in the research, as well as the view that education should not be carried out in an atmosphere of terror. A few felt that corporal punishment was a good thing and lamented its demise, feeling that it might prevent trouble at school, and deter classroom disruption and bullying. Almost a third overall took up the adult view that educational standards and provision had improved considerably. While some young people took up the adult discourse that education is more important today for employment, they were more likely than adults to reflect on the increased pressures on young people for educational achievement, reinforced by the absence of jobs for those leaving school, even when they have qualifications.

Family relationships and values

Adults talked about changes in the family and family relationships. Key themes related to changing gender roles, the break-up of the nuclear family with higher divorce rates and increasing numbers of single parent families, and a common statement was that 'divorce was almost unheard of then'. Views on the parenting relationship differed: some adults talked of a decline in the authority of parents as well as in the quality of parenting, noting that children show less respect for and obedience to their parents than in an earlier generation. But they also talked about an increasingly relaxed and open relationship between parents and children, in particular welcoming greater communication about previously taboo subjects such as sex and relationships. Here respondents developed a wider theme about a decline in family relationships and security, and invoked a 'golden era' in which family bonds were more enduring and family was viewed more positively than today. Many suggested that families were closer and stronger in the past with more shared time and activities.

A smaller proportion of young people than in the case of education took up the adult perspective on declining family values and relationships (6 per cent). Here they would also talk about the deterioration and breakdown of the family unit, increases in unmarried mothers, divorce and single parent families. But this discourse was re-articulated from the perspective of young people themselves, and they emphasized how children suffer when families fall apart: 'children get really traumatized by it'. Linked to this was the view that communications between parents and their children were failing, preventing young people from making informed decisions about sexual relationships and drug-taking. But an equal proportion of young people talked about positive changes in family life emphasizing increased and improved communications between parents and their children as a result of a decline in parental authority. Young people suggested that this brought families closer together and that families today are more loving and spend more time together.

Childhood and youth

A strong theme in adults' observations of social change was that young people have greater freedom than they enjoyed in their own youth (27 per cent of adults in the assignments drew on this discourse). Such freedom includes the freedom to go out, to return later and to socialize, with many noting that young women have made particular gains in this area. Freedom was also talked of in terms of freedom *from* other responsibilities such as earning in order to contribute to the family economy, domestic chores and childcare. Adults also regarded children today as having a stronger voice or place in society, in contrast to admonition to 'be seen but not heard' when they were young. Paradoxically, while young people were seen to have fewer responsibilities than in the past they were also considered to be 'growing up faster'. Here some adults mentioned changes such as girls wearing make-up at a younger age, but most focused on shifts in the etiquette of intimate relationships with young people engaging in romantic and sexual relationships at a younger age than in the past, when it was observed that children matured more slowly.

Generally adults considered youth to be increasingly troublesome (24 per cent), that the misdemeanours of youth had grown more serious, and there was a sense of the normality of such activities as drug use and crime for young people. This was linked to the demise in traditional sources of authority such as the policeman and the father, and here adult accounts constructed a past world of innocence, where young people did little more than cat call, the horrors of teenage sex, drugs and violence were unknown and there was a basic respect for law and order.

There was nostalgic talk of playing games such as hop-scotch, skipping, marbles, building camps, fishing, walking and of passing time reading and knitting. They talked of 'making our own fun' noting that young people today are involved in more organized forms of leisure (swimming, leisure centres, clubs etc.) and that they spend more time inside the house watching TV or playing games than the outdoor leisure activities of the past. Some also suggested that perceptions of young people's leisure activities had shifted, so that what was viewed as harmless fun in the past such as hanging around on street corners was now viewed as trouble by the police.

Young people's views on the changing nature of youth echoed those of adults but also differed in interesting ways. Not surprisingly many young people welcomed greater freedoms of movement and choice, stressing a cultural shift whereby young people now have rights, should be treated fairly and have supports and outlets to talk about abuse and other problems. However some argued that these greater freedoms were a social ill, suggesting that if young people are allowed out later and at a younger age there will be more crime, vandalism and teenage pregnancies, tending to attribute these changes to an erosion of parental authority. Yet also evident, if less prevalent, was a view that young people in fact have less freedom than in the past. Here parents, faced with an increasingly unsafe society, were forced to be more protective than formerly, keeping children inside and monitoring their activities in fear of paedophiles and abduction. As one young person noted, 'I think it's a shame we don't have much freedom but I understand why'.

'The good life'

Comments on social changes that affect the quality of life were common. Adults' views on such changes were again mixed, emphasizing advances as well as loss. On a positive note they identified the contribution of new technologies to the quality of life. Improvements in health care, housing and in a few cases the welfare state were seen as contributing to longer and healthier lives.

Some adults observed changes in styles, fashion, music, money and food. Often these were linked to wider themes around consumerism and commercialism that developed a more negative picture of decline and loss in the quality of life. For example, some stressed the importance of having the 'right' clothes and designer labels, especially for young people who, they argued, have more material possessions, take money for granted and fail to appreciate the value of things. This more general theme of commercialization, where all that matters is having the 'right' consumer goods, was contrasted with a past golden age where, because material possessions were fewer and less important, more precious aspects of human life were valued. 'Money was short so simple things in life were very important, e.g friendship.' From this perspective advances in technology were seen as accelerating the pace of life, increasing social alienation and stress: 'there seems to be more of everything: money, cars, houses, problems, people, temptations, pressure etc.' This is contrasted with a past characterized by community spirit where 'shopkeepers knew everybody, as did the policeman who patrolled the village'.

Like adults, young people took up the theme of progress citing advances in medicine, science, technology, housing, wages, community facilities and job opportunities. Technological advance was seen to have made life easier (domestic appliances) as well as more fun (computers, TVs etc.). Improvements in transport were a focus, with young people reflecting positively on not having to walk everywhere. Increased choice in the form of improved shops and a wider range of material goods and personal styles was also seen as an advance. In particular young people talked about improvements to leisure with TVs, computers, clubs and holidays abroad, noting that they would have been bored in the past without the facilities that they enjoy today. However some young people talked about the social ills that such 'progress' can bring. Again they developed ideas about the increasing materialism and consumerism: 'the world is full of greedy people'. Unlike adults young people discussed the impact of pollution on the environment, and the consequences of increased car use including asthma, accidents and the loss of countryside. Here young people also linked an increased pace of life with greater stress, more intolerance and increased selfishness. They drew on adult talk of the loss of community spirit, which 'means everybody is out there for themselves and are less willing to help others'.

A conversation between adults and children

We can see from this analysis that discussions of social change on the part of both adults and children tend to take place within competing discourses of progress and decline, and discussions of change are marked by contradictions between the two perspectives. Each of the areas of significance are seen as double-edged swords, the legacy of which can be seen as positive or negative. These contradictions capture some of the complexity of the issues involved, including differing interests of participants in the discussion (Scott 2000).

By seeing the consideration of the meaning of social change as a 'conversation' between adults and children it is possible to make sense of the contradictions between competing discourses of progress and decline, and the shifting balance of consensus and dissent between the two groups. It is clear that there are many areas in which young people and adults articulate similar ideas, for example views on the negative legacy of consumerism or on advances in education. If we regard such views as formed 'in conversation' then we can make sense of their ideas, recognizing both the areas of consensus and those of difference as being 'negotiated' between the parties. So when young people break from the consensus discourse shared with a parent to make a particular point about the impact of divorce on communication with children, the lack of physical freedom of some modern childhoods or the environmental consequences of some area of technological advance, they can be understood as making an intervention into negotiations over shared understandings of social change and the parenting practices that structure their relationship with their parents.

We suggest that the childhoods of the past are active in the present, and the childhood values of adults are made available to young people through their own parenting practice, and that this process is negotiated. The fact that memories of these childhoods are contradictory, recalling both a 'golden era' and the 'bad old days' can then be understood partly as the outcome of these negotiations. Brian Turner has recently talked about a 'generational habitus' where the cultural landscape of the 1960s may continue to dominate the tastes of today's teenagers (Turner 1999). Parenting practices could be seen to be one of the prime locations for the contestation of a generational habitus (Scott 2000). Young people may cede to, resist and/or transform these values in the negotiation process. As one of the young women in our study observed:

Kim: Parents nowadays try to, they don't realize this is the 90s, it isn't the 70s or the 60s. But they always put it back and say this is what it is.

yw, 14/15, S1, ffg

Conclusion

The analysis reported in this paper is an initial approach to understanding different temporal processes that are involved in the construction of young people's moral landscapes, and the methods we employed had different purposes in the context of the research. The two types of memory invoked here (ours and the young people's) can be regarded as providing an insight into particular childhoods located in time and space, and so bringing the past into the present. Here we find common currency in both sets of memories which include specifics such as stealing sweets, and cutting things up, and more general themes of guilt and of transgression between adult and child spaces. There were also differences both within and between our memories in the research team, and the young people's memories relating to time, age and social and geographical location. Just as these memories bring the past into the present, they also bring the present into the past, in that memory and autobiography involve a reconstruction of the past from the perspective of the present, and are important in the construction of contemporary identities.

We can also see the social through the social and cultural environment in which the individual is immersed, and in the construction of the memory in the social relations of both past and present. An example here is Adele's mother 'always remembering' her about the wee teat bottle taken to school. In the research assignments we can read through the narratives to the adults' experiences which can compare with those evoked through the memory methods. But we suggest that in the conversations between young people and adults about time past and present we can see a negotiation of meaning and relationships between the generations. In many instances in the findings from the research assignment we see both adults and children drawing on similar discourses of progress and decline. But the younger and older generations each place their own inflection on the articulation of the discourses, and in this way meaning and understandings of practices and relationships are negotiated.

Both these approaches point to the impossibility of disentangling substantive observations about time, memory and change from the methodological dimensions of their generation. Moreover, the theoretical underpinnings of memory work and auto/biographical analysis suggests that the substantive and the methodological are necessarily mutually dependent. We can never know about the past independently of biography, and individual biographies exist within historically situated networks of complementary and dissonant story-telling (Bruner 1987; Plummer 1995). Liz Stanley observes that 'from one person we can recover social processes and social structure, networks, social change and so forth, for people are located in a social and cultural environment which constitutes and shapes not only *what* we see, but also *how* we see it' (1993, 45, original italics). Children and young people are not exempt from these auto/biographical processes, and while as adult researchers we may seek reflexivity and methodological invention, we suggest that it is neither possible, nor ultimately desirable to completely disentangle past, present and future in the social analysis of childhood.

Notes

1. The study *Youth Values: Identity, Diversity and Social Change* was funded by the Economic and Social Research Council from 1996–9 on the programme *Children 5–16: Growing up into the 21st century* (Ref. L129251020).
2. There is a large and complex psychological literature on memory processes, and the recent controversy associated with 'recovered memory' (or 'false memory syndrome') has stimulated research relating this body of knowledge to the after-effects of trauma, particularly on memory (Pally 1997; Sandler and Fonagy 1997).
3. Extracts from the young people are labelled young woman or man (yw, ym), age, school number (in Northern Ireland: School 1, Turnmill, mixed religion, working class; School 2, Knowlands High, integrated, mixed class; School 3, St Saviour's, Catholic, working class; School 4, Castleglen, Protestant, working class; in England: School 5, North Park, ethnically homogeneous, working class, deprived estate; School 6, South Park, ethnically diverse, working class, inner city; School 7, Forest Green, ethnically homogeneous, middle class, commuter belt; School 8, Crossways, ethnically homogeneous, mixed class, rural) and source of data, mixed (mx) or single sex (m/f) focus group or interview (fg, ind. int.).
4. We have explored the concept of the 'critical moment' in more detail in Thomson *et al.* (2002).
5. Our thanks are due to Isabel Walter who analyzed and wrote up the data on young people's assignments, and to Helen Membry who prepared the coding frame.
6. The majority of adults interviewed for the research assignments were in the 30–50 age group, with 11 over 60 and 28 between 20 and 30. 146 were the young people's mothers, 44 their fathers and the rest mostly female relatives (grandmothers, aunts), friends or unspecified females.

Part II
Family and Household Formation

6
Young Motherhood: Family Transmission or Family Transitions?

Sarah Cheesbrough

Introduction

The high rates of young motherhood in Britain, compared to neighbouring European countries, have attracted particular policy attention in recent years with a focus on identifying those considered to be at risk of young motherhood and evaluating programmes to reduce rates of teenage conceptions (Social Exclusion Unit 1999). Although the circumstances of young mothers may be as much due to pre-existing factors as early child-bearing itself (Coley and Chase-Lansdale 1998), young mothers in Britain tend to have lower educational and occupational prospects (Hobcraft and Kiernan 1999), may be reliant for some years on social security benefits (Social Exclusion Unit 1999) and live in poorer housing (Allen and Bourke Dowling 1998). In searching for the precursors of young motherhood, British longitudinal studies confirm the relationship between the family formation patterns of a mother and her daughter (Kiernan 1997a; Maughan and Lindelow 1997). After taking this, and other background factors into account, some studies have also found living apart from a natural parent in childhood to be associated with becoming a young mother (Kiernan 1992; Manlove 1997; Ní Bhrolcháin *et al.* 2000).

There are two temporal limitations to earlier British longitudinal data on family structure and young motherhood. First, much of the current evidence comes from the National Child Development Survey (NCDS) based on a cohort of individuals born in 1958, only 10 per cent of whom experienced family disruption (Ferri 1984). As rates of divorce have increased, families who experience disruption have become a less select group and social policy responses may have cushioned some of the economic impact of lone parenthood (Richards 1997; Rodgers 1996). Also, as the experience becomes more common children may experience less stigma and individuals may be better informed of the potential impact on the family (Beck and Beck-Gernsheim 1995; Furstenberg 1987). In turn, we might expect to find fewer associations between childhood family disruption and potentially disadvantaged adult outcomes among more recent cohorts. However, evidence of educational attainment among successive British cohorts who experienced family disruption has not provided empirical support for this proposition (Ely *et al.* 1999).

Second, the NCDS only observed family structure at the surveys conducted at ages seven, 11 and 16. As information on the timing of changes in family structure between survey stages was not collected, analysis of the study has been restricted to these snapshot measures, either comparing family structure at 16 (Kiernan 1992; Power and Matthews 1997) or looking at children who have changed family structure between the three survey stages (Cherlin *et al.* 1995; Elliott and Richards 1991; Ní Bhrolcháin *et al.* 1995). More recently, it has been possible to use retrospective accounts of childhood family disruption, although these were not collected until the cohort members were aged 33 (Kiernan 1997b).

Cross-sectional measures create difficulties when examining the life course of those experiencing family transitions. For example, if we considered all those living in a lone-mother family at 16, we would conflate the outcomes for those who experienced parental separation with those born to a lone mother or those who experienced multiple transitions. Evidence from the US shows that young adult outcomes can vary substantially according to the pathway followed to particular family types and more attention should be paid to prospectively collected measures of both the type and timing of family transition experienced in childhood (Martinson and Wu 1992; Wojtkiewicz 1992; Wu and Martinson 1993).

This research uses the 1970 British Birth Cohort Study (BCS70). The BCS70 sampled all those born in Britain in the week 5–11 April 1970 totalling around 16,000 births. Children who migrated to Britain were added at later stages if they were born in the sample week. After that, four subsequent surveys of the entire cohort were conducted at ages five, ten, 16 and 26 (Despotidou and Shepherd 1998). This analysis has two aims: first, to examine the extent to which associations between maternal age at first birth and early child-bearing persist among this cohort; and second, to consider the different probabilities of becoming a young mother according to both family structure at 16 and the precise sequence of family structures experienced during childhood. This is possible because as well as collecting family structure at each survey stage, the BCS70 contained questions regarding changes in parenting arrangements between waves of the survey. This enables us to consider whether our conclusions about the outcomes of family disruption would vary according to the measure used.

The chapter begins with a review of the processes by which experiencing family transitions may be a precursor of young motherhood. Descriptive statistics are then presented showing the levels and types of family disruption experienced by those remaining in the study at 16. In the following section, the birth rates among women in the study are compared, first according to the woman's mother's age at her first birth and then according to whether the woman experienced family disruption. Here, we can examine whether the observed rate of young motherhood is higher among those who experienced disruption and analyze the size of any differences in comparison to the variation according to the woman's mother's age at her first birth.

The remainder of the chapter uses multivariate analysis to consider the associations between different types of family disruption and young motherhood after taking into account a selection of family background factors. Previous research has demonstrated the extent to which controlling for these background factors modifies the strength of the association between family disruption and a range of possibly negative outcomes (Elliot and Richards 1991; Furstenberg and Teitler 1994; Ní Bhrolcháin *et al.* 2000). The results of the multivariate analysis are then used to predict the likelihood of young motherhood according to maternal age at first birth or type of family disruption after taking other family characteristics into account.

Family transitions and young motherhood

Family transitions may act as a precursor of young motherhood through both economic and social processes which create an environment that may affect the educational career and aspirations of a young woman or predispose her to early sexual activity. Lone mothers in Britain are more likely to experience financial hardship (Bradshaw and Chen 1997; Millar 1992) than two-parent families, and those who repartner may still be financially vulnerable because stepfamilies are often larger than first families and may have child support obligations to a partner's previous children (Ferri and Smith 1998; Haskey 1994). Apart from economic pressures, lone mothers in the US have been found to be less restrictive in their attitudes to pre-marital sex and may provide a positive role model to a daughter for raising a child without the natural father (McLanahan 1988; Thornton and Camburn 1987). Separation may precipitate a two- to three-year period of lower parental control and discipline for the child as the parent adjusts (Hetherington and Clingempeel 1992; McLanahan and Sandefur 1994) but also maternal involvement with children has been found to fall after repartnering when children and the new stepfather may compete for the attention of the mother (Furstenberg and Cherlin 1991; Hanson *et al.* 1998).

Any type of change in household family structure may bring about conflict, and conflict around transitions has been shown to be more relevant to the child's response and outcomes than the actual type of parenting change (Cherlin *et al.* 1995; Rutter 1981). In particular, daughters who have spent longer durations in a lone-mother family may react negatively to the arrival of a stepfather because they feel that their previous status and contribution to the household has been undermined (Weiss 1979). Even if a transition does not involve conflict, the requirement to adapt to a new family structure may still put a strain on the daughter. In the US, the sheer number of parenting changes in childhood has been found to be associated with an elevated risk of a non-marital birth regardless of the nature of those changes (Wu and Martinson 1993). In all, the association between family disruption and young motherhood may vary according to the number and type of transitions that occurred in childhood. The next section describes some of this variation among the 1970 British Cohort Study members.

Family transitions among the 1970 cohort

The BCS70 has experienced higher levels of attrition than the 1958 NCDS, falling to a response rate of 72 per cent at age 16 and 58 per cent at the age 26 survey (Despotidou and Shepherd 1998). By the later stages of the study there are small biases against those from disadvantaged backgrounds as well as those who have experienced family disruption or moved house many times (Shepherd 1997). Given the relevance of these characteristics to the research, the descriptive statistics concerning childhood family transition are reweighted using inverse probability weights constructed by the author based on regression analysis of the probability of response to the parental interview at 16. The analysis of rates of young motherhood is also reweighted according to the probability of response to both the parental interview at 16 and the survey at age 26. Reweighting has the effect of slightly, but consistently, increasing the estimates of the proportion of children not living with both natural parents at every age and, similarly, a small increase in the estimated proportion of women who have become young mothers.

Nearly 92 per cent of the 1970 cohort were born to married parents. Most of the remainder were born to lone mothers (nearly 6 per cent) or co-habiting parents (2 per cent).[1] By the time they were 16, just over 28 per cent of the cohort had experienced some change in residential parenting, most commonly parental separation and then possibly repartnering. Those born to a lone mother were most likely to experience transitions, including nearly 30 per cent spending at least some time with the natural father living in the household.[2]

Figure 6.1 shows the distribution of family structures among children not living with both biological parents for each year from birth to their 16th birthday. Between 1970 and 1980, the annual number of children under 16 affected by parental divorce doubled as both divorce rates increased and couples divorced at shorter durations of marriage (Haskey 1990). Among this cohort, over 40 per cent of those children who experienced parental separation had done so before their sixth birthday, and 72 per cent before their 11th. This cohort was more likely to experience family disruption

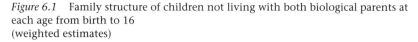

Figure 6.1 Family structure of children not living with both biological parents at each age from birth to 16 (weighted estimates)

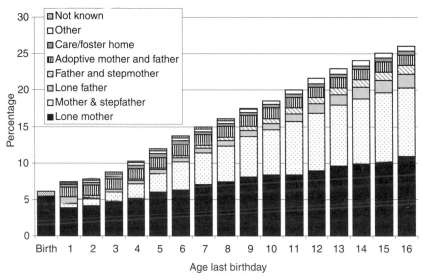

Total sample: unweighted 9,467, weighted 17,316

than their predecessors in the 1958 NCDS, it was likely to be at an earlier age and, in turn, their mother was more likely to repartner during their childhood. By the time they were 16, 10 per cent of the cohort were living in stepfather families and 11 per cent in lone-mother families. Very few children were in their father's custody, particularly at younger ages, and one-third of those that were had experienced their mother's death rather than parental separation. Whilst there was no gender difference in the likelihood of experiencing family disruption, boys were slightly over-represented in lone-father or stepmother families formed after parental separation.

The pathways through family transitions

As the number of people experiencing childhood family transition grows, we need to pay more attention to the variety of experiences within this group rather than making a dichotomous distinction between those living in 'intact' or 'non-intact' families. Table 6.1 adapts a format used by Wu and Martinson with the US National Survey of Families and Households (Martinson and Wu 1992; Wu and Martinson 1993) to examine childhood family trajectories in the 1970 study. Looking at the frequency distribution of the sequence of family structures, over 86 per cent of the cohort either grew up with both biological parents, or moved to a lone-mother and then possibly a stepfather family after parental separation (with some mothers recalling temporary periods of reconciliation before the separation became permanent). The remaining 13 per cent had a wide diversity of experiences. A further 21 sequences are required to classify just over 10 per cent of the sample and the remaining 3 per cent experienced very unusual or unique trajectories. For information, Table 6.1 contains both weighted estimates and unweighted frequencies of family sequences.

Types of family trajectory used in the analysis of the likelihood of young motherhood

Table 6.1 contains 26 different family trajectories classifying 97 per cent of the sample but many of these trajectories involved a small number of individuals. For the analysis of data to predict the chances of young motherhood, the sample was restricted to women who took part in both the age 16 and 26 surveys and, given the smaller numbers involved, it was necessary to collapse the categories of family transition. Table 6.2 presents the categories of family structure at 16 and Table 6.3 summarizes the most common sequences of family structure that were used in the multivariate analysis.

In classifying the sequences of family structure, if a child had experienced the death of either parent they were identified separately, regardless of their family trajectory, given the different circumstances and adaptations found to ensue bereavement compared to parental separation (Cherlin *et al.* 1995). Also, children who had ever been placed in statutory or foster care, even if they had returned to their natural family by age 16, are classified as one group in order to distinguish those people who are likely to have had some of the most disadvantaged childhoods. Among the other trajectories, girls who lived in a stepfather family which ever contained stepsiblings are identified separately from the majority living in stepfather families who did not. Children born to a lone mother experienced a great diversity of trajectories. Here, those who went on to live with both natural parents continuously until age 16, who comprised about 20 per cent of the group, are separated from those who followed other pathways.

Table 6.4 gives the frequencies for the other factor of interest in this analysis, the age at which the mother of the cohort member began child-bearing herself. Around 1970, the majority of women began their child-bearing by their early 20s and nearly one quarter of this cohort were born to mothers who had their first child when they were teenagers. Again, both the weighted and unweighted frequencies are presented in all three tables.

Young motherhood among the cohort

By the late 1980s, fertility behaviour had changed considerably; the teenage birth rate had fallen and the mean age at first birth was rising towards 25

Table 6.1 Frequency distribution of family trajectories from birth to 16 (among the BCS70)

Family trajectory	Weighted %	Unweighted %
Main sequences		
(bio-m, bio-f)	70.6	73.1
(bio-m, bio-f) → (bio-m)	8.1	7.6
(bio-m, bio-f) → (bio-m) → (bio-m, bio-f) → (bio-m)	0.3	0.2
(bio-m, bio-f) → (bio-m) → (bio-m, stp-f)	6.2	6.0
(bio-m, bio-f) → (bio-m, stp-f)	1.2	1.1
Other sequences		
(bio-m, bio-f) → (bio-m) → (bio-m, stp-f) → (bio-m)	0.4	0.4
(bio m, bio f) → (bio-m) → (bio-f, stp-m)	0.1	0.1
(bio-m, bio-f) → (bio-m) →(bio-m, bio-f) → (bio-f)	0.1	0.1
(bio-m, bio-f) → (bio-m) → (bio-m, bio-f)	1.0	0.8
(bio-m, bio-f) → (bio-m) → (stat-c)	0.1	0.1
(bio-m, bio-f) → (bio-m, stp-f) → (bio-m)	0.2	0.2
(bio-m, bio-f) → (bio-f)	1.6	1.5
(bio-m, bio-f) → (bio-f) → (stp-m, bio-f)	0.7	0.6
(bio-m, bio-f) → (stp-m, bio-f)	0.2	0.2
(bio-m, bio-f) → (stat-c)	0.2	0.1
(bio-m, bio-f) → (stat-c)→ (bio-m)	0.1	0.1
(bio-m, bio-f) → (stat-c)→ (bio-m, bio-f)	0.2	0.2
(bio-m, bio-f) → (gr-par)	0.1	0.1
(bio-m)	1.0	0.8
(bio-m) → (bio-m, bio-f)	1.4	1.1
(bio-m) → (bio-m, bio-f)→ (bio-m)	0.1	0.1
(bio-m) → (bio-m, stp-f)	1.4	1.2
(bio-m) → (bio-m, stp-f) → (bio-m)	0.1	0.1
(bio-m) → (bio-m, stp-f) →(bio-m) → (bio-m, stp-f)	0.1	0.1
(bio-m) → (stat-c)	0.1	0.1
(adpt-m, adpt-f)[3]	1.2	1.1
Other sequences	3.2	3.0
Total	*17,316*	*9,467*

(Base = male and female respondents with parental interviews at age 16)

Key:
bio-m	Biological mother	adpt-m	Adoptive mother
bio-f	Biological father	adpt-f	Adoptive father
stp-m	Stepmother	stat-c	Statutory/foster care
stp-f	Stepfather	gr-par	Grandparents

Table 6.2   Family structure at 16
(women only)

Family structure at 16	Weighted %	Unweighted %
Both natural parents *	76.0	79.2
Lone mother	8.3	7.3
Mother/stepfather	9.0	7.7
Lone father or father/stepmother	1.6	1.6
Other family structure (including in statutory/foster care)	0.7	0.6
Either parent died (any family structure)	4.3	3.7
Total = women with parental interview at 16 and responding at age 26	*8,232*	*3,297*

* 'Both natural parents' refers to either the biological parents or parents who adopted the child before his or her first birthday

Table 6.3   The main sequences of family structure from birth to 16
(women only)

The sequence of family structure	Weighted %	Unweighted %
Always natural parents	73.2	76.9
Natural parents → lone mother	6.3	5.8
Natural parents → [lone mother] → mother/stepfather (never lived with stepsiblings)*	5.2	4.7
Natural parents → [lone mother] → mother/stepfather (lived with stepsiblings)*	1.5	1.3
Natural parents → lone father or father/stepmother	1.3	1.2
Lone mother at birth → natural parents	1.3	0.9
Lone mother at birth → other sequences	3.1	2.1
Either parent died	4.3	3.7
Any time in care	1.6	1.2
Other sequences	2.3	1.9
Total = women with parental interview at 16 and responding at age 26	*8,232*	*3,297*

* These sequences include children who moved directly from a natural parent to a stepfather family and children who lived in a lone mother family prior to the formation of the stepfamily.

(Office for National Statistics 1998). A birth by age 21 among this cohort was less likely than a teenage birth among their mother's generation and given these changing patterns of the timing of child-bearing, women giving birth before their 21st birthday are defined as young mothers in this analysis.

Figure 6.2 shows the proportion of women in the study that had become mothers by age 21 according to her mother's age at first birth (presented in

Table 6.4 The cohort member's mother's age at first birth
(women only)

Mother's age at first birth	Weighted %	Unweighted %
Less than		
19	22.0	18.3
20–23	41.8	42.2
24 or older	36.2	39.4
Total = women with parental interview at 16 and responding at age 26	*8,232*	*3,297*

Table 6.4). Just under 5 per cent of those born to mothers who were age 24 or older at their first birth had become mothers by 21 compared to over 22 per cent of those born to mothers who began childbearing as teenagers.

Figures 6.3 and 6.4 examine the bi-variate associations between the two measures of family disruption and becoming a mother by age 21. About 18 per cent of those living in a lone-mother family at 16 and 21 per cent of those in a stepfather family had experienced a birth by this age compared to about 10 per cent of those living with their natural parents. The difference is generally less marked though if we compare the most common family trajectories of those experiencing family disruption. For example, around 14 per cent of women who lived in a lone-mother family after parental separation became young mothers along with about 16 per cent of those who went on to live in a stepfather family with no residential stepsiblings. However, a higher level of young motherhood is found among those who lived in a stepfather family which ever included stepsiblings, of whom over 25 per cent had become mothers by 21.

Among the less common trajectories not shown on the chart, rates of young motherhood among women who experienced the death of either parent were very similar to those who grew up with both natural parents. By contrast, over one quarter of women born to a lone mother had experienced a first birth by age 21, but the rates were very diverse with the higher levels of young motherhood among those who had experienced multiple family transitions or went on to live with both of their natural parents rather than remaining with a lone mother. Although a small group (see Table 6.3), over one third of young women who had spent any time in statutory or foster care had become mothers by 21.

The relationship between family background and young motherhood

Those born to a young mother are more likely to come from disadvantaged backgrounds and experience childhood family disruption (Allen and Bourke-Dowling 1998; Clarke *et al.* 1997). After taking such factors into

Figure 6.2 Percentage of women having a birth before their 21st birthday according to their mother's age at her first birth
(weighted estimates)

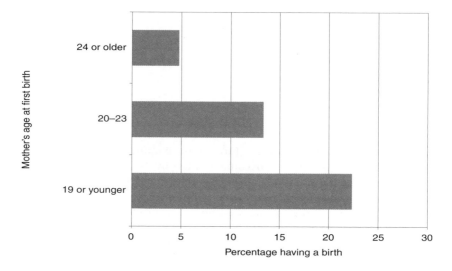

Figure 6.3 Percentage of women having a first birth before their 21st birthday by family structure at 16
(selected groups, weighted estimates)

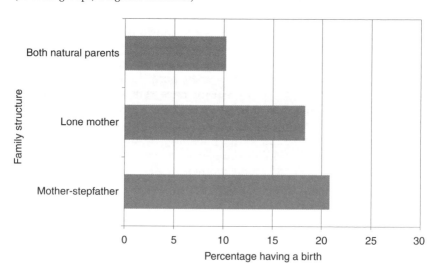

Figure 6.4 Percentage of women having a first birth before their 21st birthday by sequence of family structure (selected trajectories, weighted estimates)

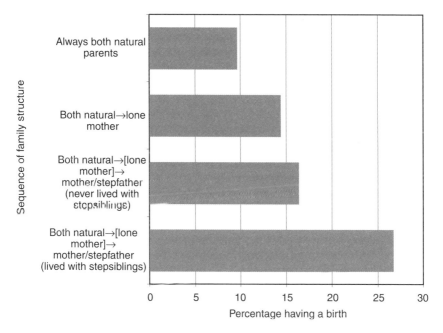

account, is there still a relationship between childhood family trajectory and the likelihood of becoming a young mother? This section examines first whether the observed differences in rates of young motherhood shown in Figures 6.2–6.4 are statistically significant. It then examines whether associations between childhood family structure and young motherhood remain after taking into account the mother's age at family formation and other measures of the family socio-economic circumstances.

To address this question, the multivariate analysis uses a logistic regression model to estimate the relative likelihood of young motherhood among those experiencing family disruption after controlling for maternal age at first birth and selected family background characteristics. Potential background factors were restricted to information collected at the birth of the cohort member. Although a wider range of factors, found in earlier studies to be associated with young motherhood, were available from later stages of the survey, these circumstances could well reflect the consequences of family disruption for the household. So, although the socio-economic information available at the birth survey was quite limited, these measures are unambiguous precursors of any transitions in the family. The final fitted model included the additional covariates of social class and parental age at completing full-time education.[4]

Results

Table 6.5 shows the results of the three preliminary logistic regression models testing separately the relative likelihood of becoming a young mother according to maternal age at first birth or the two measures of family disruption, using no background controls. First, maternal child-bearing patterns are highly associated with the child-bearing behaviour of daughters. With no controls for other circumstances, women with mothers who began child-bearing as a teenager are found to be 5.8 times more likely to become a young mother than those with mothers who had their first child at age 24 or older. In the second and third models, most types of family disruption, except those caused by parental death, are found to be associated with young motherhood. However, Model 3 in Table 6.5 already highlights the value of considering the trajectory rather than cross-sectional measure of family structure at 16. The odds ratios comparing those living in lone-mother or stepfather families (never with stepsiblings) after parental separation to those who grew up with both natural parents are both lower than the odds ratios for all the other post-transition groups at age 16 except those who experienced parental death. Instead, high odds ratios are found among those born to a lone mother, those who lived in a stepfather family that ever contained stepsiblings and women who were ever taken into care, even if they had returned to their original family by age 16.

   The next step is to examine whether these differences in the likelihood of an early birth according to family structure or trajectory persist after taking into account mother's age at family formation and the additional controls for social class and parental education level (Table 6.6, Models 4 and 5). Those from manual social-class backgrounds and those whose parents did not continue in education beyond the statutory school leaving age are more likely to become young mothers and taking these family characteristics into account attenuates the difference in the likelihood of young motherhood both according to maternal age at first birth and family structure. Women born to a mother who began child-bearing as a teenager were still over 3.5 times more likely to have a birth by the age of 21 than those born to a mother who was 24 or older at her first birth. Even those with mothers who began child-bearing between ages 20 and 23, only just under the average for the time, were nearly 2.5 times as likely to have a first birth by 21 than those whose mothers began their child-bearing at an older age.

   The relationship for those who have experienced family transitions is less clear once we have controlled for the other factors. In Model 4, which uses the family structure at 16, those in both lone-mother and stepfather families at 16 are found to be about 1.6 times more likely to have an early birth than those who were living with both natural parents. The association also remains statistically significant at the 5 per cent level. However, we can

Table 6.5 Results of logistic regression models of association between maternal age at first birth, family structure at 16 or family trajectory and becoming a mother by 21 (weighted data)

Variables (reference categories are underlined)	Model 1 Odds ratio	Model 1 95% Confidence interval	Model 2 Odds ratio	Model 2 95% Confidence interval	Model 3 Odds ratio	Model 3 95% Confidence interval
Mother's age at first birth						
Less than 19	5.77***	4.11–8.10				
20–23	3.08***	2.24–4.26				
24 or older	1.00	—				
Family structure at 16						
Both natural parents			1.00	—		
Lone mother			1.96***	1.34–2.86		
Mother/stepfather			2.31***	1.61–3.28		
Lone father or father/stepmother			2.05**	1.00–4.22		
Other family structure (including in statutory/foster care)			2.37	0.82–6.86		
Either parent died (any family structure)			1.30	0.74–2.30		

Table 6.5 Results of logistic regression models of association between maternal age at first birth, family structure at 16 or family trajectory and becoming a mother by 21 (weighted data) (*Cont'd*)

Variables (reference categories are underlined)	Model 1		Model 2		Model 3	
	Odds ratio	95% Confidence interval	Odds ratio	95% Confidence interval	Odds ratio	95% Confidence interval
Type of transitions between birth and age 16						
<u>Always natural parents</u>					1.00	—
Natural parents → lone mother					1.58**	1.01–2.46
Natural parents → [lone mother] → mother/stepfather (never lived with stepsiblings)					1.84**	1.14–2.96
Natural parents → [lone mother] → mother/stepfather (lived with stepsiblings)					3.42***	1.64–7.11
Natural parents → lone father or father/stepmother					2.13*	0.96–4.74
Lone mother at birth → both natural parents					5.08***	2.27–11.35
Lone mother at birth → other sequences					2.84***	1.59–5.06
Either parent died					1.39	0.78–2.46
Any time in care					5.13***	2.55–10.32
Other sequences					2.42**	1.23–4.74

* significant at the 10% level
** significant at the 5% level
*** significant at the 1% level

Table 6.6 Results of logistic regression models of association between family structure at 16 or family trajectory and becoming a mother by 21 after controlling for maternal age at first birth and other family characteristics (weighted data)

Variables (reference categories are underlined)	Model 4		Model 5	
	Odds ratio	95% Confidence interval	Odds ratio	95% Confidence interval
Family structure at 16				
<u>Both natural parents</u>	1.00	—		
Lone mother	1.60**	1.09–2.37		
Mother/stepfather	1.59**	1.09–2.34		
Lone father or father/ stepmother	1.93*	0.93–4.01		
Other family structure (including in statutory/ foster care)	1.77	0.51–6.11		
Either parent died (any family structure)	1.28	0.72–2.28		
Type of transitions between birth and age 16				
<u>Always natural parents</u>			1.00	—
Natural parents → lone mother			1.35	0.85–2.14
Natural parents → [lone mother] → mother/stepfather (never lived with stepsiblings)			1.27	0.77–2.09
Natural parents → [lone mother] → mother/stepfather (lived with stepsiblings)			2.74**	1.23–6.14
Natural parents → lone father or father/stepmother			1.93	0.87–4.26
Lone mother at birth → both natural parents			3.53***	1.55–8.06
Lone mother at birth → other sequences			1.99**	1.07–3.68
Either parent died			1.35	0.76–2.41
Any time in care			3.31***	1.86–7.80
Other sequences			2.02*	0.99–4.14
Mother's age at first birth				
Less than 19	3.76***	2.63–5.39	3.56***	2.48–5.11
20–23	2.46***	1.77–3.42	2.41***	1.73–3.35
<u>24 or older</u>	1.00	—	1.00	—

Table 6.6   Results of logistic regression models of association between family structure at 16 or family trajectory and becoming a mother by 21 after controlling for maternal age at first birth and other family characteristics (weighted data) (*Cont'd*)

Variables (reference categories are underlined)	Model 4		Model 5	
	Odds ratio	95% Confidence interval	Odds ratio	95% Confidence interval
Family background factors				
Social class at birth				
I/II	1.00	—	1.00	—
IIINM	1.46	0.85–2.49	1.45	0.85–2.48
IIIM	1.54*	0.97–2.43	1.52*	0.95–2.42
IV/IV	2.25***	1.38–3.68	2.20***	1.34–3.62
Parents' ages at completing education				
Neither beyond age 15	1.00	—	1.00	—
Either age 16+	0.62**	0.38–0.99	0.61**	0.37–0.98
Both age 16+	0.15***	0.05–0.45	0.15***	0.05–0.44
Not known	0.66***	0.50–0.88	0.64***	0.48–0.86

*   significant at the 10% level
**   significant at the 5% level
***   significant at the 1% level

draw different conclusions by using the measure of the sequence of family structures prior to age 16 shown in Model 5. After controlling for pre-existing family characteristics, women who were living in a lone-mother or stepfather family (without residential stepsiblings) after parental separation were not found to be more likely to become young mothers.

Women who experienced less common, or multiple transitions, were generally more likely to have an early birth. Also, those who lived in a stepfather family that ever contained stepsiblings were over 2.5 times more likely to become young mothers than those who grew up with both natural parents. The odds ratios for the group of women who were in their father's custody after parental separation were higher than those who lived with their mother but the results did not achieve significance at the 10 per cent level. Overall, those born to a lone mother had a relatively high risk of young motherhood but the results presented here show the diversity of pathways that these women could follow. Those who went on to live with their natural father actually had higher odds of young motherhood than those who followed other trajectories. Similarly, although nearly half of the group had returned to living with their natural family by age 16, children who had spent any time in statutory or foster care had the highest likelihood of young motherhood even though controlling for socio-economic background did attenuate the differences. If family structure at 16 was only used in this analysis, the results would have conflated the experiences of the more disrupted minority with others living in the same family type at 16 after more common transitions. If these more unusual groups are shown to have a higher risk of young motherhood then analysis based on a cross-sectional observation which includes these different trajectories would possibly draw different conclusions about an association between the more common types of family transition and young motherhood.

The predicted probabilities of young motherhood

Maternal age at first birth and young motherhood

Although Figure 6.2 presented the different levels of motherhood by age 21 according to maternal age at first birth, the analysis has shown that some of those differences are explained by the potentially more disadvantaged or disrupted childhood circumstances of those born to young mothers. Figure 6.5 uses the results of the logistic regression model (Model 5, Table 6.6) to calculate the predicted probabilities of becoming a mother by 21 according to the mother's age at first birth whilst holding all the other background and family trajectory variables at an 'average' level. This predicts the extent to which maternal age at first birth might affect the likelihood of becoming a young mother if the women had grown up with otherwise similar backgrounds. If the observed differences according to maternal age at first birth were entirely explained by the other background factors such as parental education, social class and family disruption, there would be little difference between the predicted probabilities across the groups.

The chart shows that for those born to mothers who were teenagers at their first birth, the predicted probability of a first birth, if family circumstances were held at an artificially average level, is 0.15. This is considerably lower than the observed rate of 22 per cent showing that a proportion of the increased risk of young motherhood among this group is explained by other family characteristics. However, although taking other background factors into account has reduced the differences between the categories, those born to this youngest group of mothers were still over three times as likely to become young mothers than those born to mothers who began child-bearing at 24 or older who have a probability of 0.05. So, although the overall rates of young motherhood are lower among this cohort than their mother's generation, differences in the relative likelihood of an early birth according to their mother's age at first birth persist.

Figure 6.5   Predicted probability of having a first birth by exact age 21 according to mother's age at first birth whilst holding all other independent variables at their average level

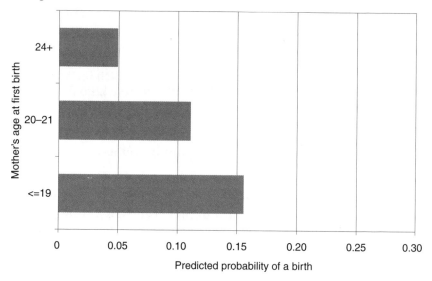

Family transitions and young motherhood

Figures 6.6 and 6.7 again present predicted probabilities of young motherhood derived from the results shown in Models 5 and 6 in Table 6.6, this time according to the main family structures at 16 or family trajectories, whilst holding all the background factors at an 'average' level. Again, if the association between family disruption and young motherhood was largely due to differing levels of parental education, social class or maternal age at first birth then we would expect the predicted probabilities for those in post-transition families to be much lower than the observed rates given in Figures 6.3 and 6.4, and to be similar to the probability for those living with both natural parents.

Figure 6.6 shows that the difference in predicted probability according to family type at 16 ranges from about 0.08 among those living with their natural parents to 0.13 among those living with either a lone mother or in a stepfather family. Although the differences were found to be statistically significant, in substantive terms they are relatively small. The greatest fall between an observed rate of 21 per cent and predicted probability of 0.13 occurred among women living in a stepfather family. In other words, the higher rates of young motherhood among these women compared to those in lone-mother families had more to do with the socio-economic circumstances of the family and the mother's age at family formation than the transition to a stepfamily.

Most of the differences according to the sequence of family structure are even smaller than those according to family structures at 16 (Figure 6.7). Here, the probability of young motherhood of 0.10 among women who experienced parental separation followed by lone motherhood or a stepfather family without stepsiblings is only slightly greater than the 0.08 probability among those who grew up with both natural parents and, as discussed for the model, the differences are not statistically significant. In this case, the greatest reduction between the observed rate and predicted probability occurred among women who lived in stepfather families without residential stepsiblings. The reduction was not quite as large among women who had ever lived with stepsiblings who still had a predicted probability of 0.18 after controlling for other family characteristics.

Among the less common family transitions, not shown in the chart, there is generally a higher risk of young motherhood. In particular, although socio-economic circumstances were important, even after taking these into account, those who had spent any time in statutory or foster care, regardless of their family structure at 16, had over a 0.20 predicted probability of becoming a young mother.

Figure 6.6   Predicted probability of having a first birth by exact age 21 according to family structure at 16 whilst holding all other independent variables at their average level

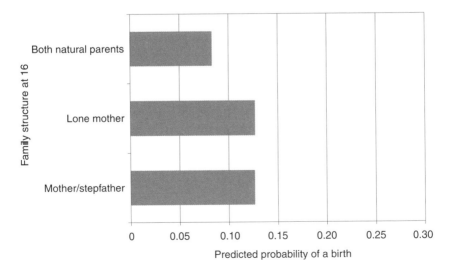

Figure 6.7   Predicted probability of having a first birth by exact age 21 according to family trajectory whilst holding all other independent variables at their average level

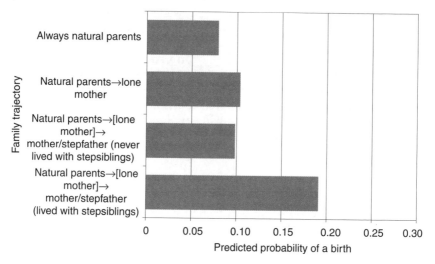

Conclusion

This research confirms the well-established association between maternal age at first birth and a woman's own family formation patterns. It has, however, supported the US evidence about the limitations of drawing conclusions about the effects of family disruption on children based on cross-sectional observations of family structure in late childhood. In addition to using family structure at 16, the analysis adopted a more dynamic measure of family transition reflecting the type of transitions experienced by the child. The models deliberately tested a very limited number of background controls that unambiguously predated any transitions in parenting arrangements in order to avoid confusing the precursors and possible consequences of family disruption.

The model using family structure at 16 produced results that continued to find a small, but statistically significant, increased risk of young motherhood among women living in lone-parent or stepfamilies at 16. Although the observed rates of young motherhood among women living in stepfamilies was higher than among those living in lone-mother families, controlling for other family characteristics eliminated any differences between these two family types. However, when using the more dynamic measure, women who lived in a lone-mother or stepfather family (without residential stepsiblings) after parental separation were not found to have a higher likelihood of young motherhood, even when only controlling for the very limited number of background factors used in the analysis.

Twenty per cent of young women living with a lone mother at 16 were either born to a lone mother, experienced multiple family transitions or had been in and out of care. All of these women were found to be at an increased risk of young motherhood and not distinguishing them from women living with a lone mother after parental separation could have led to the conclusion that all women living with a lone mother at 16 were more likely to become young mothers. Similarly, the model of family structure at 16 found women in stepfather families to have a small increased likelihood of an early birth. However, the model which considered the type of family transition in more detail found this only to be the case among women who had ever lived with stepsiblings. This is possibly a very select group and we do not know whether the stepfather came to have custody of his children after parental separation or the death of the mother. Stepfamilies with stepsiblings tend to be larger, placing a strain on household resources, and also more conflict has been found to occur in these families (Hetherington *et al.* 1999).

Those born to a lone mother showed a great diversity of family trajectories and outcomes about which it is hard to draw conclusions. However, identifying the sequence of family structures revealed a higher rate of young motherhood among those living with both natural parents at 16 who had not done so for all of their childhood. Finally, the high risk of adult social exclusion that was previously found among those taken into care in the 1958 NCDS (Cheung and Buchanan 1997) was repeated in the context of young motherhood among this cohort. Using the dynamic measures to identify anyone who had spent any time in statutory or foster care, even if they had returned to their natural family by age 16, separated out some of the more disrupted childhoods from the experiences of the majority. Even after controlling for their family background circumstances women in this group were over three times more likely to become young mothers than those who grew up with both natural parents.

Further investigations in this research include examining whether factors associated with very young motherhood differ from those associated with motherhood at later ages as well as adding measures of the timing of childhood family transitions. The analysis presented in this chapter already shows how sensitive conclusions about the outcomes of childhood family disruption may be to the measures used.

Acknowledgements

I am grateful to Ann Berrington and Mac McDonald, who supervised the original PhD research that this chapter draws on. I would also like to thank the editors of this book plus Nicole Stone and Rachel Partridge for their valuable comments on earlier drafts.

Notes

1. Marital status rather than family structure was asked at the birth survey. Mothers who were married were assumed to be living with the natural father. Mothers who were not married were classified as lone mothers if they gave no information about the father. Retrospective information from later stages of the survey was also taken into account in order to classify whether or not the parents were cohabiting at the birth.
2. Although this may seem high, and could reflect some stepfathers identifying themselves as the natural father, it is consistent with results from the 1958 NCDS where a considerable minority of natural fathers moved in with lone mothers shortly after the birth of the child (Clarke *et al.* 1997).
3. These children were adopted at birth. Those adopted after their first birthday were allocated to other sequences.
4. The logistic regression model estimates the probability of an individual *i* having a birth before her 21st birthday given a vector of independent variables X_i so that:

$$\log\left(\frac{p_i}{1-p_i}\right) = \beta_0 + \beta_1.X_i$$

where β_0 and β_1 are unknown parameters. A number of independent background variables thought, from previous evidence, to be potential precursors of young motherhood were selected for the model using a combination of forward selection and backward elimination techniques. Given the research question, the measures of family disruption and maternal age at first birth were retained in all of the models, regardless of their statistical significance. These included: the parents' ages at completing full-time education; the mother's occupation prior to the birth of the child; her age at the birth of the cohort member; social class according to the father's occupation (or the mother's social class background if there was no information on the father); as well as the number of siblings living in the household when the cohort member was born.

7
Young Adults' Household Formation: Individualization, Identity and Home

Elizabeth Kenyon

Introduction

Increasing numbers of 20- and 30-something young adults in the UK are rejecting early partnership formation, and are instead living alone or in multi-adult shared households unconnected by marriage, co-habitation or family ties (Bynner *et al.* 1997; Jones 1995; McRae 1999). Similar shifts have been observed in the USA and across Northern Europe (Goldscheider and Goldscheider 1993; European Commission 1997). Sociological explanations for such changes have largely focused on the determining influence of structural economic factors on the housing options available to young adults. In line with a decrease in the welfare benefits available for young people over the 1980s and 1990s, the growing insecurities of the youth labour market have been argued to disrupt or fracture transitions to adulthood, and to create prolonged periods of dependency on parents and guardians (see, for example, Coles 1995; Hutson and Jenkins, 1989; Jones 1995; Roberts 1993). Reflecting the predominant cultural belief that home is somehow less authentic and meaningful if an individual lives with his or her peers into adulthood (Anthony 1993; Somerville 1997), those living in shared houses are viewed as experiencing an extended transitional period of 'making do', where adulthood is placed 'on hold' until a truly independent adult home can be established. Yet this assumes that young adults' expectations and ideals of housing are static and remain the same as those of previous generations, despite the changing reality of their housing careers. What has not been considered in the same detail is what such changing housing experiences signify to those involved.

Following Heath (1999), this chapter considers whether recent sociological theorizing on the changing nature of contemporary social relationships (Beck 1992; Beck and Beck-Gernsheim 1995; 1996) provides an alternative starting point from which to develop an explanation for changing patterns and experiences of household formation among young adults. While not concerned with the experiences of young people *per se*, Beck and Beck-Gernsheim's work argues that alongside recent economic and structural transformations (often beyond the control of the individual) wider social shifts are underway; social shifts that may be transforming our images and expectations of home and domesticity. Indeed, taken one step further, it could be argued that under the conditions of *individualization* (Beck 1992) young adults may be choosing to live in households that previous generations considered unconventional and transitional. They may be active in redefining the settings for their developing adult status and identities, and may not feel compromised by such living arrangements.

Drawing on recently completed research on the experiences of young adults aged 18 to 35 living in non-familial and non-student shared households,[1] this chapter examines these theoretical claims in order to further our understanding of contemporary household formation patterns and the role that domestic space plays in the transition to adulthood. Focusing on six young adults' narratives of the meaning and experience of home, and the processes by which they have come to live in their current houses, the chapter explores the personally and socially embedded nature of their housing biographies and choices. It moves on to consider whether attitudes of young people towards their domestic space are indeed changing, as Beck predicts, and the implications this has for their developing sense of adulthood and identity. However, before such a discussion takes place it is important to establish why a study of home experiences and meanings is such a useful tool with which to explore contemporary experiences of young adulthood. The brief overview of research that follows provides a clear indication as to why home takes on such an important role in the entry into adult life, and why an exploration of the meanings and experiences of home proves central to discussions of changing patterns of household formation amongst young adults.

More than just a shelter

In recent years there has been a growing recognition that the places we inhabit are more than static backdrops. Rather, they are key components of the socio-cultural world we create and play a part in the process of our everyday lives. As Bartlett (1997, 169) states: 'Human life is embedded in a concrete physical world. We shape this world and endow it with meaning and in return are shaped, stimulated, restricted and supported by the places we occupy.' Home is understood to form a particularly special place in our everyday lives (Perkins and Thorns 1999); a space which is imbued with meaning and value beyond its market or material value (Birdwell-Pheasant and Lawrence-Zuniga 1999). Most significantly it is seen to provide individuals with a sense of place, identity and status in the world. Two recent reviews of the literature on home (Despres 1991; Somerville 1997) have acknowledged that while studies of the meaning of home exist across a variety of disciplines, the same recurrent themes have emerged: home as a projection and realization of self-identity and social and cultural status; home as a centre for family life; home as a place of retreat, safety, relaxation and freedom; home as a space of privacy; home as a social support mechanism; and home as a place of familiarity and continuity. Moreover, studies on the meaning of home ownership have shown that home can also be seen as a financial asset and a space of ontological security, 'for a home of one's own offers both a physical (hence spatially rooted) and permanent (hence temporally rooted) location in the world' (Saunders 1990, 293).

While it is not within the scope of this chapter to explore this literature in any great depth, one idea that is worth highlighting further, and to which I will return later, is the recognition that home can be both an ideal and a reality, and that the experiences of inhabiting, and meaning given to, a particular dwelling can involve both (Kenyon 1999; Somerville 1992). It should not be assumed, however, that either of these aspects of home is singular, permanent and static. An individual can hold more than one ideal of home, and such ideals may adapt over time. For example, an individual might believe their current living arrangements to be 'ideal' for the present, but may hold another 'ideal' image of home as a future aspiration.

Earlier findings that expectations and ideals of home can act to frame an individual's everyday experience of dwelling there (Kenyon 1999) appear a useful starting point for an evaluation of the contrasting theoretical assumptions made in relation to shared housing: that, on the one hand, young people are constrained by structural factors into living in such conditions; and, on the other, that young people are consciously choosing such housing and households due to a fundamental shift in their needs and expectations. In the analysis that follows I will explore these connections further. The competing theoretical explanations for changes in household formation among young adults have been well reviewed by Heath (1999) and will not be repeated at length here. However, a brief summary is necessary if they are to be reconsidered in the light of evidence provided by the case study material presented below.

Theories of constraint

Sociological explanations for the changing dwelling patterns of young adults have largely been dominated by theories that attribute changing patterns of household formation to a number of structural shifts. In particular, evidence has been found to suggest that global economic restructuring, the casualization of the UK youth labour market, and a series of social policies that have prolonged the financial dependency of young adults on their parents and guardians (Jones and Wallace 1992; Jones 1995), have proved central to the growth in young people remaining in the parental home or moving into the shared household sector for longer periods of time. As Berrington and Murphy (1994, 242) state:

> The ability of young people to plan their future has been substantially reduced and lack of confidence about future income prospects is likely to be a major deterrent to some young people undertaking long-term commitments, including setting up a home of their own (especially purchasing a house), marriage and childbearing.

However, as Heath (1999) argues, while constraint theories have provided youth researchers and policy-makers with a sound understanding of the impact of current economic trends and social policy on young adults' home-leaving experiences, such explanations can remain only partial. First, in focusing on the structural factors that have contributed to the narrowing of housing and household choices for young adults, youth research has tended to neglect more agency-oriented explanations. While researchers have remained aware of economic, political and ideological changes affecting experiences of purchasing or renting a house (see, for example, Ford 1999), there has been little recognition of the impact of wider social transformations on experiences and perceptions of home. Second, youth research has largely focused on the experiences of young people in their late teens and early 20s. What then of those who are continuing to live in shared houses into their late 20s and early 30s? Is their adulthood compromised and are they still in a transitional state? Third, research findings support the idea that young people continue to aspire to a home and family of their own (see, for example, Jamieson in this volume), with any other form of housing falling short of this ideal. Yet this appears to contradict the finding that ideal notions of home are often situationally defined and, in practice, are usually neither static nor singular (Kenyon 1999), and contrasts with recent representations of shared houses in popular culture that depict 'sharing' as an enjoyable and fashionable life-style choice.[2] Finally, there has been a tendency for youth sociologists to focus on disadvantaged youth and to neglect the study of those who are continuing to experience relatively smooth transitions into adulthood. Yet analysis of individual-level data from the 1991 Census of Population conducted as part of the *Shared Household Living* project reveals that 48 per cent of sharers aged 20–29 were located in Social Classes I and II and 39 per cent had at least one degree-level qualification. Whilst not denying that shared household living remains strongly associated with economic constraint at one end of the spectrum, it would also seem that it is becoming increasingly associated with more affluent young people of graduate and/or professional and managerial status. Why, then, are those who appear to be in a position to afford a home of their own continuing to share?

A fully mobile society of singles?

In *Risk Society* (1992, 105), Beck argues that increasingly '... men and women are released from traditional forms and ascribed roles in the search for a life of their own'. This is, in part, due to changes in the global economic structure which place pressure on individuals to remain flexible and adaptable to labour market demands. If this process continues onwards, as Beck predicts, a 'fully mobile society of singles' will develop as individuals reject family, marriage, parenthood or partnership in order to make their own life-choices and decisions. Such changes will, in turn, have implications for future household formation patterns, as

> *a broad spectrum of variations* on familial and extrafamilial forms of living together will arise and continue to exist side by side. Characteristically, many of these – single life, living together before and during marriage, living in communes, various parenthoods over one or two divorces, etc. will be integrated as different phases into *one* overall biography.
>
> Beck 1992, 119, original emphasis

Due to the 'individualized' conditions in which we now live, the biography to which Beck refers is somewhat different to the structured and ordered biographies experienced by previous generations. Beck stresses that due to the need for flexibility in the writing of biographies – most clearly influenced by the need for geographical mobility in the labour market – the family becomes less desirable as a social grouping in society, and the 'basic figure of *fully developed* modernity' (*ibid.*, 122, original emphasis) becomes the single person. This is further compounded by the welfare state which Beck and Beck-Gernsheim (1996, 27) view as 'an experimental apparatus for conditioning ego-related life-styles'; an apparatus directed towards supporting adults who remain flexible within the labour market and free from domestic and family ties and responsibilities. Under such conditions, individuals feel the need to place themselves in the driving seat in order to make sure they are not disadvantaged by the rapidly changing socio-economic order. Beck therefore rejects the notion of inflexible and undifferentiated housing and household trajectories, believing that a variety of households will serve to support the individual during different life phases.

Beck argues that in order to avoid the almost inevitable social isolation that this life necessitates, friendships are now taking on more importance and are actively nurtured in our lives (see also Pahl 1998; 2000). The growing importance of friendship is further supported by Allan and Adams (1998, 193) who suggest that in a world where identity is less tied to social position than before, 'Who you are becomes even more marked by who you spend time and socialise with.' Perhaps, then, non-familial shared households provide a domestic space in which friendships can be nurtured and take on new importance? And if such processes of individualization are underway, and individuals are becoming increasingly 'self-reflexive' with a greater capacity to write their own biographies than ever before, then it should follow that they will be increasingly conscious of the choices they are making as they progress through life. As Beck (1992, 135) states:

> The proportion of life opportunities which are fundamentally closed to decision-making is decreasing and the proportion of the biography which is open and must be constructed personally is increasing ... Decisions on education, profession, job, place of residence, spouse, number of children and so forth, with all the secondary decisions implied, no longer can be, they must be made.

As individuals, for the sake of survival, are compelled 'to make themselves the centre of their planning and conduct of life' (*ibid.*, 88), perhaps the role and meaning and ideals associated with home and home life will also change. The appeal of 'the single life-style' may act to refocus notions of the ideal home as 'the lifelong standard family ... becomes the limiting case, and the rule becomes a movement back and forth among various familial and non-familial forms of living together, specific to the particular phase of life in question' (*ibid.*, 114). So too, shared households may provide a domestic space in which young adults, aware that conventional forms of 'living together' and the permanence associated with purchasing a house cannot support their present individualized life-styles, can explore and forge their own individual identities and biographies free from the trappings associated with conventional home and family life.

From theory to methods

Data from recently completed ESRC-funded research into the experiences of young adults living in non-familial and non-student shared households are presented below. The research aimed to advance understanding of processes of household formation in contemporary Britain by undertaking a detailed multi-method analysis of shared household living amongst young adults. This included secondary analysis of Samples of Anonymised Records from the 1991 Census of Population, 25 group interviews with shared households involving 77 residents (36 male and 41 female) and one-to-one interviews with 61 shared household members. The characteristics of our sample reflect our explicit concern to explore the growing association between shared living and young people of graduate and/or professional and managerial status. Fifty-eight per cent have a highest qualification of degree level and above (including 18 per cent with a Masters degree). All but ten are in employment and, of these, 82 per cent are located in Social Classes I and II with a further 10 per cent in Social Classes III and IV. The mean age of our respondents is 25.5 (26.9 for men and 24.3 for women).

This chapter focuses on data collected during the one-to-one interviews. For this 'individual' phase of the research we were drawn to approaches that have been loosely categorized as 'interpretive-biographical methods' (Denzin, 1989). This form of qualitative enquiry appeared most apposite as it claims to offer insight into the biographical processes by which individuals construct and make sense of their lives. Due to the fundamental belief guiding interpretive-biographical methods – that respondents set the interview agenda and highlight the issues and processes of significance to them – we felt that they would prove effective not only in highlighting how young people make sense of their adult housing and household choices and experiences, but also in assessing Beck's claims about the 'individualized' and 'reflexive' nature of these experiences.

Following the lead of Holloway and Jefferson (1997) respondents were asked a series of focused narrative-inducing questions. As we had hoped this approach prompted a variety of diverse story-telling techniques. The analysis and discussion below draws on six of the 61 narrative interviews. These particular cases provide examples of the way in which respondents took control of their narratives, set the interview agenda, and in doing so revealed the embedded nature of their housing and household choices and the role that their dwellings played in the formation of their identity and status. In all cases, rather than a straightforward description of where and with whom they had lived, each respondent made sense of and evaluated their homes in the light of personally relevant circumstances.

Six housing biographies

An analysis of young adults' experiences of home and the meanings they attach to domestic space is fundamental if we are to further existing debates on changing household formation patterns amongst young adults and contemporary transitions to adulthood. The six housing biographies detailed below provide evidence with which to assess whether the attitudes of young people towards home and household formation are changing, and to address the claims of Beck and Beck-Gernsheim that a process of individualization is underway, and that young adults are becoming active in creating and writing their own (housing and household) biographies.

Coming out

Brad (age 24) and Rick (age 26) met at university and lived together in the first and final years of their degrees. Both returned to their parental homes after graduation. Brad spent some time 'temping' before securing a permanent job, and had bought and moved into a new house near his parental home three months before the first 'household' interview took place. In the meantime Rick had decided to continue with his studies and had been applying for Masters degrees. On receiving news of his acceptance on a course in Brad's home area, he rang to tell Brad and found that he had just bought a house and was looking for a lodger. Rick moved into Brad's house two months before the first 'household' interview.

In his narrative, Brad discussed how the various houses and households in which he has dwelt have been significant in stifling or providing space for his developing gay sexuality and identity. Unless a dwelling could provide him with a space in which this could be acknowledged and fostered, then it could not become a true adult home. After a year in university halls of residence where he felt unable to reveal his sexuality to so many strangers, he purchased a house in his second year using money he inherited from his father, and let rooms out to his friends. It was in this dwelling that Brad established a physical and social environment in which his identity and sexuality could emerge into public view for the first time:

> once I had my own place it was very much my place, it wasn't my parents, it wasn't me living with someone else. It was my house and to a certain extent ... I felt 'this is my place and people live by my rules, I want to be at home in my own home'. And so it was during that first year [as a homeowner] that I came out.

Indeed this is contrasted sharply with his experiences of returning to his mother and stepfather's home after university. Despite being 'out' to his parents, he still felt it was important to live by their rules and according to their values when living in their house:

> it was very hard to meet people because you could meet somebody and strike up a friendship but at the point at which you wanted it to develop and you wanted to start an intimate relationship I couldn't possible invite anyone back to my parents' house.

After some months 'temping' on his return home he was able to secure a permanent job and became a homeowner again. At this point Brad felt able to return to expressing his sexuality on his own terms. Speaking of his new house he told me:

> it's my house and I know that I'm safe, if you like, here. If people come round and they don't particularly like me or the way I live my life, my sexuality whatever, then it's their lookout and they can go and accept someone else's hospitality.

Rick similarly evaluated the houses and households in which he has lived in terms of the space they provide for the expression of his adult identity. Rick spoke of the extent to which he could be himself in each of the houses and households in which he had lived in terms of the freedom each afforded him to 'come out' about his transvestism. Rick and Brad had met at university in halls of residence in their first year. Like Brad, Rick found that university halls of residence were not an environment in which he could be open about his sexuality: 'I felt horribly standardized in a box, literally, physically in the sense that I was in a box room. Box in the sense that I had to be standard white male heterosexual bloke.' During his second year at university Rick lived apart from Brad in a rented student house. However, this year was marred by illness, damp living conditions and a burglary. Consequently, Rick chose to move into Brad's house in his final year of study. And it was here that he felt comfortable enough to be open about his identity for the first time. However, his developing openness about his transvestism was held in check by his impending return to his mother and stepfather's home after graduation, where he would have to 'hide away the make-up and all of that kind of business again'. Indeed, before Rick knew of Brad's second house purchase he felt that his suppression of his transvestism would have to continue when he moved to take up his place on the Masters course:

the one thing I was really dreading was finding somewhere to live with people. I'm sure it's everyone's biggest worry, but I was absolutely dreading it, especially 'cos I'd decided I wanted to be more 'out' about being TV [transvestite], and I thought 'I'm not going to be able to introduce it again for like eight months at least, until I've sussed these people out.'

Living again with Brad, Rick felt he could return to being himself and expressing his true identity in his home. For both Rick and Brad their various housing and household experiences were therefore evaluated and chosen in terms of each dwelling's ability to house and foster their respective adult identities. This need was reflected in both men's vision of the future, and their wish to live in tolerant domestic environments.

Breaking away

Sarah was a 25-year-old software trainer who worked for a large electronics firm. She lived with her 29-year-old co-worker, Pippa, in a rented two bedroom house. Both women told long and varied housing histories during which they described their gradual and purposeful withdrawal from their parental homes and expectations. Sarah, a South African and Pippa, a British Asian, had moved into their shared house four months before we first interviewed them for the project.

Pippa left home to attend university at the age of 18 and had never returned. Her story revealed her twin goals of career and relationship. As a result of her family's expectation that she would return home to an arranged marriage, her eight-year relationship with her white boyfriend, and to some extent her career goals, had remained a secret. In essence she felt that her childhood and adulthood comprised two very distinct and separate periods in her life.

Even before attending university, Pippa knew that she wished to study away from home. However, despite enjoying the freedom that going to university entailed, it was only with hindsight that she was able to reflect on this time as the beginning of her new life. Although she began her relationship with her current partner while at university, she stated that she did not tell her parents as she was unsure whether she would be returning to an arranged marriage. Indeed her parents assumed she would return home after university, fitting back into the life she had left: 'They expected little old Pippa who had gone away three years ago to slot into place again, you know, but plus a degree, and that was it.' Pippa admitted that they would never be close again and she could never return home to live with her parents: 'You know, I'm just like, sort of, gone out to sea and its like, you know, I'm waving at them. I'm here still, but not so close to them now.'

Since leaving university Pippa had lived in various shared houses, and had lodged on three occasions with her boyfriend Ray's parents. On the second time she returned to their house, the bedroom she had occupied was unavailable and she moved in with Ray. Pippa continued to share Ray's bedroom on all subsequent visits to the house and saw this as a turning point in both her relationship with Ray and his parents. She now felt that she was seen as part of the family. Indeed, she believed that Ray's parents' house was more of a home to her now than her parental home. When musing about where 'home' was she stated:

> I think its almost neck and neck Ray's house and here ... [But] if I go up there I would say 'well where's my work?' I miss that. And there's the fact that it's not quite my place. So I actually would say this place would pip it, pip it to the post, this place is my place.

What is interesting about this quotation is that it hints at the priorities in Pippa's life. Her career took first priority in her decision-making about where to live and with whom. Indeed, when contemplating her move to her current job, an opportunity arose to work near to her boyfriend but: '... it wasn't the right job. So I thought "there's no point living here just for the sake of being with you".' As a result, Pippa was clear that their respective careers must be sorted before she and Ray could commit to living together: '... we just both want to get our careers sorted out and if it means being apart from each other to do it, we'll do it. Because we know we're going to end up together no matter what.'

Sarah's housing history crossed three continents. It began with childhood memories of growing up in South Africa where her father was a church minister. At the age of 18 Sarah followed in her sister's footsteps and left the family home to attend a denominational university in America. After graduating she remained in America to work for two years before moving to the UK where she chose to live with a grandmother whom she barely knew. Around a year later she felt the need to establish her own independent space and moved into a bedsit. However, this did not work out as well as she had expected. Pippa joined the company as Sarah's housing contract was coming to an end, and they decided to look for accommodation together.

Notwithstanding stories of her nomadic life so far, or of her strong connections to her church, Sarah had one other clear story to tell when she narrated her housing and household history. This centred around her wish to break away from the expectations of her family and to establish her own independent identity and life-style. In particular Sarah felt the need to separate herself from her older sister, Jane, who had set a precedent within the family about how daughters should behave. Put simply, Sarah felt that her own housing and household trajectory was seen by the rest of her family as non-conformist.

Within moments of beginning, Sarah introduced Jane to me: '... we never got on that well together because, for me, she was always the older sister. I was always sort of living in her shadow.' As she continued her story Sarah told of how Jane always took the lead, and of how Sarah was always expected to follow in her footsteps. This problem came to a head when Sarah moved to the United States to attend university:

> first year [at university] she suggested that I go and room with her in the dorm. Which wasn't a brilliant idea because, of course, she probably thought of me as she left me two years previously. And that's the way she still sort of treated me, as her baby sister.

It was not until Jane graduated, at the end of Sarah's second year at university, that she finally felt that her own adult identity began to develop. However due to the fact that Jane had returned to South Africa to settle down and get married, her ghost continued to haunt Sarah still. She believed that, in returning home to marry, her sister had conformed to her family's expectations in such a way as to place her in a difficult position. In short, she felt pressured to return home and to 'settle down in terms of finding a mate'. In the face of such pressure she viewed her shared home with Pippa as a haven, and as a space in which her own independent adult identity and life-style could be developed and displayed. In contrast, she saw her parental home and family as stifling, and somewhere she could not be her own person if she returned. Due the economic and social benefits gained from sharing a home Sarah stated that she could see herself continuing to share until she felt ready to live alone or to marry.

A means to an end?

The final two housing histories to relate are those of Sean and Mark, two 31 year olds who were joint owners of a three-bedroomed house. Both men were the eldest sons of large families and a series of factors including lack of space in the parental home, the coincidence of both ending serious relationships at a similar time, and promotion into settled and well-paid employment had combined to prompt them to buy a house together eight years earlier. The arrangement had always been viewed as temporary and as something that would come to a natural end when one or the other moved out to live with a partner. In relating their housing histories both Sean and Mark were clear that their move into the shared house was a calculated step towards independence and adulthood.

After leaving school at 16 and an aborted attempt to study at college, a series of casual labouring jobs led Sean to realize that a permanent job with career prospects would be necessary to facilitate his move away from the parental home. This, in turn, was necessary to gain some adult independence:

> There was every reason to move, socially it was going to be a lot better 'cos we could have our own pad ... Financially it makes sense 'cos you've got on the housing ladder, and domestically in terms of your relationship with your family ... if you're living at home after 25, that's got to be bad news.

However, the reasons for moving into the house were very different to his continuing rationale for living there. Sean was clear that over the eight years of living with Mark a number of other benefits had arisen. First of all their home provided him with a haven from which his work and adult life could be conducted:

> Everyone spends all day, if you're working, out and about, other people are constantly influencing what you do ... you're constantly reacting to what other people are doing ... Whereas you get back to the house, the home and that's not the case ... there's a certain amount of comfort, relaxation, karma, in not having to react to other people.

Sean saw the fact that he and Mark had built up routines and a relationship to support this growing adult need as adding to the homely atmosphere of the house. In addition, perhaps as a result of their long stay in the house and/or the fact that their needs were changing, Sean felt he was now prepared to make some investment in the fabric of the dwelling; something that had not previously occurred over their eight year period of living together. Such investment would bring his current home nearer to the 'comfort zone' he would ideally associate with adult home life.

Sean had recently emerged from a three-year relationship and reflected on the fact that single life exemplified true adult independence. Indeed, he was quite philosophical about the idea of settling down with a partner and felt that the time was now right to invest in his career. Consequently, he did not discount the possibility of moving for work. However, he reflected on the fact that he would strive to make future dwellings and households more settled and comfortable, as this was something he now required from his home:

> I've always felt you settle down when you've accepted that you're happy with the standard of living that you have, the environment that you're working in. You really are in a comfort zone and that's where you want to be ... Now whether that's with a wife and family, or whether that's whatever, I don't think it matters.

For Mark the ending of a period of apprenticeship as a furniture-maker led to a salary increase and an awareness that he could now leave home. Sharing provided Mark with the space and independence he craved, while allowing him to maintain a life-style to which he had grown accustomed: 'The main reason for sharing with Sean was so that we had more disposable income to do all the things we were doing ... You know, the social side of it: two holidays a year, cars, motorbikes.' Moving in with Sean had developed and reflected Mark's sense of adulthood in a variety of ways. In particular he had been able to renegotiate his relationship with his father and brothers on an adult basis:

> My brothers are almost like my mates ... My relationship with my father as well, that's changed 'cos he's not really my father any more. He's my mate. He doesn't tell me what to do. I ask him for advice instead of him telling me things and that's great ... I have to admit I didn't feel fully independent for the first few years I moved away, 'cos I was so close to my parents. But now I am fully independent.

Like Sean, Mark had seen the ways in which they used their home, and the identities that it reflected, change over the period of their residence there. Initially their home was seen as a space in which to party and to display their freedom. However, over time he has realized that it provided more than this. In particular, he and Sean had developed a supportive adult friendship. Over their eight years together their household and home had thus adapted to suit their changing life-styles, and their changing work needs. Mark was less ambivalent about the future than Sean. Although he stated; 'I'm quite happy here for the moment', he hoped that his future would replicate his parent's 'great' marriage and believed that he would share his home with a friend until this came to fruition.

Conclusion

Our use of interpretive-biographical interviewing techniques led respondents to reveal the personal and social values that frame and have framed their housing and household experiences and choices. While each narrative has proved personal in its focus and direction, all of the stories that were told were underpinned by a common awareness that sharing a home was a choice that had been consciously made due to the various benefits involved. Four of the young adults discussed above – Sean, Mark, Pippa and Sarah – were in a financial position to be able to set up a home of their own, yet felt that their present living arrangements were ideal for their current needs. All were aware that living alone would not provide the social support currently gained from their shared households. A further benefit of this arrangement was that sharing a dwelling cut costs and provided a greater disposable income for spending on leisure and holidays. Those who had chosen to invest in property had also benefited financially from shared living arrangements as they were able to buy larger properties than would have been possible if they were financing a mortgage on one income.

While all six respondents were aware that at some point their housing and households would change to suit their future needs, none believed his or her shared arrangement to be a compromise, or a stop-gap. In describing what made them homely, respondents' stories consistently highlighted the fact that their dwellings supported and reflected their developing adult identities and provided them with the space to grow. A further factor that was found to be of key importance in young adults' home lives was the existence and development of supportive adult friendships. Thus, in support of Beck (1992), non-familial shared houses certainly appeared to provide our respondents with domestic spaces in which adult friendships could be nurtured and could take on new importance. The fact that each of the three shared houses discussed in this chapter had become meaningful adult homes for those dwelling there also supports the idea that ideals of home can be both multiple and flexible. As stated above, although there was a general recognition that future homes would adapt to suit future needs, this did not detract from the day-to-day experiences associated with respondents' current dwellings. Shared houses were viewed as an ideal arrangement for those who were not in a position to settle down with a partner, or to commit to an area, yet wished to develop a supportive adult home environment.

While the conclusions that can be drawn from six housing biographies are necessarily limited, all six respondents viewed their shared houses as sources of, and arenas in which they could develop and display, their adult identities. The young adults we interviewed were aware that increasing skills and/or geographical flexibility were now required in order to build a career. Thus while many still valued the domestic aspirations of earlier generations, and clearly believed that co-habitation (and in most instances marriage) was a desirable long-term goal, they were also aware of the need to establish their own niche in the world before this could be achieved. Accordingly, our respondents appeared to be active in appropriating the space of home to support these changing needs. In such circumstances it would seem fallacious to assume that those who fall short of the domestic ideal of family life will somehow fail to gain full adult status and identity.

It thus appears that the process of individualization is indeed underway, evidenced by the fact that many young adults are choosing singledom and career flexibility over the idea of settling down. Yet some caution should be exercised when drawing such conclusions. The majority of the 77 young adults who participated in the shared household living research, including the six cases detailed above, had a much more static view of the future than Beck (ibid.) anticipates. Most respondents imagined their ideal future in terms of a permanent partnership in a single family owner-occupied dwelling. For example, Pippa was clear that the flexible single life she was embracing was necessary in order to strive towards this more permanent goal. When asked why this goal was desirable, respondents indicated that they wished to avoid loneliness and uncertainty. Indeed, our research reveals that loneliness is one of the most feared outcomes of faulty housing choices; whether the result of choosing to live with the wrong people, or to live alone at the wrong time. Thus, although increasing numbers of separations, divorces, stepfamilies and lone-adult households may make such fixed future ideals uncertain and unpredictable, the fact that they were still viewed as desirable by the young adults in our sample is of interest. While striving towards this ultimate goal, many young adults are happy to choose the flexible arrangements provided by shared houses and the single life that such households support. Yet this 'fully mobile society of singles' appears to be desirable for young people only insofar as their peers entertain similar life styles and are available to form friendship groups and households. In such circumstances 'single' life is both fun and practicable. However, our respondents believed that such support was unlikely to exist in the longer term as their peers, like themselves, would ultimately aim towards forming couple households and buying a property alone or with a partner. Consequently, planning to share in the future was deemed both impracticable and undesirable.

Possible explanations for such trends can be found in recent writings on gay and lesbian *families of choice* (Weston 1998), contemporary experiences of intimacy (Jamieson 1998) and the meaning of home ownership (Gurney 1999a; 1999b). Weston (1998, 92) argues that although same-sex partnerships make the headlines, legal briefs and publications, intimate, family-like relationships with friends 'fail to find a place in these representations'. She goes on to state that if such relationships do not find 'authenticity' in public representations, they may lose appeal for those who have created them. Despite Weston's focus on non-heterosexual intimate friendship groups, the insights that she provides appear useful for a general understanding of intimacy amongst friends and, in particular, our respondents' failure to see such intimacies as realistic and authentic in the longer term. A lack of authenticity could also be argued to result from the non-sexual nature of intimacies amongst friends. The intimacy of friendship stands in stark contrast to idealized images of permanent partnerships founded on sexual intimacy. As Jamieson (1998, 105) states, 'Given that friendship is culturally defined as a non-sexual relationship, and a pervasive public story is that adults need a sex life, then friendship is not all you need.' Finally, Gurney (1999a; 1999b) discusses the ways in which commonsense metaphors and language in support of single family owner-occupation appear to override many of the negative experiences that have come to be associated with home ownership in recent decades (for example, repossession and negative equity). The pervasive ideology that renting is 'dead money' and that getting onto the property ladder is an important personal investment in one's future leads to an almost unquestioned acceptance that there is no other tenure that would be more desirable.

Reflecting on these insights, it is unlikely that the authenticity and legitimacy accorded to households comprising partners living in a home of their own will be transferred to households comprising 'impermanent' friendship groups living in fully, part-rented or joint-mortgaged homes. Indeed, several respondents talked of the need to justify their decision to live in shared housing to bemused older colleagues and family members. While public and political discourse appears to lag behind changes in the lived experiences of individuals, and continues to promote an 'ideology' of stable and permanent coupledom and single family owner-occupation, it seems unlikely that alternative adult household forms and tenures will be viewed by young people as desirable in the longer term. Thus while the young people in our sample appeared to be embracing many of the ideas discussed by Beck (1992) and Beck and Beck-Gernsheim (1995; 1996), they tended to see these experiences as realistic and desirable largely in the here and now. Ultimately they aimed to construct futures characterized by happiness, security and permanence. In the light of fears of loneliness and uncertainty, the appeal of the single life-style appears unlikely to counter such ideals and to refocus young adults' long-term housing and household aspirations.

Beck and Beck Gernsheim's (1995, 40) recognition that individuals can find themselves under 'considerable pressure to conform and behave in a standardised way' as their decisions remain 'heavily dependent on outside influences' is thus of key importance. In identifying that outside influences can become internalized and influence individuals' personal decision-making strategies, we can begin to understand why young adults appear to be making plans that may not materialize in the settled form they imagine. If we consider the lack of authentic housing and household alternatives available to young adults, it is somewhat unsurprising that they continue to strive towards the notion of creating permanent social and sexual bonds, and putting down temporal roots in homes of their own. The loneliness and unhappiness that could potentially result from the breakdown of such socially sanctioned household forms and housing tenures appeared to be viewed as less probable and problematic than the isolation our respondents associated with remaining single in a society of couples. Thus, while our research certainly provides evidence in support of the growth of a new ethic based on 'one's duty to oneself' (Beck and Beck-Gernsheim 1996, 43), the fixed ideals of home life and intimacy that exist in contemporary society provide one possible explanation for young adults' failure to contemplate and plan for *individualized* futures. Such evidence of conformity should, however, not detract from the fact that our respondents were aware that they were eschewing pre-determined routes into adulthood and were making conscious and active decisions about education, work, domestic life and parenthood. While continuing to embrace the social goals of co-habitation and/or marriage, they clearly only intended to pursue these goals when the time was personally right.

Notes

1. The *Young Adults and Shared Household Living* project was funded by the Economic and Social Research Council (Award reference R000237033) and was directed by Dr Sue Heath, University of Southampton.
2. The TV programmes *Friends*, *This Life*, *Flatmates* and *Men Behaving Badly* and numerous newspaper and magazine articles documenting real 'Friends' or 'This Life' households (e.g. Neustatter 1998; Robson-Scott 1999) provide the impression that sharing is fashionable and, most importantly, is fun.

8
Negotiating Difference: Lesbian and Gay Transitions to Adulthood

Sara McNamee, Gill Valentine, Tracey Skelton and Ruth Butler

Introduction

The concept of transition has been at the heart of social science work on youth for several decades. In the late 1970s and early 1980s, a time when the labour market was severely depressed, structuralist explanations dominated understandings of the routes that young people follow into adulthood. The emphasis was on the way that young people's class positions shaped their transitions from school to work. However, at the end of the twentieth, and the beginning of the twenty-first centuries, changes in the labour market, familial relations and class cultures are creating new life situations and biographical development patterns. Beck (1992) points out that the life course is no longer organized around employment history with the consequence that the possible pathways that young people can follow after school are becoming more diversified. Social change is eroding traditional forms of knowledge and communication. Faced with a proliferation of choices young people's biographies are becoming increasingly reflexive, with young people being able to choose between a wider range of life-styles, subcultures and identities. Yet, with these opportunities also comes increased risks for young people, in the form of guilt or blame if they end up on the margins of society as a result of their choices.

This emphasis on the significance of individual action has contributed to a recognition amongst researchers that youth are not a homogeneous group (Cohen 1997). Rather, there is increasingly acknowledgement that some groups of young people find the transitions to adulthood particularly difficult and as such are at risk of homelessness, unemployment, estrangement from their families and social isolation (Coles 1997). The term 'vulnerable youth' has been coined to describe those who have a greater likelihood of becoming socially excluded as they attempt to make employment, domestic and housing transitions (*ibid.*, 81). 'Vulnerable' groups of young people that have been subject to recent attention include those with special needs and disabilities and those in care.

This chapter focuses on a further, and generally neglected group: lesbian and gay youth. In doing so it draws on material from a research project about the processes through which vulnerable groups of youth[1] are marginalized and the ways in which they resist this marginalization.

The findings are based on in-depth interviews with 30 young people aged 16–25 who self-identify as lesbian and gay. These participants were recruited via support groups and snowballing within two British towns: one in the North East (Lisby) and one in the Midlands (Sheldon). The interviews, which took place in a range of different settings including the interviewees' homes, workplaces and 'community' or social settings, lasted between 45 minutes and nearly two hours. These were taped and transcribed using conventional social science techniques. In order to protect the confidentiality of those who participated in this study all the names of people and places referred to in this chapter have been changed.

In addition, the study also involved participant observation and focus group work with a lesbian and gay youth group; e-mail interviews with some young people who preferred the anonymity offered by this disembodied form of communication (Valentine, Skelton and Butler, in press), retrospective interviews with 30 'older' lesbians and gay men about their memories of their youth, and how their experiences as young adults' shaped (or did not) their subsequent lives, interviews with service providers for sexual dissidents (for example, HIV support workers, those who run drop-in centres and support groups etc.), and finally a large-scale questionnaire survey about young people's self-esteem administered through schools and colleges to all pupils/students.

Transitions to an adult sexual identity

Morrow and Richards (1996) note that the transition to adulthood has traditionally been marked by: the finishing of full-time education; entry into the labour market; leaving home; marriage/co-habiting; and parenthood. Each of these transitions is affected by structural factors, such as 'race', gender, disability, class and geography. However, Morrow and Richards (*ibid.*, 9–11) contend that since the 1980s these stepping stones to adulthood have changed, and instead offer four categories of contemporary adulthood: political/legal (for example, ages for voting, marrying, criminal responsibility); financial/economic (limited for those under 18); social/sexual (life-styles and identity becoming different from those of parents); and parenthood (which they say is 'central to adult feminine identity'). While each of these transitions raises specific issues for lesbian and gay youth (for example, until recently when the age of consent for gay men was reduced from 21 to 16, the age of consent for heterosexuals, the political/legal transition was problematic for young gay men), it is the social/sexual transition which is most pertinent and underpins many of the difficulties young lesbians and gay men incur in making the other transitions.

Lesbian and gay sexualities are largely stigmatized identities. In most western countries anti-discrimination legislation does not cover sexual minorities, lesbian and gay relationships have only limited recognition before the law and homophobia is still commonplace (Valentine 1993a; 1996). Such negative attitudes to homosexuality are also evident amongst children and young people. Numerous studies have documented the hegemony of heterosexuality within the classroom, highlighting the way that labels such as 'poof' are used by children to police gender and heterosexual identities, as well as serving as more general terms of abuse (Epstein and Johnston 1994; Haywood and Mac an Ghaill 1995; Holloway, *et al.* 2000; Valentine 2000).

When young people begin to develop a lesbian and gay sexuality they often find it hard to come to terms with, or to understand, these feelings and begin to question who they are. Most of the young people in this study claim that they began to become aware of their sexual orientation between the ages of ten and 16, in other words around puberty (although some young people say they knew they were gay as early as five or six years old). This is often a time of confusion and stress. Indeed, many of our interviewees pinpoint the emergence of their sexuality not in terms of an attraction to, or a relationship with someone of the same sex, but rather in terms of feeling different from their peers without necessarily realizing why this was so. These feelings are often only understood, or made sense of, retrospectively. Peter, aged 19 from Lisby, recalls: 'I'd say I finally admitted it [that he was gay] to myself at 15, but although I wouldn't admit it, I've known from being about 11.'

Given that peer groups are so important during childhood and adolescence, and that the pressure for conformity is intense (James 1993; Holland *et al.* 1994), this sense of being different is often accompanied by feelings of alienation and isolation. While some young people take their sexual feelings in their stride, 'coming out' to friends or families or seeking out lesbian and gay support networks, it is more common for most lesbian and gay youth to go through a period in which they recognize they are different but do not identify as lesbian or gay before they develop the knowledge or confidence to connect with the lesbian and gay community.

Most young people do not know where to find information about lesbian and gay groups and are fearful of being seen buying lesbian and gay magazines or of going to gay venues. There is a lesbian line and a gay switchboard available in Lisby, yet only one of the young people interviewed had known about it and used it. Even when young people know about support services available, actually making use of them can be difficult. For example those living at home with their parents may not feel safe to use the telephone to call help-lines or to give their phone number out to lesbian and gay contacts because they are afraid of their families finding out about their emergent sexuality, as Peter explains: 'I would have liked a phone service that I could have rang that wouldn't have appeared on the phone bill, I was very scared of my family finding out and thinking me a pervert, I never rang anyone.'

Likewise, Lynne from Sheldon recalls the problems she encountered trying to find someone to talk to:

> I did, I remember once – I must have been about 14 or 15 and phoned the Samaritans and had this awful conversation with a woman who I, kind of, visualize in a sort of 40s kind of twin set and pearls – who said to me – You will be alright, you just need to find a boyfriend. And it was, you know, the antithesis of what I wanted to hear. I wanted to hear something confirming, something positive and I remember coming away from that conversation feeling really awfully fed up with her response and just generally fed up I think. Because there didn't seem to be anywhere obvious that I could turn to. And I think – I remember, actually I remember going down the road to the phone box and I think – I must have been phoning lesbian line – yes I did do, I spoke to them a few times. And it was, it was very much, yes – I mean going down the road to the phone box I suppose is kind of quite telling, that I felt that I needed to do that.

Such experiences of isolation have a number of consequences. First, because most lesbian and gay youth have heterosexual parents, their families do not usually serve as a guiding norm for them. Unable to seek advice about sex and relationships from heterosexual parents or friends, and without the opportunities that heterosexual young people have to pick up sexual knowledges from everyday television programmes or newspapers and magazines, young lesbians and gay men are potentially vulnerable when they become sexually active.

Second, without support or positive role models it is quite common for lesbians and gay men to internalize negative representations of homosexuality which in turn makes them vulnerable to low self-esteem, depression and self-hatred. Although, the majority of interviewees who participated in our study were not suicidal (only one young man had taken an overdose, but some had thought about it, or were self-harming), there are indications in the literature that lesbian gay and bisexual youth are at high risk of making suicide attempts (McBee and Rogers 1997; Savin-Williams 1998). For example, in a study of members of lesbian, gay and bisexual youth groups in the US and Canada, Proctor and Groze (1994) found that over 40 per cent had attempted suicide at least once, while a further 26 per cent had seriously contemplated it.

In the circumstances it is not surprisingly that some young people deny or suppress their same-sex desires and seek out heterosexual relationships in the hope of becoming 'normal'. Indeed, 'coming out' is not a one-off linear process, rather young people may experiment with their sexuality reconceptualizing their identity not only in the transition to adulthood but throughout the life course.

Riva (a 24-year-old woman from Sheldon) was disowned by her parents at the age of 18 when she told them she was a lesbian. As she struggled with her sexuality she suffered a breakdown and attempted arson which led to her receiving a prison sentence. She describes below how she then got pregnant in a bid to redress her feelings of rejection and isolation:

> And then – then what did I do – oh yeah, I decided to have a baby, so I thought I'd have a baby, but I had to sleep with a man, and that weren't a good idea, but I still managed to do it. (Laughter) I didn't want to, but I was that drunk, it didn't really matter at the time, I just wanted a baby. 'Cos I felt real rejected, you know, by my family and everybody else, and I wanted somebody to love me without any reasons, so I thought the baby was – having a baby was the answer, but it wasn't.

Since then Riva has had counselling at a youth drop-in centre and is now more confident of her sexuality, but she recalls the difficult period she went through:

> I feel so much better in meself now, but I've been struggling really, with having the kids, I couldn't – me family couldn't understand why I was gay, if I could have a baby, do you get what I mean? So, there was a real confusion and it confused me as well, you know – 'Well, am I – well, I know I like it, so – so I must – there must be something there, but I don't want to go that way 'cos me family don't like it' – So, it was – it pulled me apart a bit, because I didn't know which direction I was going in, if you get what I mean?

Riva's children are currently in the care of her mother, who refuses to let her visit or have them back until she 'stops being gay', although she is trying to fight this through the courts at present. In this way, while Riva has found the transition to an adult sexual identity as lesbian difficult, she has not been a passive victim of circumstance. Rather, she is a strong young woman who made an active choice to pursue her sexual identity, is now in a stable relationship with a woman, and feels optimistic for the future. Indeed, she currently works as a volunteer at a youth drop-in centre, helping to empower other young people in similar circumstances to herself. Thus Riva's experiences demonstrate, that while the transition to an adult sexual identity as a lesbian or gay man brings with it potential risks and problems, processes of marginalization can also be resisted and overcome.

Lesbian and gay transitions within the family

'Youth transitions are not voyages of the single-handed mariner, but founded in social relationships' (Allatt 1997, 92). Several studies in particular have highlighted the crucial importance of parents, relatives and friends in shaping, supporting and sustaining young people through employment, housing and domestic transitions (Coles 1997; Jones 1995). Yet for lesbian and gay youth the overwhelming and taken for granted heterosexuality of the family home can be experienced as oppressive and alienating (Elwood 2000; Johnston and Valentine 1995). In particular, young people can feel guilt and discomfort at concealing their sexuality from family members. This can serve to drive a wedge between young people and their parents.

Lesbian and gay youth therefore face a difficult choice about whether to disclose their sexuality to their families or to pass as heterosexual. Coming out may produce more understanding, honesty and increased familial support but also carries with it the risk of rejection. As Nardi and Bolton (1998, 141) explain, 'frequently, gay youths are rejected and abused by parents, siblings and other kin because of their homosexuality. Thus, where other minority youth generally do not face problems with racism and religious intolerance within their own families, for gays and lesbians often abuse begins at home.'

The risks inherent in coming out to heterosexual family members are evident in Fiona's story. Fiona, a working-class, unemployed young woman, says that she knew she was lesbian from the age of seven, but she that felt unable to come out to her family until she was 19 when she moved from the small Scottish community where she grew up to Lisby. When she was ten her brother had suspected she was a lesbian and challenged her about her sexuality but she did not dare tell him because, in her words, 'he would have battered me'. When she was 14 she took the risk of coming out to a friend, with distressing consequences. Her friend was horrified and told her she was evil and began to pray for her. Fiona recalls her sense of isolation:

> Alone, I did, I felt really isolated ... I was just at home ... just like really convinced that I was just evil and that I was just ... just pure sin and that, 'cos it's like an old Christian community and there's loads of churches and that, and it was like oh shit.

When she did eventually come out, her father disowned her, and she has had no real support from her family since. As a consequence, Fiona has had suicidal thoughts and is still occasionally self-harming as she comes to terms with her lesbian identity.

A fear of such reaction prevents many lesbians and gay men from disclosing their sexuality to their families even though they may be 'out' to other people in their lives such as friends, teachers or colleagues. Peter (a working-class student, aged 19, from Lisby) receives a lot of support from his friends but is not yet 'out' to his parents, and does not intend coming out until he has a steady boyfriend. He describes the risks he has to weigh up:

> My mother would be fine, but she would tell my Dad. My Dad is okay sometimes, other times he sounds off, in the recent debate about gays in the military he said that all gays should be destroyed. He wasn't serious, but it still hurt. I need to work out if he hates gays more than he loves me ...

In contrast, to Fiona's experience and Peter's fears, Hilary, an 18 year-old undergraduate from a middle-class family in Lisby, describes her positive experience of coming out to her family:

> Yeah I've pretty much come out now. I told my sister not long after I told my best friend, she was fine ... and then I told my parents just after I turned 17. That was a very unplanned thing of 'why are you acting like this, you're being a pain in the backside, you've changed so much, you're always mardy' and I said 'Well, it's because I'm gay' and then burst into tears. This was only to Mum at that point and she just said 'It doesn't matter, it doesn't matter.' I mean I'd kind of broached the subject with her before but only sort of 'Mum what would you say if I said I was gay?' – this was when I was 14/15 and we'd just been sort of talking about the subject and I said 'Well what if it was me?', you know, and so she guessed and my Dad – she'd said stuff to my Dad as well. My Dad I was very worried about because of his reactions to people on television who were – mainly men I have to say – I hadn't seen a bad reaction towards a woman on television who was gay but I sort of didn't want him to know so, I mean, I said to Mum 'Please don't tell him ...' She said 'Of course I'm going to tell him, he's your father.' [laughs] 'He'll be fine about it.' And he was great. You know he said 'Well as long as you're not mardy and not a pain in the backside basically and you're sensible about it then you know it doesn't matter to us.'

Most experiences of 'coming out' fall somewhere between the two extremes of Fiona's and Hilary's stories. Coming out does not necessarily bring with it increased understanding, honesty and support. Rather, some parents go into denial or avoid acknowledging the young person's relation-ships and everyday experiences. Lynne, a middle-class postgraduate, aged 24, from Sheldon, was not rejected when she came out to her family but found that her sexuality was never really mentioned by them again. She explains:

> And I remember for about five years I worked on Lesbian Line and periodically my Dad would say 'Where have you been tonight and what have you been up to?' And I would say 'I have been to Lesbian Line.' But it kind of was a conversation stopper rather than a – right well tell me more about it [laugh]. That kind of thing. Rather than thinking – oh great, wonderful, you know, we will have a discussion about this topic, it tended to close things down.

While Lynne frequently challenges her parents' head-in-the-sand attitude and forces them to confront and talk about her sexuality, other young people are more protective of their parents' feelings. Young people are often presented as emotionally immature, less competent than their parents and in need of protection from the turbulence of adult relationships. Yet, many of the young people who participated in this research represented themselves as more worldly than their parents, arguing that they passed as heterosexual in the family home in order to protect their emotionally vulnerable parents from the hurt or disappoint-ment of discovering their sexuality, and from having to make similar choices about whether to disclose this information to other relatives and their friends. Amanda, a postgraduate, middle-class woman from Lisby, describes the way lesbian, gay and bisexual youth often take responsibility for their parents in a reversal of the traditional child-adult relationship:

> it's a curious thing where we're brought up with the idea that parents look after their children and this is the natural order of things but in this kind of like emotional area I know a lot of people who are not out to their parents because of what it would do them. How they would react to it. What it would do to the family. And you, you do see younger people taking control over information because it's not in their parent's best interests to know ... but we, I don't think we voluntarily do it I feel, I think we feel as if we have to do it, yeah. I don't know, maybe there are similarities there with young people who look after disabled parents, yeah. There's a substitution of parental role if you like, yeah.

As such, depending on individual and family circumstances, young people develop a complex range of strategies to conceal their sexual identity and pass as heterosexual (Valentine 1993b). For example, Tony, a working-class young man from Sheldon, pretended to his family that his best friend was actually his girlfriend because they were having difficulty dealing with his emergent gay identity. He and his friend would share a bed at his parents' house after a night out, and would bounce up and down on the bed groaning before going to sleep to give the illusion that they were having sex. The strategy of pretending to have an opposite-sex partner is one that many of our interviewees reported adopting while at school in order to fit in and to resist marginalization and exclusion within their peer groups.

Discussing the notion of 'passing' (that is, concealing one's sexual identity and passing as heterosexual) Babuscio (1988) argues that it is due to oppression in, for example, housing, employment, law and in wider society. He contends that passing shows the ways in which lesbian and gay people are marginalized: he states that 'passing is largely motivated by an assumption of failure, a conviction that one has failed to measure up to society's concept of "man" and "woman"' ' (Babuscio, 1988, 41). We suggest, however, that passing is not necessarily motivated by failure, but is usually a conscious strategy, adopted at particular times and in specific places in order to resist marginalization.[2] In other words, lesbian and gay young people are not always marginalized within the family, rather coming out to parents and making the transition from asexual child to lesbian/gay adult sexual identity is something which is dealt with through particular strategies in which 'passing' may be used by individuals for their own benefit or to protect their parents and siblings.

Lesbian and gay identities in education

In a study of 307 schools commissioned by Stonewall and the Terrence Higgins Trust, Douglas *et al.* (1997) found that 82 per cent of the schools contacted were aware of homophobic bullying within the institution. Although, 99 per cent of the schools had an anti-bullying policy in place, only 6 per cent had a specific anti-homophobic bullying policy. In part this reflects the confusion that the introduction of section 28 of the *Local Government Act* (1988) has caused in British schools. This states that 'a local authority shall not (a) intentionally promote homosexuality or publish material with the intention of promoting homosexuality; and (b) promote the teaching in any maintained school of the acceptability of homosexuality as a pretended family relationship'. As a result many schools report being unsure about how this law should be interpreted and whether they can provide for the needs of lesbian, gay and bisexual pupils.

In this institutional context coming out as lesbian, gay or bisexual can make the time spent in compulsory education difficult. Bob, a 19-year-old college student in Sheldon, describes how his experiences of homophobic abuse at school prevented him fulfilling his academic potential and led him to make an early exit from the education system:

> it [homophobic bullying] started up in year ten and it put me right off my studies, I used to really enjoy school up until I got into secondary school, I used to, I used to love it but then I got to secondary school and I hated it, I just wanted it to be over, I just thought, I just can't do this, I was glad the day I walked out, I know I got really, really poor grades ...

Almost without exception, the young people who participated in this study did not enjoy secondary schooling. While clear cases of homophobic bullying were not evident in all their accounts, the stress of wondering if anyone at school suspected their sexual orientation was ever present. Those young people who did attempt to talk to teachers felt that their experiences were ignored. Bob describes the failure of his teachers to deal with the way he was treated by his peers:

> They did, they'd hear it, they, they'd sort of half-heartedly tell the students off, but they didn't mean it. Deep down they weren't bothered, either way. It was like 'Oh stop being homophobic,' but they wouldn't take the, they'd say 'Oh stop saying that about that person,' or whatever, but they wouldn't say 'Stop being homophobic.' They'd just say 'Oh you shouldn't say that about people,' so they, they weren't really bothered. I think there was one or two teachers that knew about homophobia but again they were scared, I think they were scared of saying anything. I know as I moved up into year nine we got a new biology teacher and he was gay. You could tell he was gay, everybody knew and everybody took the mick out of him. I thought to myself 'Maybe I could talk to him, maybe,' but then I thought, 'Well okay, he's probably gay but he's a teacher, I've got a problem what do I do?' so I never mentioned it to him. I never, I never did anything ...

Indeed, most of the young people interviewed reported receiving no information about lesbian and gay sexualities at school, even in sex education classes. None of the young people had ever heard a teacher mention homosexuality at school. In the absence of any information about their sexuality some young people turned to the Internet for support. Peter explains how the Internet eased his sense of isolation:

> [I felt] isolated, very isolated. When I thought of gay I thought of Julian Clary and blokes with handle-bar moustaches in leather harnesses. I didn't want to become like that. Fortunately, when I got to college, I had Internet access, so I could look for gay-related sites. I found a lot of homepages that made me feel not so alone.

Andrew, a 16-year-old boy, from Lisby, although keen to take part in the research, refused to be interviewed face-to-face because he was not out (except within a small group at college) and elected instead to be interviewed by e-mail. Yet, despite being very closeted in off-line space, on-line Andrew was posting to a gay website, and even had a photograph of himself displayed there. Hinkinson-Hodnett (1999, 8) argues that young men in particular often find it easier to deal with their emerging sexuality through a computer screen rather than by talking face-to-face. He writes: 'forget a locked diary full of secret heartbreak – the new way to deal with being teenage and gay is through the Net. It's healthy; it's about expressing yourself and it doesn't require any embarrassing heart to hearts.'

Andrew uses the spatial strategy of performing his gay identity in cyberspace while maintaining a heterosexual front in off-line space as a way of negotiating his sexuality without coming out to his family and friends. In the same way other lesbians and gay men often use similar spatial and temporal strategies to manage their sexual identities in off-line spaces (Valentine 1993b). For example, some lesbians and gay men regard going away to college or university as an opportunity to come out in a place where their family and friends have no connections, yet, when they return to their home town they go back into the closet and resort to performing a heterosexual identity. However, while going to university is liberating for some, others feel just as inhibited about articulating their sexual identity in this new environment as they did at school, avoiding lesbian, gay and bisexual support groups through a fear of being outed to friends and academic staff.

Transition to the lesbian and gay community

Faced with experiences of marginalization or rejection at home and at school many young people eventually seek support from the lesbian and gay community. The provision of venues and support groups varies widely between places, with bars for gay men usually being more prevalent and visible than the lesbian scene (see, for example, Adler and Brenner 1992; Castells, 1983; Valentine 1995). Sheldon has a better-developed commercial gay 'scene' than Lisby, with a number of venues for young people to meet others.[3] Lisby, a more working-class city, has at present only two commercial gay venues (and one of these is only open one night a week). According to most of the people interviewed in Lisby there are certainly pockets of what might loosely be termed 'community' in the town, but these are divided by geographic area (that is, there might be a small gay community on several city estates, but the members of one community do not mix with members of another); and by class. As such it can be almost impossible for a young person just coming out to find others with whom they identify.

In Sheldon it is easier for young people to find gay venues because the gay scene is more developed. Bob, from Sheldon, used a copy of the *Gay Times* (a gay magazine) borrowed from a friend to find gay bars in his town:

> Yeah, managed to get a copy, looking I thought 'Ooh that's a gay, might go in there one night,' and go in, and you go in and at first everybody looks at you and thinks fresh meat and you think 'Ooh, it's a bit, it's a bit disorientating.' But you get used to it after a while, and you think to yourself 'Well I can see where this scene starts and see where it ends' ... It's great to go out and be who you are and do what you want to do basically.

For those young people who do not simply identify as lesbian or gay, participating in the gay community can be more problematic. Gareth explains his experience of marginalization on the scene:

> Bisexuals is actually a funny camp because, well, straight people traditionally don't like it because they're gay. But gay people sometimes – you get the gay people that don't like the straight people and they don't like bi's so often you get – I don't know I've discovered an awful lot of bi's, a lot of them haven't – when you go to the LGB everyone just assumes you're gay sort of thing and no-one ever clicks unless well maybe if you ask directly but no-one jumps up and says 'Oh I'm bi' sort of thing. So a lot of people hide like that sort of thing 'cos they're not sure how – I know I did – well, no, I didn't, well, yeah, I did – I don't know, you're just assumed to be gay or lesbian really by a lot of people I think.

Ponse (1978) argues that bisexuals are paradoxical in lesbian subculture, on the one hand occupying a legitimate position but on other hand being stigmatized for maintaining heterosexual privileges. She goes on to suggest that lesbian communities 'police' the performance of identity within their ranks, excluding, for example, women who have sex with women but who do not accept the signifier 'lesbian'. Likewise, other studies suggest that lesbian communities are also often fractured by other differences (such as class, 'race', age, politics etc.) which can generate exclusions (Taylor 1998; Valentine 1995).

The same is also true for the gay men's scene. Here, young men also described a lot of pressures to be sexually active and to consume alcohol and drugs to excess. Indeed, the police in Sheldon expressed concern about the number of young men being drawn into prostitution as rent boys. Terry, a 16-year-old college student from Sheldon, describes his experiences of being on the 'gay scene':

> I'm the youngest there as far as I know, but there are people, you know, roughly my age, but not as many ... I get more attention of I'm young,

but that tends to be off older people ... I have found that difficult ... if people offer to buy you drinks and stuff like that, you kind of think that you've got to owe them, or you kind of think there's something underlying behind that. Yeah, so I mean there is a tendency to like, oh, I'm really nervous so I'll drink a lot to give me the confidence.

As a consequence of these sorts of pressures, some young people undoubtedly find integrating into lesbian and gay communities difficult. There can be little space for them to question their sexuality in safety (which is also often denied in the home and at school) because they are expected to be sure of who they are by others who are more clear in their own sexual identities; and there are many pressures to be sexually active. As such some young people are vulnerable to being pressurized into making a 'forced' transition to a lesbian or gay sexual identity.

Conclusion

In this chapter we have focused on the transition young people make from the asexuality of childhood to an independent sexual identity as a lesbian/gay man. In doing so we have examined how young people negotiate this transition within the spaces of the family home, the education system and lesbian and gay communities.

Our interview material clearly demonstrates that young gay people find it difficult to make the transition to an independent adult sexual identity as a lesbian or gay man because of the homophobia they encounter, or are fearful of encountering, in everyday contexts. Young people receive a lack of information about lesbian and gay sexualities and issues at home and at school, they do not know where or how they may access this information from other sources, and commonly perceive there to be little emotional or practical support for their needs. As such they face risks and forms of marginalization which are very different from those faced by heterosexual young people, and are perhaps most vulnerable within social institutions which are commonly deemed to be among the most supportive for young people – the family and the education system.

In particular, lesbian and gay youth often experience a profound sense of isolation in the parental home and at school. This can make them vulnerable to self-harm, to destructive sexual experimentation in a bid to be 'normal', to difficult and sometimes violent familial relationships, and to making a premature exit from the education system. Such pressures are captured in this quote from Bob, from Sheldon. He was bullied at school and, unable to turn to anyone to discuss his dawning awareness of his homosexuality, took an overdose:

Yeah, it was everything, it was everything at once, it was a cumulative affect, it was like the bubble burst basically, everything spilled out. I was like 'Oh, can't gather it up, can't gather it up', so you had, you do something that's you think at the time's a bit rash, or afterwards you think it was a bit rash, but it's, it's not. It's everything. I felt like I was drowning, I felt that I was really drowning and nobody was there and it was a really, really bad experience.

In pointing to the need for more information to be made available about lesbian and gay issues within schools and the wider community, and the need for heterosexual society to be both more aware and accepting of 'other' sexualities, our findings are similar to other studies conducted in both the UK and North America (see, for example, Perry 1999). Our research also exposes however, the risks young people encounter in lesbian and gay spaces. While many young people receive a lot of positive support from lesbian and gay communities when they first come out, there is some evidence that young people are also vulnerable to sexual and social pressures in what are often quite socially and politically fractured environments.

Yet to conclude on a more positive note, our research does also highlight the strength and resourcefulness that many young lesbians and gay men demonstrate in recognizing and making the transition to an adult sexual identity and their ability to resist very difficult situations. As Savin-Williams (1998, 233) warns:

Viewing all sexual-minority youths as overwhelmed or defeated with problems in living diminishes the reality that such individuals are a minority of gay youths. Indeed, many youths with same-sex attractions have unique skills that allow them to cope and even thrive in a culture that seldom recognises them and actively attempts to suppress them. To deny their diversity and resiliency is, in short, to silence gay, bisexual and lesbian youths.

Acknowledgements

We are grateful to the Economic and Social Research Council (award no. L134 25 1032) for funding the research on which this chapter is based. Gill Valentine also wishes to acknowledge the Philip Leverhulme Prize.

Notes

1. The study involves work with hearing lesbian and gay youth, D/deaf lesbian and gay youth and D/deaf heterosexual young people. The term is written like this to indicate that our research involved work with D/deaf people who identify and

communicate in a range of different ways. Some of our informants regard deafness as a disability, others understand Deaf people to be a cultural and linguistic minority. Some informants use oral forms of communication, for others their first or preferred language is British Sign Language. The study was funded under the ESRC's Youth, Citizenship and Social Change Programme.

2. It should be noted that 'passing' is not something which only lesbian, gay and bisexual people do, rather it has been noted that disabled people often pass as able-bodied in some circumstances (Butler 2000).

3. However, the commercial provision is based around clubs and bars, therefore excluding the under 18s.

9
Single 20-something and Seeking?

Lynn Jamieson, Robert Stewart, Yaojun Li, Michael Anderson,
Frank Bechhofer and David McCrone

Introduction

The demise of marrying as the rite of passage that coincides with exit from the parental household, solemnizing the establishment of a new household and commitment to a sexual partner is well documented across a range of wealthy western countries. It is less certain whether being single is simultaneously being 'talked up' (discursively produced) and lived as a positive social category for women and men. It has previously been argued that never-married women cannot easily escape a sense of being marginalized (Gordon 1994) and that the 'symbolic and material influences' of marriage 'stretch to shape the lives of those furthest from marriage, as with never-marrying, never-co-habiting women' (Chandler 1991, 3). This paper explores the meaning of 'single' for young people in their 20s. The early 20s is now an age group in which not being married is statistically normal. Hence, this paper explores the attitude to being single and partnership plans of young people who are somewhat less in the shadow of marriage than either older unmarried people or young people of their age 30 years ago.

In Britain, over the 1980s the popularity of marriage seemed to decline from its all-time peak in the 1960s and 1970s. In both Scotland, and England and Wales, the average (mean) age of first marriage has climbed to 30 for men and 28 for women. During this same period, there was a significant increase in the number of couples living together without being married. Most couples marrying today have lived together before marriage and there is a growing number of longstanding unmarried co-resident couples. In the same period, there has been some increase in the minority of people who remain unpartnered, neither co-habiting nor marrying, a trend predicted to continue (Shaw and Haskey 1999). The proportion of young people living alone has increased, particularly in cities (Hall *et al.* 1999).[1] Families in which women are bringing up children alone have also increased in recent decades, including an increase in the 1990s in the proportion who have never married or co-habited with the father of the child (Berthoud *et al.* 1999; Haskey 1998).

If there is a resurgence in being single in the sense of never having married or co-habited, this is outstripped by the growth in being single as a consequence of more frequent exiting from marriage and co-habiting relationships. Divorce rates rose across the second half of the twentieth century and levelled out in the 1990s at between one in two and one in three marriages ending in divorce. Co-habitation has a higher rate of dissolution than marriage and this is true even controlling for duration of co-habitation (Haskey 1999).

Some sociological theorists suggest that permanent partnerships are in decline as a set piece of adult life. Such claims are variously based on general theoretical understandings of the enhanced fragility of personal life at the turn of the twenty-first century (Giddens 1992), fears about excessive self-obsession (Bellah *et al.* 1985; Bauman 1990) and heightened gender antagonisms (Beck 1992), or specifically laddish 'flights from commitment' and destructive crises of masculinity (Lees 1999). By contrast, many researchers of personal relationships emphasize continuity in the patterning of personal relationships such as a continued sense of family obligations and continued gender inequality and gendered conventions that constrain couple's room to manoeuvre (Finch 1989; Finch and Mason 1993; Jamieson 1998; Silva and Smart 1999). Explanations for the high rate of dissolution of heterosexual relationships often debunk the notion of a more general turning away from marriage-like arrangements, instead suggesting heightened expectations of relationships and lowered stigma of failing and trying again.

The question of the balance between remaining single and partnering has attracted less attention than the balance between marriage and co-habiting on the one hand and partnering and divorcing on the other. However, the propensity to remain single has long been a topic for demographers employing costs and benefits analysis. As Kravdel (1999, 7) puts it 'It is not obvious that a pooling of resources is more beneficial compared to life as single in a population where all have good economic prospects.' It is widely assumed that the abandonment of marriage-like arrangements was opened up as a practical possibility for women with the financial independence offered by their greater participation in paid employment and the back-up of state income support. It is salutary to note, however, that a recent study of women's earnings suggests that significant numbers of women have insufficient earning power to support an independent household (Rake 2000, 86).

There is surprisingly little research that addresses what single young people seek, want and expect of relationships. Is the experience of being single still in the permanent shadow of marriage? How gendered are young people's partnership plans and expectations about the future of their personal life? Is there an increase in 'laddish' flights from commitment among young men (Lees 1999)? Are there gender differences in balancing paid employment and personal life? Are young women more mindful of the economic difficulties of going it alone? In this chapter, we examine young people's accounts of the desirability of being single, their partner-ship plans, and the ways in which they refer to employment plans or other thoughts about the future.

The data

Our data consist of a survey of young men and women in the 20–29 age group living in the Kirkcaldy district of Fife in Scotland. Interviews were conducted in 204 households, resulting in 246 interviews with young people and their partners aged 20–29.[2] The initial respondents included 109 people in their 20s, 48 men and 61 women, who were not living with a partner at the time of interview. The data collected from these 109 'single' young people during the survey are drawn on in this chapter. (In what follows, we term this the 'survey' data.) Twenty-four had previously co-habited and 12 had previously been married, so a third had lived as a couple. Twenty-six of the 'singles' were mothers, three of the 'singles' were fathers. We also conducted intensive follow-up interviews with selected respondents from the main survey. In this chapter we make extensive use of the responses from the 14 interviewees who were not only single (in the sense of not living with a partner) but also either not in a relationship at all or else in a relationship which they described as not a partnership and having an uncertain future. (We refer to this data as the interview data.)

Choice, voluntarism and temporality

In her study of single women over 35, Gordon (1994), drawing on the work of Stein (1981) and Simon (1987), tries to draw a distinction between actively and consciously 'choosing' to be single and a broader category of women who have not consciously steered this course but she nevertheless classifies as voluntarily single. These are women who recognized that they may remain single as the unintended but preferred consequence of other choices, such as prioritizing work, finding the possible partners encoun-tered unattractive, or exiting from a particular relationship or relationships. They saw being single as a better alternative than not having made those choices. Gordon argues that the majority of women in her study were voluntarily single in this sense.

In contrast to her study, younger people are less likely to interpret choices in this way because they are not yet of the age in which being partnered is the norm. In Peter Stein's typology 'young never-married people' and 'never-marrieds' with an interest in partnership are 'voluntary temporary singles'. The statistics of partnership formation suggest that, for these young people, the passage of time will result in the majority becoming partnered, with a small, albeit growing, minority remaining single. In our study, both young men and women typically described being single as temporary. In answering the question 'Ideally by the age of 45, which would you prefer to be: married, living with somebody, single', the modal choice was 'married', with 'living with somebody' some way behind and only 8 per cent of single men and 3 per cent of single childless women picked 'single'. Intensive interviews also suggest that young women were more equivocal about declaring being single as a positive choice, even a temporary one, than men. In the survey a much larger minority of lone mothers (23 per cent) said their preferred status at age 45 was 'single' and again interviews illustrate their greater ambivalence about being partnered.

'Singles', gender, partnerships and partnering plans

Young people who are 'single' in the sense of not living with somebody, may, of course, nevertheless be 'in a relationship'. Sixty per cent of the 'single' young men in the survey and 54 per cent of the 'single' young women described themselves as in a relationship of some sort. A gradation of choices was offered leading up to 'partner' with the intention of discriminating between degrees of involvement in and commitment to a long-term relationship. The answers revealed gender differences in choice of description. The majority of young women 'in a relationship' (70 per cent) opted for 'I do think of this person as my partner'. This is also the top choice for young men, but a matching number distributed their answers evenly between the other choices, 'a steady sexual relationship, but with no emotional ties or commitment' and 'a steady sexual and romantic relationship but I don't think of this person as my partner'. Those who described themselves as having no relationship were asked if they were looking for one. Women were much more likely to say that they were 'not actively looking for any kind of relationship' than men.[3] 'Singles' in a relationship were asked about its future and although more women described the other person as 'a partner', young men were no less likely to say they were planning to progress to living together or marriage. Just over half of both young men and young women saw their relationship as involving such a plan. Single mothers were less likely to see the future as involving a partner than childless women or young men.[4] Interviews suggest that the gendered pattern of answers may be about gender differences in socially acceptable vocabularies of motive as well as divergence in behaviour.

   Thus, the survey of single young people indicated that just over half were not currently oriented to a long-term commitment, either not being in a relationship and not looking for either a partner or a romance or else being in a relationship which they viewed as short-term. While the same proportion of childless women and young men were neither seeking nor planning a partnership, this was true for a higher proportion of lone mothers. Overall, there was no notable gender difference. The propensity of men without relationships to be seeking one translated into a higher proportion of men than women seeking a romance or a partner, despite a higher proportion also seeking relationships without commitment. The group of men interested in seeking a partner-like relationship balanced the greater number of women describing an ongoing relationship as a partnership. However, the interviews revealed that what 'not looking' means in terms of commitment can be very different for men and women and undermined the apparent gender symmetry.

Perceptions of the advantages and disadvantages of being single

Single people were asked if they thought there were any advantages of living on their own rather than living with a partner. The majority of both men and women said 'yes' (69 per cent of the men and 77 per cent of the women). Slightly more agreed that there were disadvantages (73 per cent of the men and 82 per cent of the women), although childless women were more emphatic about the disadvantages of living on their own than single mothers. In exploring this further, respondents who said they saw some advantages were offered a list of advantages from which to select, and similarly with disadvantages.[5] In terms of disadvantages, the one item identified by the majority of men and women was 'loneliness/lack of companionship'. No other disadvantage was picked out by a clear majority. Women were more likely to pick 'financial insecurity' than men. In terms of advantages, the overwhelming majority[6] chose 'nobody else to please'. Many other items were chosen by more men than women. There were also differences, albeit not statistically significant, between childless women and lone mothers who had an intermediate position between childless women and men on all the advantages. For example, among those who saw advantages, 67 per cent of men chose 'money is your own' compared with 47 per cent of women overall but 55 per cent of single mothers. In general, men were more likely than women to pick negative items about partnership and less inclined to pick items indicating benefits.

Accounts of being temporarily single

'Enjoy freedoms, let yourself grow'

The interviews confirmed a greater emphasis on the constraints of partnership among young men than young women. Alan, for example, emphasized the constraining effect marriage has had on the activities of his friends:

I ken a lot o' freends that have been married eh, and you, that's it, you just dinnae see them again. Start gettin a lot o' money worries and a lot o' problems and ... Totally different people eh. And they, they gie up everything. Ken, maybe they were a' into like daein a lot o' sports and that. Daein a lot o' things, ken, but I just, I dinnae ken, they just seem to gie up. Ken, they get into a routine efter that eh. They just dinnae gang oot. I ken loads o' boys like that.

Walter, who had lived with his girl-friend for six months, described the break-up of his relationship with the girl-friend as a lucky escape from loss of freedom to come and go:

A' the thoughts and the plans that I had when I was wi' [girl-friend] just sort o', I forgot aboot. Ken. I thought, I'm kinda glad I didnae dae that and, because that would've been me tied doon. I would, I wouldna have had a life, ken. I wouldnae have been able to sort o' pack up and say, 'Right. I'm goin abroad to work.'

Walter emphasized freedom to roam in terms of geographical mobility. Roger made reference to the joys of sexual freedom when he talked about the importance of making up for time lost on steady girl-friends:

I've been away on holiday loads o' times wi' my mum and my dad and, eh, once wi' my friends up north and that, but I never actually done the Ibiza thing, you know what I mean. Eh, so I think, I'm 25 now, I want to, I want to experience what it's like. I want, I want to just live this single guy's life for a wee while. Do you know what I mean? Enjoy myself. ' Cause I've, I've sorta been in relationships since I was aboot 18 19, I always had the steady sorta girl-friend the whole time.

Women who were not in relationships and who said in the survey that they 'are not looking' did not present constraint in quite the same way. For example, Jane did refer to the constraints and negative possibilities of marriage but this was not underwriting complete temporary avoidance of partnership. She was explicitly open to and hopeful of 'meeting somebody'. She stressed that she above all was going to avoid a marriage like her mother's in which her mother was treated very badly. Her concern to 'better herself' and 'do things for me' meant being careful not automatically to follow the conventional partnership sequence: 'I don't want to just fall into a routine, you leave school, you get married, you have children, I never wanted that.' However, she had been on the verge of engagement at 21 expecting to be married at 22 when her boy-friend got engaged to somebody else. Wanting to avoid the constraints of doing the conventional thing did not mean having to avoid a relationship. Rather than presenting her failed relationship as a lucky escape she presented it as an experience that helped her grow as a person, more able to know herself and 'do things for me'.

The importance of personal growth was also stressed by Kirsty who had a boy-friend but was wary of living with him and uncertain about the future of the relationship because she was determined to work abroad and was unsure whether her boy-friend would go with her or that this could be successfully managed. She felt that he had not achieved an equal footing with her, not yet being fully mature:

> I think, at the moment he doesn't really know what he wants from his life, he doesn't have his own ideas as much as I do and sometimes I try and encourage him and say to him, well what is it you want, you know tell me really, without thinking about me, be selfish, really what is it you want. He says 'I just want to be wi' you and be happy you know and ...' I don't know maybe in time he'll come to something. I mean he's maybe in his head at the same stage I was when I was 19 or whatever, I don't know ... He needs to prove to me how he is as a person away from his family for instance.

'Get established in your career/job, gather some resources'

Young men's notions of travel also contained themes of personal growth but the emphasis was more often on 'the good life'; their reflections concerning the implications for partnership choice were more in terms of resources than the quality of relationship. For example, Alan's and Walter's accounts of travel, seeing things and doing things also blend into accounts of needing to get settled in employment and gather resources before settling down:

LJ: Yeah. But yet you said you thought maybe by the age of about 45 you'd be married, so.

Alan: Oh, I totally, I thought so. It's just that I'm wanting mair money, eh. Ken, like I couldnae just go and live in a Cooncil hoose, eh. I'd hae to go and buy a guid hoose, eh.

LJ: Right. It sounds like you're imagining yourself as, well, a single man for a while.

Walter: Yeah. Well I think I'd like tae, just tae sort o' get a, a bit o' career, a bit o' experience behind me. Eh, I suppose in the long term I'd like to get my own place. I'd like to start my own restaurant or something sort o' in the catering side or, eh, but that's no, that's years, that's, we're talking aboot 20 year away or maybe when I'm 40, 40, late 40s. Get settled into a place of my own but. Until then I want to sort o' travel a bit and see a bit, and different cultures and ...

LJ: Yeah. Would you be quite happy to not have a steady relationship with anybody until maybe your late 40s or?

Walter: Yeah. That's, that's what I want, what I want the noo Lynn, just tae sort o' no have any ties, just be my own person ...

LJ: But I mean if in the end, like well say by your 40s you want to be more settled, I mean if at that point you wanted to have children do you, do you think you would, you might end up feeling you've left it too late or? I mean, well obviously if you had a partner the same age as you, it would be too late, really. Em, would that matter or would you be quite happy never to have children?

Walter: Eh, I'd like to have children. Eh, I mean I would like to have children but I'd like to get settled first, I wouldnae like tae have tae sort o' have kids and then have to settle and stick into one job and make sure that the kids looked after well ... I mean you've got a secure home, a secure base for the kid and, eh. I don't know it's a tricky question that Lynn, it's, I do, I do want children but I dinnae want them sort o' in the near, in the next decade like.

A number of young men and women talked about how their work left them very little time for a relationship. Most saw this as a temporary phase that they would transcend once on top of the job or established in their career. Fiona and Laura as teachers both noted how time-consuming the early years of developing lesson plans were and how little time was left for a social life. When asked about future plans for children, Fiona noted:

Fiona: But, I reckon I would like to have kids. When I have them. I mean I know it won't be when I'm in my 20s unless something happens and I don't think anything like that will. 'Cause eh, if I do have a relationship I'm probably that careful that nothing would happen. And I'm not likely, I'm not of the, the way I've been brought up; I'm not likely to bedhop, as they say. You know, I'm not into that. So I reckon it would probably be a late one. Whether it be the 30s or even early 40s, I don't know.

LJ: Yeah. Yes, I mean more women are putting it off till quite late aren't they?

Fiona: Yeah. I mean I wouldn't like to have one just for the sake of having it. I would like to be sorted ... but, when I don't know. I mean at the moment the main thing is getting my career start, started. 'Cause I am still proving myself along the road, that I can do it.

While Fiona loved her work, Laura was already disillusioned and dreamed of establishing her own business. As a peripatetic teacher, she did not have her own classroom, with a stable pattern of classes, and was not convinced that the job would get easier. However, thinking about the fit between her current work and a future relationship and child-rearing encouraged her to shelve her desire to leave teaching:

I then started thinking about sort of, oh God it does sound like I plan things eh? But I thought like if you're married or babies come into the picture again, I thought teaching's quite a good job to be in for that 'cause the holidays, you know and ... By the time you, and then you sorta go back to part-time, still be working still in the same sorta career and things, sort of more fit it into what you can do. So that kinda sprung to mind as well and I thought maybe I should wait until I'm a bit older, know.

Mohammed, who worked long hours in his parents' business, and Nigel, a sales rep, both saw themselves as becoming established in their work so that they can relax and have more time in the future. Nigel described his job as tailored to single men:

We've had women work there but for some reason they've all left. It tends to, the job I do tends to take up a lotta your time I think ... And eh, it's all males. Eh, two o' which are married, out of about ten. So. I mean most of us, most of us are in our sorta mid- to late 20s, all very similar people although we come from different corners of the country. But it's almost like that might be a prerequisite for the job. You know I could be on a plane to London tomorrow for the next three or four days. If you have a wife and children to throw into that sort of equation, it becomes more difficult to do your job as well as you're doing it, so.

'Need for recovery'

The interviews contained a number of accounts of failed relationships and co-habitations. Both men and women talked about not wanting to rush into living with somebody again but only women stressed the need for recovery rather than the opening up of new opportunities: 'I've been with someone quite seriously and, and it just, it's, when I split up I thought no I'm not doing that for a long time and I didn't realize it was gonna be this long but ...' Here Trudy was referring to two years as a long time. Similar periods of time were remarked on by two other young women interviewees as a 'long time' to sort their lives out.

'I have a child now'

Single parents also expressed wariness about a new relationship because of their child. Lucy is single parent who was previously married and explained her caution about looking for a relationship:

> *Lucy*: It's too scary, I've got another person to think about now eh.
> *LJ*: Right. Do you think that'll be ...
> *Lucy*: I think it'll hold me back. Especially my ... [child interrupts]
> *LJ*: What is it about that that puts you off, I mean.
> *Lucy*: I'm just scared in case nobody's interested really, wi' somebody with a child. You know, I don't want to hurt myself ... I mean I suppose there's still is a lot o' men out there that are interested in, in somebody with a child but you've got to be careful, eh ... Cannae trust anybody these days.

Jill, another single parent, also worried about her child having too many fathers. She still saw her ex-boy-friend and he remained a friend although she no longer slept with him. She stressed the importance of her ex-boy-friend taking the role of her daughter's father, although he was not the biological father:

> Wi' [daughter's] situation, ken what I mean, if I have another boy-friend, she's gonna be going like that, know what I mean, 'How many daddies have I got?' Ken what I mean. So, there's just gonna be me and her and [ex-boy-friend]. But he's no gonna be there as like, sleeping the gether eh. He's gonna be there for [daughter]. But I dinnae want naebody else like.

Roger, a non-custodial father, focused his concern about the impact of future relationships on his child on whether his own relationship with her was sufficiently established not be damaged. He wanted a period of being single in which to have a good time before another 'steady' relationship and 'settling down'. He planned to create a suitable space between himself, the child's mother and his child in order to make this possible:

> I mean at the end o' the day I'd be away somewhere else, she'd [daughter] probably be here and I'd probably be (pause). I mean this is where I can see mysel' in a few years time. She gets away to school. I'm away to Edinburgh. [I] come through and see her now and again

or she comes through and sees me now and again. [I] meet somebody in Edinburgh and then you'd never know what can happen, sorta thing.

'I've not met the right one'

Women who said they were not 'looking' for a relationship often presented themselves as constantly open to a relationship. They were only 'not looking' because they had a general rule against ever 'looking'. Fiona, who gave an account of being single in terms of giving priority to work, made it clear that although she was 'not looking' she was open to a relationship. She took it for granted that the way of finding the relationship she wants was not to look but to build up her social life. This was something she had difficulty doing because of moving and the demands of a new teaching job:

> You're that busy with what you're wanting to do, your career and whatnot, that when you come back [after being at college] all your friends have moved off. I mean I've got friends in America and whatnot. That your social life is absolutely zilch. So. It's a case o' building up your social life, building up your circle of friends and then, they keep telling me, 'That man's out there somewhere'. (laughs)

Jane had this to say about her reasons for not actively looking for a relationship:

> I never go out looking for to find 'Mr Right' or to find anybody. I think, I just don't think you can do that. I go out to have fun and if I meet somebody fine. If I don't, then I'm still having a good laugh. I think if you go out with the expectation you're gonna meet somebody and you don't you're disappointing, you're ... you're having a bad night 'cause you're looking for something. But I think, I mean I've, I'm quite positive that I will meet somebody.

Jane is quoted above as emphasizing the importance of personal growth. She suggested that self-confidence would help her negotiate a good relationship when she found the right person. At the same time, she recognized that she had become quite fussy and that there were not many suitable candidates. So while emphatic about finding somebody, she was also rehearsing some of the explanations of being single made by Gordon's 'voluntarily single' older women:

> *Jane*: Em, but like I say I won't just go out wi' somebody so that I'm going out wi' somebody.

LJ:	Right, yeah. And in terms of kinda negotiating the sort of 50–50 kinda relationship that you want to have, do you think that'll be difficult? I mean.
Jane:	I think it's very difficult to find. I feel a lot of people are threatened by my independence in a lot of ways. And because I am very independent em, and some people think because in my suc, well my success really in my job, they feel threatened by it. Whereas I think in all honesty to be with somebody I'd need somebody on an even level intelligence-wise em, no disrespect to anybody else but I feel I, I need to sit down and be able to talk to somebody who understands what I'm talking about. Em, have an intellectual conversation as it was. Em, so I need, I think I'd need to find somebody on an even scale. Em, but it, I think as you get older it does get harder. Em, because I expect an awful lot … I'm quite particular I think I'm quite fussy. That's probably why I'm still single.

Some of the respondents who were more emphatic about remaining single sometimes also acknowledged that this position might be abandoned if they 'met somebody'. They did not want to 'find somebody' because they had other priorities but, nevertheless, tossed in a qualifying phrase about 'the right one'. The idea that it might be possible suddenly to meet a person who would change a planned period of remaining single was not necessarily associated with any detailed sense of what this person would be like. For example, when Alan mentioned the possibility of 'the right person' I asked:

LJ:	What would the right person have to be like, have you got any idea?
Alan:	Eh. I dinnae ken. I dinnae ken, nut.
LJ:	So how would you know when you met them.
Alan:	I dinnae ken. As long as she was good looking eh.
LJ:	Is that the most important thing, good looking?
Alan:	Well it helps eh.
LJ:	Yeah, yeah.
Alan:	I dinnae ken. You just, you just ken eh if it happens eh.
LJ:	What, because you'd be *in love* sort of thing.
Alan:	Well maybe aye.

Lucy a single parent who was previously quoted as wary about looking for a relationship, goes on to say:

Lucy:	I mean I suppose there's still is a lot o' men out there that are interested in, in somebody with a child but you've got to be careful eh … Cannae trust anybody these days.

LJ: Yeah, sure, yeah. So, do you think that'll be true for the next couple o' years, five years, ten years?

Lucy: I cannae really plan 'cause you don't know what's ahead o' you … You know, I might meet somebody tomorrow. You know, if it's gonna happen it'll happen. I'm not going out looking for something to happen.

LJ: Right. So you're not …

Lucy: I'm quite happy on my own just now you know. Making a life for myself. If I did meet somebody I suppose it would be a bonus.

LJ: Right. So it's not like completely a no-no, totally off the agenda?

Lucy: No, but I'm not looking for it. If it happens it happens.

Notions of the 'right one' who might change things were not obliterated by experiences of failed love relationships and could persist despite love relationships that have not had a transformative effect. While talk of finding the 'right one' or special person was common, young women were generally more likely to also emphasize that you have to work at relationships.

Partnership plans and economic security

In the survey, childless women were more likely to choose economic benefits as an advantage of being partnered than young men. The interviews provided some further insight into the perceived economic consequences of partnering. While it was not unusual for young women to emphasize becoming 'established' in paid employment, only young men stressed gathering resources prior to marriage in a way that assumed that the man would be the main provider. The earning power of both male and female respondents varied considerably. Some were already home owners while others defined themselves as simply not able to afford to buy a home. It is interesting to note that among those who could afford to do so, young women were not less likely to have purchased their own home than young men and, in this real material sense, no less likely to have begun gathering resources.

While a number of young women without relationships stressed that they would wish to continue to work if they did find a partner, two respondents outside of relationships expressed willingness to be a dependent upon a partner. Fergus joked about finding a rich girl-friend who would pay for him to travel round the world and Laura, who was already unhappy and feeling trapped in her job, expressed hypothetical willingness to give this up for part-time self-employment taking private pupils, if she had the security of a partner's support:

LJ: Right. So even, say you weren't enjoying teaching that much and, he had a reasonably well-paid job it wouldn't, that wouldn't tempt you to …

Laura: Oh yeah, if he was gonna offer me just to go and live and, if I could just go live with him and teach privately sort of, I would do that in a minute. Well ... I don't know if I would. I would certainly consider it.

LJ: Right. It wouldn't worry you to be slightly financially dependent or?

Laura: Oh no, I'd quite happily. (laughs) As long as I had some ... personal sort of. No, I'd spend anybody's money. I'm not proud.

At the same time, the survey suggests that the most economically vulnerable young women, lone mothers, valued their financial independence more than childless young women and were no more likely to see marriage or a partnership as bringing them financial security. Among our interviewees, Sheila was a single mother on benefit who had been engaged for three years to an employed partner who still lived with his parents. Her boy-friend could fit the stereotypical suitable provider/partner but they had no definite plans to marry or live together. Had they married or co-habited, as a couple they would possibly be poorer and certainly each have less financial independence than they had seeing each other on a regular basis. Living together might also have meant the reallocation of any domestic work being performed for her boy-friend in his parent's house to her, or at least new negotiation of divisions of domestic labour. Sheila refers to 'convenience' and getting 'peace':

Sheila: But, I cannae really say, em. Marriage isnae everything, nowadays marriage doesnae mean nothing. I'm, as far as I'm concerned people get married and then, the next time you see them they're divorced so, I don't know. I'm quite happy the way I am.

LJ: And would you rather live on your own with [your son] than live with somebody?

Sheila: No. No it's just that, that's mair convenient the now.

LJ: Right.

Sheila: Staying on my ane, I get peace and that the noo.

Discussion

Being single was not being described as a way of life that remains good across the whole life course, although single people in their 20s offered a rich variety of accounts for temporarily remaining single, some more celebratory of singleness than others. Focusing on being single allows us to examine the ways in which, for a substantial group of young people, aspects of their work, partnership and leisure practices are dovetailed. While theoretically our study enables us to explore in particular how partnership plans are framed in the context of personal ambitions and perceived life trajectories, in practice most single young people share the same long-term ambition to become partnered. The overwhelming majority of the respondents continued to think of their long-term futures in terms of committed relationships and living with a partner. While more currently saw advantages in 'living together as a couple' as opposed to getting married, most respondents still thought that they would be married by the age of 45. The majority wanted children and the notion that marriage is the best arrangement for bringing up children remains strong. Among the childless single respondents only 13 per cent of men and 8 per cent of women said they did not want children. At the same time young women emphasized that they could never imagine rushing into a relationship just because they wanted a partner in order to have children. Most childless young men and young women expected to be married in time to have children, a time-scale that was vaguer for men than women. In this sense, being young and single is still in the shadow of marriage.

Among those who were not in a relationship, more young men than young women were very committed to a period of voluntarily being single. This includes a 'laddish' group who wanted to pursue a 'singles life-style' of sexual freedom and freedom to roam. Pleasure, travel and new experiences were high on their agenda. Young women committed to personal growth also stressed the importance of not rushing into commitment and the value of experience in both work and leisure. There were both young men and women who emphasized the need to establish a career or a position of material security before partnering, and single mothers who weighed the needs of their child against the likelihood and benefits of a new or co-resident partner. These accounts did suggest hierarchies of plans that placed the possibility of partnership among other priorities. At the same time, many, perhaps most, thoughts about the future were tentative and open to revision rather than a definite programme of action. For example, young women who were 'not looking' for a relationship generally admitted more openness to the possibility than young men, despite saying that they were 'not looking'. Moreover, both men and women qualify emphatic statements about not wanting a relationship with the possibility of meeting somebody special who will change their mind.

In terms of exercising forethought and planning their personal lives, young men had more emphatic accounts of being single as a chosen temporary stage in a sequence of personal life stages. Women's accounts of 'not looking' and of positive reasons for 'being single' as a stage in a particular desired sequence were undermined by constant openness to finding 'Mr Right' and acknowledgements that he had not yet been found. Young women who were mothers typically already admitted defeat in terms of managing stages and sequences in their lives. Young fathers did not see fatherhood as a necessary constraint on their future management of personal life-stages in the way that young mothers did.

Gender differences persist beyond these particular subtleties. Success in work can be a time-consuming business for both men and women but the notion that success makes you intimidating and unattractive is a worry for women, but not for men. A committed relationship for young women did not mean constraint first and foremost in the way that it did for a group of young men. Women were more likely to see the need to negotiate as a way of having a good relationship while some young men thought of a relationship primarily as a constraint. Women did not start from a position of assumed unwillingess to negotiate and had less vague notions of what the 'right one' might be like. More young women had thought about the detail of how they wanted a relationship to be and were concerned about equality in their relationship. However, among both young men and young women there were references to a special person for whom rules might be broken. More young men than young women talked of past relationships which were conveniences and distractions rather than 'real relationships'.

While most saw their justifications for being single as resulting from the fact that they saw it as a temporary phase, this was likely to change if they continued to be unpartnered into their late 30s. Then the same accounts of being temporarily single might have to become the raw material for justifying a future that anticipates the possibility of remaining single. This would leave some of our respondents as 'voluntarily single' in Gordon's sense: arriving by accident having made choices to the best of their ability concerning work, 'getting established', the possible partners they encountered, bringing up their child, their need for self-development or 'a good time'. Some further shifts would need to take place before many would be able to unequivocally celebrate a permanent future of being single.

Authorship

Like all papers arising from these projects this is the product of collegiate fieldwork, analysis and discussion. Our normal practice is for the person responsible for initially drafting and subsequently revising the paper to be the first author with the rest of the team placed in random order.

Acknowledgements

We thank all of our respondents for their generous participation and gratefully acknowledge ESRC funding. The study is an ESRC-funded project (R000238020) 'Telling the Future: Individual and household plans among younger adults' (M. Anderson, F. Bechhofer, L. Jamieson, D. McCrone). This complements an ESRC-funded study (R0002396922) of adults aged 30–70, 'Individual and Household Strategies: A Decade of Change?' (M. Anderson, F. Bechhofer, D. McCrone) which follows up a sample of respondents from the earlier ESRC 'Social Change and Economic Life Initiative'. Survey questionnaires were designed by the research team and administered by Public Attitude Surveys. Interviews of single people were conducted by Lynn Jamieson and of couples by Robert Stewart. We are grateful to the Institute for Social and Economic Research at the University of Essex for help in commissioning, piloting, cleaning and checking

Notes

1. Although note that changes in census definition have resulted in the reclassification of some households from shared household to multiple single households and that this has also inflated the numbers.
2. There were also a small number of partners outside this age range who have been excluded for the purposes of this paper.
3. Twenty-two out of 28 women not in a relationship versus 10 out of 20 men. The men who described themselves as 'looking' were equally divided between a search for a 'partner' and a search for a 'sexual relationship with no emotional ties or commitment'. Women were more likely to say they were looking for a partner or a romantic relationship.

Table 9.1   Looking at the options on this card, which one would best describe what you are doing now?

	Males	Females
I'm not actively looking for any kind of relationship	47% (9)	79% (22)
I'm looking for a sexual relationship without emotional ties or commitment	21% (4)	4% (1)
I'm looking for a romantic/loving relationship but not a partner	10% (2)	7% (2)
I'm looking for a relationship that I hope will be a partnership	21% (4)	10% (3)
Total	100%=19	100%=28

4.

Table 9.2   Relationship plans among those 'with relationships'

	Males	Females	
		No child	With child
Plan to live with	5	3	4
Plan to marry	10	9	2
No plans	14	8	7
Total	29	20	13

5. The whole list of advantages was:
      'Nobody else to have to please/personal independence';
      'No legal ties';
      'Keeping options open';
      'It is possible to move to another town/place more easily';
      'Sexual freedom';
      'More time for friendship';
      'Money is your own/financial advantages';
      'Other' (specify).
    The whole list of disadvantages was:
      'Loneliness/lack of companionship';
      'Lack of sexual relationship';
      'Financial insecurity';
      'Having to do everything yourself';
      'Parental disapproval';
      'Other financial disadvantages';
      'Other' (specify).
6. Ninety-seven per cent of men and 89 per cent of women asked; that is 66 per cent of all men and 70 per cent of all the young women.

Appendix

Alan Aged 29, lives with his parents. Has never left home. Has a secure job as a machine operator but has trained to become a body-guard and is seeking a new position. He described himself in the survey as having no relationship and looking for a sexual relationship with no emotional ties or commitment.

Fergus Aged 25, lives with his parents having returned home after a career change and going to university as a mature student. He is now applying for jobs overseas teaching English as a foreign language. He described himself in the survey as having no relationship and looking for a partner.

Fiona Aged 24, lives with her parents having returned after training to be a teacher. She is in her first secure teaching job after replacement and supply teaching. She described herself in the survey as having no relationship and looking for a romantic relationship not a partner.

Jane Aged 25, lives in her own house, which was for sale at the time of interview. She works as a financial advisor and insurance agent and is looking for a new job and house. She described herself in the survey as having no relationship and not looking.

Jill Aged 23, is a lone mother with her own tenancy in local authority housing. She co-habited with her boy-friend from 16. Her pregnancy followed the break-down of this relationship and she does not see the father of her child. She has no employment. She sees her former boy-friend as a friend and has no other relationship.

Kirsty Aged 24, lives with her parents having previously worked abroad following college. She is working in a local office until doing a TEFL course and plans to work abroad. She described herself in the survey as having a romantic relationship but not a partner and 'planning to live with this person but I have not thought beyond that'.

Laura Aged 25, lives in her own home and is a peripatetic teacher. She described herself in the survey as having no relationship and not looking.

Lucy Aged 21, is a lone mother who was previously married, marriage having been hastened by pregnancy. She still sees her former partner who takes the child at weekends. At the time of interview she was about to start a job as a care worker. In the survey she described herself as having no relationship and not looking.

Mohammed Aged 21, lives in the parental home, never having left and works in the family business. He described himself in the survey as having a steady sexual/romantic relationship but not a partner and expecting the relationship to end.

Nigel Aged 27, lives in his own home. He is a business rep and expects promotion or a job change in the next year. He described himself in the survey as having no relationship and looking for a sexual relationship with no emotional ties or commitment.

Roger Aged 25, lives in his own home which he purchased when his girl-friend was about to have his child. However, the relationship broke down and he 'threw her out'. He has a secure, skilled job in a service trade.

Shella Aged 23, is a single parent with her own tenancy in local authority housing. She described herself in the survey as having a partner but with no plans to marry or live with him because 'I have not thought about the future'. She does not see the father of her child and was not employed at the time of interview.

Trudy Aged 26, has migrated to Edinburgh and lives in a shared flat. She does telephone debt collection work. She described herself in the survey as having no relationship and not looking. She has previously co-habited.

Walter Aged 28, lives at home with his parents having previously lived away from home with a girl-friend and also having served a prison sentence. He was unemployed at the time of interview but was planning to use his trade to get work on cruise ships. He described himself in the survey as having no relationship and not looking.

Part III
Re-formulations

10
'Making It Their Home': In-migration, Time, Social Change and Belonging in a Rural Community[1]

Catherine Maclean

In this chapter, I seek to demonstrate how time and the life course combine with other factors including age, generation and social change, to affect the chances In-migrants to a rural community have of successfully making it their home. I begin by outlining developments in the literature pertaining to 'belonging', migration and social change, focusing largely on rural Britain. I go on to examine a particular rural community, the parish of 'Beulach' in the Highlands of Scotland. I show how in Beulach, the personal characteristics and behaviour of any individual in-migrant were set within a specific context of social change which had resulted in the community being relatively open to newcomers, but more so to those with time and life course factors operating in their favour. The concluding section of the chapter compares the Beulach case with the wider literature in a discussion of the relative salience of a range of factors in processes of migration and belonging.

In-migration to rural communities

Sociological accounts of community divisions and conflicts have a long history of positing a dichotomous opposition between 'insiders' and 'outsiders', and while the exact terminology varies from study to study (and from community to community), it appears that everywhere, there are those who belong and those who do not (Crow and Allan 1995b). The insider/outsider distinction is found in many classic sociological studies of community (see Elias and Scotson 1994; Frankenberg 1957; Stacey 1960; Williams 1956; 1963). The clear-cut distinction is perhaps easier to maintain in distinctly bounded locations such as islands (Bennett 1990; Cohen 1987; Forsythe 1980). It has also been observed that 'belonging' has become a dominant theme of the anthropology of Britain (Macdonald 1997). The work of Cohen (1989) has been very influential in this

157

development, including the now well-established concept that people are most sensitive to their culture at its boundaries with other cultures. There has been a growing awareness that the cultural boundary between locals and incomers is flexible and that 'belonging' can be a contextual, fluid, varying, constructed and contested process (see Gilligan 1987; Macdonald 1997; Phillips 1986). It is rarely the case that 'belonging' is tied simply to ancestral links and length of residence, with individuals moving along smoothly over time from 'outsider' to 'insider'.

Community has for some time been understood as involving dimensions of place, social structure and meaning. Crow and Allan (1995a, 149) add to this the fourth dimension of time, arguing that it mediates the connections between these other aspects of communities. Time has a major influence on the ways in which community processes are interconnected, and neglecting it reproduces static typologies that fail to capture the dynamic nature of community formation and development (*ibid.*, 147). The conceptual replacement of dichotomy by continuum had the effect of introducing a more temporal dimension to theories about 'belonging', although attempts to place a figure on the amount of time it takes to move along the continuum from outsider to insider vary considerably from study to study (Crow and Allan 1995b, 2). It is likely to take less time to become an insider in communities where there has been considerable in-migration. Where there are many incomers, someone who has been a resident for only five years can seem relatively local (Jones 1999; Maclean 1997). However, as Jones found in the Scottish Borders, 'meeting time criteria does not automatically lead to acceptance as a local' (1999, 15). It thus does not seem particularly valuable to attempt to set time-scales for 'belonging', but a wider appreciation of the role of time can benefit analysis of the interrelationships between other significant factors in this process. Kenyon (2000) argues that attempts to categorize communities rigidly are doomed to fail, and 'lack of fit' must be accepted as normal. She emphasizes 'the adapting and changing nature of community, and the centrality of "time"' in the process of bringing together and pushing apart communities (*ibid.*, 21). Appreciating the centrality of time was crucial to understanding the experiences of incomers and locals in her research in Sunderland. She states that it is necessary to be flexible in approach, and recognize that the different aspects of communities (e.g. place, sense of belonging) can combine in different ways and be of greater or lesser significance over time.

Awareness has also grown that there has been a tendency to treat 'belonging' as an unqualified good and a goal desirable to all, and this may not always be appropriate. Jamieson *et al.* (1996) found a category of 'detached stayers' who, although remaining in the Borders after leaving school, felt excluded and voiced negative feelings about the locality (see also Albrow *et al.*'s 'dispossessed local' 1994). Not all in-migrants will wish to be involved in village life (Burnett 1998, 207). It is easier for the newcomer to maintain detachment (unless their livelihood depends on others) than for the person who belongs to become more detached (a reason for many locals, particularly young adults, to leave – see Jamieson *et al.* 1996; Jones 1999; Maclean 1997).

In some localities, the definition of 'villager' potentially encompasses all people who participate in local life (Strathern 1982a; 1982b), or a person can become an 'honorary local' if they marry someone who belongs (Wight 1993). In others, opportunities are not so open. Socio-economic status is a significant factor in acceptance of in-migrants in many cases. Certain in-migrants have had a disproportionately high profile, the type referred to by Bolton and Chalkley (1990, 40) as 'bees, beans and brown bread', and by one of my informants as 'the wood stove and crunchy Granola biscuits crowd'. In the Highlands and Islands this type of in-migration is often associated with being middle-class and English. Elsewhere in Scotland, Nadel (1986) found that 'True Ferrydeners' had developed a fierce commitment to egalitarianism amongst themselves in opposition to stigmatization by middle-class Montrose people who had moved to Ferryden. Retirement migration ('coming here to die', Gilligan 1987, 77) is often viewed more negatively than migration by younger people and families including children. In terms of gender, in-migration can be hard for women if they do not fit conventional expectations, but conversely, one of the easiest routes to 'belonging' is for a woman to marry a local man (thus even acquiring a local-sounding name) and have locally born children (Maclean 1997; Macleod 1992).

Personal characteristics and behaviour have been relatively neglected in the sociological account of belonging, with a few exceptions. Burnett (1996) argued from her Hebridean research findings that personal attributes, such as how friendly someone is, are important indicators of potential for 'belonging'; and that this status can be worked on and negotiated, but always remains fragile, with a risk of it being lost. In a study of young people in the Borders, some respondents thought that incomers have to take responsibility for inclusion or exclusion, and distinguished between 'fitting in', 'putting something into the community' and 'taking over' (Jones 1999, 16). There is a degree of agency and choice in 'belonging' which is perhaps a more managed process than has generally been recognized in the literature. However, this should not be overstated, as there are also constraining factors and 'limits to the possibilities within the repertoire that can be achieved by any individual: neither localness or strangerness are equally open to all' (Macdonald 1997, 156). There are also people whose ambiguous status blends elements of incomer and local simultaneously: those who marry in to a community; those who work locally but live elsewhere (Crow and Allan 1995a); those from a community who no longer live there but retain a social presence through gossip networks (Macdonald 1997; Mewett 1982a; 1982b); and those who move to a community as a small child (Maclean 1997).

The range of research has thus shown that categories such as incomer and local are not very meaningful or accurate labels in the sense that real individuals do not often, if ever, fit neatly into them. Indeed, Burnett argues the incomer/local distinction is of increasingly debatable worth (1998, 217) and that we should resist using such divisive categories (1998, 204). Moreover, caution should be exercised in translating directly from the terms as used by residents in a community to social science terminology. Phillips (1986) argues that dichotomous idioms such as local/incomer are 'cultural shorthand' and in the 'longhand' practice of gossip and conversation, people represent themselves and others in less dualistic, more qualified ways. Jedrej and Nuttall argue that the commonsense terms 'locals' and 'incomers' are not a literal description of reality, and cannot be equated to the technical terms and definitions of demography. They conclude that the incomer/local vocabulary 'is a complex and deeply embedded metaphor providing the terms through which people express and give meaning to the experiences which constitute their lives' (1995, 116).

It is easier, however, to say the categories incomer/local are problematic, than it is to move beyond them. Crow and Allan remark that an 'outsider to insider' continuum risks losing the relational quality of the insider/outsider distinction (1995b, 10). Increasingly subtle theories of belonging allow a more sophisticated understanding than the dichotomous insider/outsider model, yet unequal claims on the status of 'belonging' are clearly still an important feature of life in many communities, including the case study locality discussed in the current chapter.

Discussion of in-migration and 'belonging' is often underpinned by moral assumptions, associating those who belong with certain entitlements, which may be represented as being eroded or denied. This is particularly noticeable in discourse about access to rural housing. Mention the Highlands and housing in Scotland and the likely response would encompass housing shortages, second homes standing empty for most of the year, and locals being priced out of the market by incomers (Jedrej and Nuttall 1995, 115). The media have had an influential role in the debate about in-migration and in the negative portrayal of the in-migrant (Blain and Burnett 1994; Jedrej and Nuttall 1996). Tensions over housing are seldom mentioned in the earlier community studies: it would appear that feelings of scarcity, price inflation and unequal competition with in-migrants are linked to the phenomenon of 'rural renaissance' in the developed world from the early 1970s (Champion 1989). Conflict over ownership and occupation of rural housing is widespread in Britain (Shucksmith 1990, 211). In the Scottish Highlands, Gray found 'mutterings of hostility' (1993, 463) about the issue, and Skiffington concluded that young people living in mobile homes were particularly resentful of second home owners (1991, 268). Similar feelings have been documented elsewhere including Cornwall (Burton 1997; Gilligan 1987), Wales (Day and Murdoch 1993) and Orkney

(Forsythe 1980). Likewise, in rural East Anglia, Coleman identified a negative 'second home mythology' (1982, 102). However, he found that second home owners did not wholly conform to the stereotype: fewer were planning retirement to the area and more were actively contributing to the local society and economy than expected. Several studies including Coleman's have found that many in-migrants buy and restore buildings not suited to local needs, that would otherwise be (or already had been) abandoned (see also Caird 1972; Newby 1979). Macdonald found that many 'white settlers' in Skye moved into property vacated by other 'white settlers', leading to a high turnover of in-migrants which co-existed with local perceptions that in-migration was a cumulative invasion (1997, 136). On Arran, Damer found that it was common for second home owners to have strong connections to the island stretching back over many generations (2000). Occasionally, more popular accounts point out that incomers cannot shoulder all the blame (see A. Maclean 1984, 192). McAlpine argued in an article on Ardnamurchan that 'the natives are also responsible for the darkened windows and locked doors': because they work in the south and come back for holidays, let out their cottages to visitors, or sell them at high prices (*The Scotsman Weekend* 19 February 1994).

The research

The case study presented in this chapter draws on data collected during three years' research examining migration and social change in remote rural areas. The data comprises fieldnotes and semi-structured tape-recorded interviews from 18 months' ethnographic fieldwork conducted during 1995–6 in 'Beulach', a parish in the north of Scotland. Other data sources utilized were the Population Census, the Census Small Area Statistics, the Register of Sasines,[2] and local sources such as health centre records. Methodological issues are dealt with in greater depth elsewhere (Maclean 1997; 2000a; 2000b), but I wish to summarize four points here. First, at the outset of the research, I had a status somewhere between 'insider' and 'outsider' (Jenkins 1984). I had prior knowledge of the area and relationships with people there, developed through time spent on family holidays and working in the tourism sector, but had no kin connections, and no-one in my family had ever lived permanently or owned property in the parish. Second, the anonymity of the research participants has been protected in accordance with the British Sociological Association's Ethical Guidelines by giving places and people pseudonyms, and altering certain unnecessarily specific and revealing details. Third, I use the past tense when referring to data in this paper, to avoid the artificiality of 'the ethnographic present' (Davis 1992; Wight 1993). Several years after the fieldwork, many aspects of life in Beulach remain the same, but communities do change, even if only in the minutiae of individuals' lives, and I wish to emphasize that my research took place in a particular period of one community's history. Finally, in researching issues surrounding migration, there is considerable value to an approach that does not rely on one method of data collection alone. For example, much of the literature does not distinguish or explore the differences between what is felt or said by local residents about the housing market and what is actually happening in terms of house and land sales. The combination of ethnographic methods and the use of statistics from the Register of Sasines and the Population Census threw many issues into relief. Analysis of various statistical records subsequent to the fieldwork revealed some interestingly counter-intuitive data. Equally, comprehending the significance of much of the Sasines data, or assessing the validity of Sasines and Census entries, would have been impossible without the extensive knowledge gained during 18 months' fieldwork. It was the *combination* of the two approaches which was so fruitful.

Belonging to Beulach

In this section, the Beulach case will be examined in more detail. Focusing on the interconnections between in-migration, housing, belonging and social change reveals the role played by time and the life course, in conjunction with several other significant factors.

In common with the Highlands in general, and also with many other remote rural areas, Beulach has experienced a process known as 'population turnround' (see Bolton and Chalkley 1990; McCleery 1991; Smailes and Hugo 1985). There was a population decline from the later nineteenth century until the 1960s. Thereafter, population stabilized and increased slightly for a combination of reasons including Beulachers' decisions to stay in or return to the parish, and the in-migration of more people from further afield in the UK and abroad. At the time of the research, there were around a thousand inhabitants, mostly located in the coastal areas of the parish, in or near the main village, Bailemór. At the 1991 Census, 74 per cent of Beulach residents had been born in Scotland (many outwith Beulach) and 21 per cent had been born in England. Of the remaining 5 per cent, three-fifths were born in other European countries, including Wales, Northern Ireland and the Irish Republic.

In Beulach, there was to an extent a received wisdom that incomers have pushed up house prices, expressed not only by 'real locals' but also by those with fewer or no kin ties to the area. For example, Harry, born in the 1930s in a working-class, urban area of southern Scotland, lived in Beulach from the early 1960s. He met and married a woman who was a regular summer visitor to the area. They left in the mid-1980s in order to live in close proximity to a hospital. I interviewed Harry when he returned on holiday in 1995, and he told me:

There was resentment about holiday homes, the white settlers especially. Especially the English, the middle-classes coming up – solicitors, doctors – so many of them came up, they were nice when they were having a holiday home, or trying to get a home, but once they got it and they were moving here full-time, then they tried to act lord of the manor, as though they were the real millionaires, the landowners, and they, most of them weren't popular, probably a lot of them are still not popular. They were sort of resented. And then of course they pushed the prices of houses away up. If there was any empty croft houses, they'd pay in those days 10–20,000 for it and no local people could afford that, so they were resented very much for that. But the ones that were coming up, younger people living and making it their home and working in the place, most of them were welcome. Most of the local people saw that they had new ideas and they helped to develop the place … most of them were welcomed, I think, and integrated very well into the community

This short excerpt encapsulates many of the most salient factors at issue, and their interconnections. The first point to be noted is Harry's use of the term 'white settler'. Contrary to Jedrej and Nuttall's judgement (1996) that the term 'white settler' is heard as frequently as 'incomer', Beulachers generally avoid using the former as it is viewed as derogatory and offensive. I heard it most frequently in mocking self-reference by certain in-migrants, and occasionally during particularly heated conflicts. When asked, people usually said a 'white settler' was quite easy to define: someone from the south, with plenty of money, who did not fit into the local way of life, either not taking part at all, or interfering and trying to 'take over'. If I then named a person with those characteristics who was quite well liked by the person I was speaking to, the response would be denial and an attempt to explain why my example was not a 'white settler'. Three or four people at this point said straightforwardly that a white settler was someone you did not like, who had these characteristics. In Harry's case, he was an in-migrant whose in-migrant wife sold an expensive house further south in Scotland, which provided them with capital to acquire land and build a new house in Beulach. However, he does not think of himself or his wife as white settlers. Rather, when he uses the term he is referring to middle-aged, middle-class, male English professionals. He also associates it with a particular type of behaviour and attempted social climbing. These are the people to whom he attributes house price increases and the engendering of local resentment. On the other hand, people at an earlier stage of the life course, with a definite commitment to the area expressed through time spent taking part in local life, working and making Beulach their home, were welcomed. He has placed himself, his wife and their circle of friends in a category of unresented in-migrants, who apparently did not affect property prices although they bought or built houses in the area.

Another interviewee, Liza, also described 'incomers' as a category apart, but realized as she spoke that her own daughter and son-in-law, Ella and Johnny, would seem to fit the category she was describing, and amended it accordingly to encompass 'connection'. Liza herself was born in Glasgow in 1910, but spent most of her childhood living with relatives in Beulach. When she left school she returned to the city to work and subsequently married and settled there. I interviewed her on a return visit and she explained:

> When I come up here [now], the people that I know, and the way of living is quite different to what it was. A lot for the better, mind, I'm not condemning it, but ... there's as many Glasgow people here as there are the ones that Johnny and Ella know – well they're from Glasgow themselves [laughing] – but then they have some, Ella had some connection with the place. I'm amazed at the number of people who are up and they don't seem to have any connection with the place at all. But Johnny and Ella have been up 13 years I think. Och, when they used to talk about it, I thought, och, they'll never do it, they'll never come up. Johnny used to say, well, if I don't go up before I'm 40 I'll not go up at all. And they've made a life for themselves. Oh yes. Quite a change.

Many Beulach residents and former residents, both in-migrants and those with more claim to 'belonging' through kin connections, talked about it being a pity that 'the real locals are dying out'. At the same time, most also expressed an awareness and appreciation that in-migration has made the community more populous and lively, and that many incomers 'do up' houses that young local couples would not want to take on. A good example of a narrative on these sometimes ambivalent and contradictory views comes from Peggy. She was born in 1922 and brought up in a quintessentially 'real local' family, and spent all her working life in southern cities before returning to Beulach upon her retirement. She said:

> There were no houses for sale, as such, here, for years and years ... there was always somebody away from home who wanted to hold on to the house. It just all depended on whether the croft[3] houses were occupied and if they had relatives who, quite naturally, wanted to hold on to them, that they would come back when they retired. It all depended on that ... And then the grants for doing up houses and building houses improved, provided it was on a croft. If a couple got a croft, they could then build a house on it or build up the ruin ... but ... that's all changed now of course, houses go on the market and they're so expensive the local people can't buy them. But ... while a lot of people say it's dreadful, there's hardly any local people, it's all strangers that you see in Bailemór in the store now, if somebody hadn't come, the place would be derelict, there'd be nothing.

Peggy, like Harry, defends in general terms her own circumstances, saying it was 'quite natural' that many houses should stand empty, effectively the second homes of local people who spent their entire working lives elsewhere. Despite identifying a long period in which housing was monopolized by locals, she then describes houses going on the market at prices too high for locals – without indicating any agency in this process. There is no expressed awareness that responsibility might rest as much with the locals who were choosing to 'hold on to the houses' or sell them at these prices, as it does with the in-migrants who were buying them. However, Peggy also recognizes that in-migration has brought positive advantages to Beulach.

Similar sentiments were articulated many times during the fieldwork. Ambivalence was often expressed about the type of in-migrant most likely to be referred to as a 'white settler' – as we have seen above, someone who is relatively affluent, often not resident year round, and remaining detached from local life or conversely, attempting to 'take over' (cf. Gilligan 1987). Anxieties were also apparent about in-migrants referred to in Beulach as 'problem families' or 'undesirables' (cf. Wight 1993, on council tenants viewed as undermining local respectability in Cauldmoss). This was a particular concern in the late 1960s and 1970s when council house provision increased dramatically, and resurfaced during the fieldwork, in response to active collaboration between the local social work department and a number of housing associations. The anxiety seemed to relate to critical mass – the feeling being that a small village could only cope with a limited influx of such families. (Of course, it was not the case that there was no 'local' alcoholism, domestic violence or mental health problems.)

A range of different sorts of housing, and the availability of Crofters Commission loans to build new houses, meant that the issue of competition for housing stock was not as severe as it could otherwise have been. In addition, because Beulach had become more demographically and economically healthy, there were at least some locally resident families (such as those who had made money in fishing or tourism, or had secure professional jobs) who were able to compete with in-migrants on fairly equal terms. Incomers were certainly not always the 'winners' in the property market, riding roughshod over local housing needs at the expense of naïve natives. Return migrants or those from wealthier local families had successfully bought and renovated desirable houses.

An examination of the Register of Sasines revealed that in fact very few houses appeared to fit the stereotypical image of dramatic price increases tied to incomer demand. The numerically significant sales (bits of ground and council houses) were certainly not the high profile ones in village gossip. The Sasines also revealed that migration was in evidence earlier in the century than popularly supposed (see also Maclean 2000a; 2000b)

There were several cases of middle-class, retired professional in-migrants buying Beulach property before the Second World War. Properties had evidently been going in and out of Highland hands during the later twentieth century, but there were occasional cases of 'incomer houses', which experienced a high turnover of different in-migrants (cf. Macdonald 1997, 136). During the fieldwork period, the Beulach housing market was quite active, and houses did not tend to languish unsold for long, or go for very low prices. While house prices were not too unreasonable, it was a hard market for first-time buyers such as less affluent young couples (cf. Shucksmith 1990, 224–5), given the scarcity of secure, well-paid, year-round employment. There were certainly groups of residents who were disadvantaged by comparison both with new in-migrants and with more financially secure residents.

Analysis of the Census Small Area Statistics revealed that a substantial 28 per cent (n = 550) of houses in the Beulach area came under the heading of 'accommodation not used as main residence'. This was not evenly distributed throughout the parish, with the consequence that in five of the more picturesque townships, the proportion of holiday homes rose to nearly half of all houses. Closer examination of the parish as a whole revealed that there were at least as many holiday accommodation dwellings owned by Beulach residents (which in many cases made staying in Beulach financially viable for them) as there were second homes.

In general, however, housing was not highly contentious, and there did not seem to be particularly strong hostility towards in-migrants on those grounds, or feelings of direct competition between 'locals' and 'incomers'. Hostility expressed in terms of incomers/white settlers was far more likely to surface in relation to specific events and behaviour. Conversely, being a well-liked and respected individual over-rode what would seem to be typical 'white settler' characteristics (for example, affluence, Englishness).

To give one example, during the fieldwork period a crofting township in Beulach experienced a conflict over planning permission. A 'real old local' called Jessie was in the midst of this disagreement, in which rights to protest were linked to claims to localness. The township had 18 permanently occupied dwellings (two of which were caravans) and seven holiday/second homes. Many of the permanent residents were in-migrants of recent or long-term residence. Jessie was very fond of and had good relationships with several of these in-migrants, notably a young couple who were actively crofting, and a middle-aged neighbour. Jessie's niece had a non-local husband, and she herself was married to a non-local man, and had a non-local mother. So, actual objective in-migrant characteristics did not trouble her. However, this did not prevent her from being a key figure in a dispute with and about 'incomers'. A young couple who had recently built their own house planned also to build a pub/restaurant. A campaign against this was started by the Jacksons, a couple who had recently bought a cottage across from the proposed site. They were vociferously supported by another couple, early retirees who had lived full-time in the township for two years. When Mrs Jackson brought round an anti-pub petition, Jessie lost her temper with her, and declared that no-one had asked them to come and live there, and incomers should not be interfering with young locals setting up businesses and providing employment – if they wanted peace and quiet they could go elsewhere for it. This story was related round Beulach with some amusement, as Mrs Jackson was native to Ardrhu, only an hour's drive to the south. A typical comment was 'Whoever heard of a white settler from Ardrhu?!'

What was *not* voiced, either in general gossip or by Jessie herself when relating the story after I interviewed her, was that the other 'incomer couple' opposing the pub had connections in terms of duration that were of similar status to the 'local couple' who wanted to build the pub. The incomer couple were former teachers who had followed the common pattern of regular holidays in Beulach for many years, followed by the purchase and renovation of a traditional croft-house, ending in early retirement and a permanent move (see Table 10.1). In the local couple, the husband did have kinship ties with a 'real local' family, but was born and brought up in England, and retained his English accent. His wife was from southern Scotland and had only been living in Beulach for a few years. However, relative to the other people involved, this couple 'belonged', for the sort of reasons Harry outlined in his interview: they were younger, working (the husband owned many sheep and was thus a 'real crofter'), and 'had new ideas that would help develop the place', providing local employment.

In Beulach, tension and conflict did not arise straightforwardly between a category of 'incomers' and a category of 'locals'. Disputes took place between all sorts of people regardless of their status in relation to 'belonging'. However, in situations of conflict, insults about lack of local status were thrown in to add weight – but these were not straightforward, objective demographic characteristics. Rather, 'incomer' and 'local' were labels that were mobilized and deployed selectively. Not only was there no straightforward dichotomy, there was no straightforward continuum along which individuals could be placed at fixed points, or move along in a smooth unidirectional progression taking a certain length of time. The significance of life course factors in in-migrants' attempts to make Beulach their home is particularly apparent when examining incidences of discord, as has been seen above. Time spent in Beulach, or connection across generations, mattered, but valued more highly were in-migrants at a life course stage in which they were likely to be actively involved in the community, engaging in paid employment, and bringing up children locally. Middle-aged or elderly retirees, especially those potentially keen to preserve a 'village-in-the-mind' (Pahl 1968) that did not encompass social and economic change, were less welcome.

Conclusions

In Beulach, personal characteristics and behaviour were critical in the process of status negotiation and allocation. This is modelled simply in Figure 10.1, where 'personal characteristics' refers to the way in which

Table 10.1   The dynamics of in-migration – two examples

Tourist →	Summer visitor →	Second home owner →	Full-time resident
Edward's parents 'took a lodge' in the area from the turn of the century until the outbreak of the First World War	Edward married Louisa in 1941. After the war and the birth of their two eldest sons, they began spending summers staying in Beulach hotels, angling and hill-walking	By the early 1960s, they had five children. They decided to buy a substantial tract of land and build a house on it, which they stayed in during the summers from 1964	Edward and Louisa retired to their Beulach house in 1980. In 1985, Edward died, and their eldest daughter Jane moved to Beulach to live with her mother. The other children (and grand children) continue to spend summers there
Susan went on holiday to Beulach just before the Second World War	From 1950 onwards, she returned with her husband and son Richard every summer	Richard bought a semi-derelict cottage with his girl-friend Pam in 1970, renovated it and stayed there a few times per year	Richard and Pam's daughter Judith came to live in the cottage in 1990, getting a job in the knitwear factory and marrying Joe (who was born in Beulach to non-local parents)

Figure 10.1   Belonging trajectory

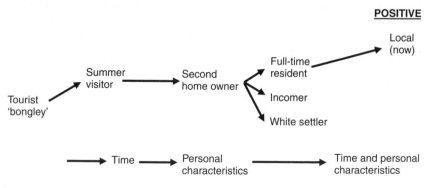

individuals behave and, related to this, the characteristics (such as gender, class) that affect how they interact with and are perceived by others. There were common patterns of moving along an 'outsider to insider' continuum over time, depicted in Table 10.1 and Figure 10.1. An individual could move faster along this continuum if s/he was liked and behaved appropriately, or equally, could be stalled or relegated to 'white settler' if s/he did not 'fit in'. Appropriate behaviour was the vital factor in speeding or stalling this process, and it centred on the ideal of taking part (which was positive and almost essential to belonging) but not taking over or 'lording it' (which was negative and led to resentment). This was a fine line for outsiders to tread. Ability to recognize and negotiate it was inevitably affected by factors including age, class and personality.

Belonging to Beulach was an easier status to achieve if an individual married a local or had children. Commitment to the area was valued, so socially detached owners of second homes were the people most likely to be viewed unfavourably, especially by those in outlying townships where up to half the housing stock could lie empty for much of the year. Beulach residents of all backgrounds tended to indicate a general preference for in-migrants who would live all year round in the parish, rather than second home owners, and were particularly positive in principle towards in-migrant families with children. However, other factors such as socio-economic status affected these judgements: the generally derogatory term 'second home owner' was reserved for those who had bought a house with little if any land attached to it, and whose behaviour led people to suspect motives of social climbing (cf. Skiffington 1991, 268). It was not used to refer to those who owned large estates, who were generally spoken of more positively or deferentially, even though their properties were also typically used only as summer residences (Maclean 1997). In general, though, in-migration and belonging was facilitated for individuals at a life course stage in which they were working and/or had young children.

Despite these apparently delicate structures and processes, belonging to Beulach was a possibility more open to in-migrants than in many localities documented in the literature. In general, Beulach people had a fairly open definition of what constituted 'connection' and 'belonging'. Understanding why this was the case requires a knowledge not just of daily life in contemporary Beulach, but also of the broader demographic, social and economic picture of social change over time. Beulach is situated in an area that appeared only 40 years ago to be virtually at the nadir of a long-term and irreversible decline. In-migration may be regarded with some ambivalence, but cannot be viewed with outright hostility when the bleaker alternative of 'dereliction' (as Peggy put it) is within living memory. In-migration – of those at the right age and life course stage – has played a key role in restoring population levels and a 'healthy' demographic profile, increasing associated services which have provided employment opportunities and thus also made it possible for more people born in Beulach to stay in or return to the parish. Moreover, the Beulach case does not parallel some areas where population was more polarised between clear-cut categories of 'incomer' and 'local', and in-migration was a sudden influx concentrated in a short period of time, associated with rapid social change (Forsythe 1980; Lumb 1980). Beulach has a long historical experience of migration. There were in-migrants in the nineteenth and twentieth centuries, and members of Beulach families have always moved away from the parish for work, but maintained connections and sent offspring back to Beulach to live for periods (see Maclean 2000a; 2000b). The more substantial in-migration of people 'without any connection to the place' (as Liza put it) began 30 years before the fieldwork took place. Moreover, many summer visitors had holidayed in Beulach over several generations of their family (cf. Damer 2000). Thus, in-migration was a phenomenon that over time had become the norm. Linked to this were life course and generation factors; by the time of the research, many original in-migrants had adult children who had been born in Beulach, had married members of 'real local families' and had their own young children. It was therefore nearly impossible in many cases to categorize individuals straightforwardly as an insider or an outsider.

Becoming seen as connected to Beulach was indeed something that could be established more firmly given time, as was demonstrating credible commitment to 'making it your home' and taking part in local life. However, time, kinship and the 'centripetal' and 'centrifugal' forces (including the labour market and housing) by which some groups and individuals are pushed to the margins of local social life, and others are drawn to the centre (see Crow and Allan 1995a; Warwick and Littlejohn 1992) are on their own insufficient to account for in-migrants' success or failure to make a community like Beulach their home. This chapter has sought to demonstrate how salient factors interact in relation to belonging, for example in the intermingling of class, age, appropriate behaviour and Englishness in Harry's account of incomers. Crucially, the significance of these factors is not straightforward – they come into play in certain circumstances. For example, on the infrequent occasions in which anti-English sentiment was expressed in Beulach, it was always connected to 'taking over' or other inappropriate behaviour, despite the fact that many non-English people might behave in identical ways, and many English people might never behave in this manner. Insider/outsider status was mobilized selectively, in certain situations, to fit these situations, regardless of independent 'realities' such as the demographic characteristics of the person under discussion. An example was given above in which a young man was regarded as a 'local' and a 'real crofter' despite his English accent. Attributes such as valued skills or personal characteristics that led to an individual being well liked and respected could over-ride or mitigate what might otherwise be seen as 'incomer' or 'white settler' characteristics, and smooth the process of making Beulach home. These appropriate personal characteristics and behaviour were set in a particular context of social change, which resulted in Beulach being relatively open to in-migrants, particularly those with time and life course factors operating in their favour.

Notes

1. I would like to thank Graham Allan, Graham Crow, Lynn Jamieson, Gill Jones and David McCrone for their comments on earlier versions of this chapter; the Carnegie Trust for the Universities of Scotland for the financial support of a doctoral studentship; and last but not least, the residents of Beulach.
2. A register of the ownership and transfer of land and houses in Scotland. For further information, see Williams and Twine (1991). I would like to thank David McCrone for drawing my attention to this data source.
3. A croft is a smallholding, and a 'crofting township' is roughly equivalent to a 'hamlet', although often the houses are scattered across quite a wide area. For further information, see Hunter (1976; 1991).

11
Family and Community Ties in Space and Time

Fiona Devine, Nadia Joanne Britton, Peter Halfpenny and Rosemary Mellor

The community studies of the postwar period in British sociological research were an important source of empirical research on people's every-day lives and how they were structured by class (Crow and Allan 1994; Eldridge 1990; Kent 1981). That is to say, they highlighted the different patterns of sociability among the working and middle-classes. It was found, for example, that in their leisure time members of the working class socialized with family and longstanding friends from their community (Dennis *et al.* 1956; Stacey 1960). Members of the middle-class, by contrast, socialized with colleagues from their jobs and more recent friends (Bell 1968; Pahl and Pahl 1971). These divergent patterns were the consequence of different migratory practices among the working and middle classes. The working classes usually took manual jobs locally and they could maintain relations with family and friends in the communities in which they lived out their lives. In contrast, the middle classes moved in search of high-level non-manual employment and they had to forgo family and community ties in new cities and towns (Bell 1968; Pahl and Pahl 1971). The working classes were 'local' while the middle classes were 'cosmopolitan'.

Of course, this is not to say that examples of working-class movement and middle-class immobility could not be found or were entirely neglected. Goldthorpe *et al.'s* (1969) affluent workers and Mann's (1973) workers on the move were significant counter-examples of working-class geographical mobility. That said, one of the authors of this paper conducted a restudy of Goldthorpe *et al.'s* affluent workers but came to very different conclusions about the effects of geographical mobility on working-class life-styles in Luton (Devine 1992). The *Affluent Worker* team argued that geographical mobility led to separation from family and friends. The severance of family and community ties accounted for the decline of a traditional working-class community and the rise of more privatized life-styles among a new working class. In contrast, Devine (*ibid.*) argued that geographical mobility did not lead to the inevitable decline of close family and community relations. Patterns of chain migration, whereby family and friends followed each other and regrouped in new towns and cities, meant that frequent and casual contact was not lost. Devine's informants did not lead privatized lives even though they were not engaged in the extensive socializing associated with occupational communities of the past.

Similarly, Watson's (1964) and Bell's (1968) 'burghers' were important counter-examples of middle-class immobility. Since then, unfortunately, there have been few intensive studies of the middle classes that might provide some insight into local middle classes and patterns of sociability with family and friends. Savage *et al.'s* (1992) analysis of the Longtitudinal Survey confirmed that the middle classes are more geographically mobile than the working class. The South East, and especially London, attracts those in search of high-level careers although middle-class careers are enjoyed in other regions of the country too. These findings were not linked, however, to their discussion of middle-class life-styles with its focus on culture and consumption. The most recent qualitative research on the middle class also says very little about their family and community ties (Butler 1997; Wynne 1998). In his case study of the life-styles and leisure practices of the new middle-class in the Cheshire green belt, Wynne (*ibid.*) makes only passing reference to the fact that the majority of his sample (59 per cent) came from the North West and a further 11 per cent previously resided in the North. Consequently, he did not consider that his informants were probably in close physical proximity to family and friends and might spend their free time with them.

This chapter considers middle-class life-styles and, in particular, the migration practices of a sample of middle-class professionals working in Manchester. The next section highlights the importance of Manchester as a regional centre in the North West and outlines the typical routes by which our informants flowed in and out of the region. The third section considers the 'locals' who were born and bred in the region although we shall see that many of them had been geographically mobile before returning to the area later. The fourth section considers the 'cosmopolitans' who moved into the region from other parts of the UK at various points in their lives. Despite the divergent routes in and out of the region, the importance of family and friends over the lifecourse – especially during changes in household structure and family formation – will be emphasized. The findings suggest that the middle classes – whether 'local' or 'cosmopolitan' – do not necessarily forgo family and community ties as a result of geographical mobility. The ability to sustain close ties with family and friends by working in professional employment locally – in this instance, Manchester – also suggests that the life-styles of the working and middle classes might not be so different after all.

Manchester and the respondents

The data presented are derived from a project that forms part of an ESRC programme of research on 'Cities: competitiveness and cohesion'.[1] The aims of the programme are to improve understanding of how cities develop and mobilize distinctive economic assets to secure competitive advantage and to examine the associated implications for social cohesion. Our research considered the interplay between economic regeneration of the city centre and the 'good' suburbs of Manchester which is the regional centre of North West England. During the nineteenth century, as centre of the textile industry, Manchester controlled a world market and was able to challenge the dominance of London (Mellor 1992). Today, as a regional business centre, it grows (albeit in the capital's shadow) and competes for business with other regional centres such as Leeds.

Like many old industrial cities, Manchester has experienced a sustained period of deindustrialization with the decline of its manufacturing base. It has also experienced a significant resurgence of its service sector with the rise of professional business services (Peck and Emmerich 1992). Between 1971 and 1989, the number of manufacturing jobs in the city was reduced by 249,000 whereas the number of jobs in the service sector increased by 107,000 (Beynon *et al.* 1993). Manchester's new economic strategy has concentrated on a service sector-led recovery, including property redevelopment. This has contributed to the expansion of secondary services such as accountancy and stockbroking (Quilley 1995). Mirroring trends in other regional centres, Manchester's rejuvenated city centre economy is dominated by a sought-after, prosperous professional service core and the knowledge industries, such as education and media (Mellor 1997).

This chapter focuses on the city centre dimension of our research. This comprised six case studies of sectors well represented among Manchester's professional business and financial services. These six were accountancy, the actuarial profession, advertising, architecture, corporate finance and law. The corporate finance case study included corporate banking, venture capital and stockbroking and the actuarial profession included a large insurance company, a 'Big Six' accountancy firm and three international actuarial consultancies. We carried out 59 semi-structured interviews with employees from 32 companies, including large and small, multinational and local firms. The interview was designed to establish how the respondents' professional careers had developed over time and how career-related decisions were influenced by family, life cycle and life-style factors.

The sample included professionals at different stages of their career and life cycle. Forty men and 19 women were interviewed, reflecting that women remain under-represented in the sectors studied (especially at the higher levels) despite a general increase in the number of women professionals, particularly in accountancy and law (Crompton and Sanderson

1990). Eighty-three per cent of the respondents were aged 35 or under but many had attained senior positions despite their relative youth. For example, six solicitors and five accountants had reached salaried partnership or high-level managerial status. Eighty-five per cent of the respondents had partners (married, engaged or co-habiting) and the majority (73 per cent) were childless. This reflects their young age but is also indicative of a general trend towards having children later. As Table 11.1 shows, two types of mobility were discernible among the sample. A small majority (58 per cent) of the respondents were born and bred in the North West, which includes Greater Manchester, Merseyside, Lancashire and Cheshire. These 'locals' were, on the face of it, non-migrants but we shall see that they included people who both went to university and stayed in the region, those who went to university outside the region but returned immediately afterwards and those who moved away (invariably to London) before returning. High levels of mobility, therefore, became apparent on examining the migration histories of even the 'locals' among the respondents. A large minority (42 per cent) of the respondents came from outside the region. These 'cosmopolitans' either came to the region to attend one of its universities and then stayed in Manchester and the North West, moved to Manchester from another region to start their first job after leaving university elsewhere or moved there, again usually from London, in mid-career. The following sections describe the two types of mobility in greater detail.

The 'locals'

Over half (58 per cent) of the sample had been born and bred in the North West although the circumstances which had led to their working in

Table 11.1   Types of geographical mobility

Types	Number of respondents
The 'locals' (born in the NW)	34
University and first job in NW	8
University elsewhere and first job in NW	16
University NW, first job elsewhere, return to NW	1
University elsewhere, first job elsewhere, return to NW	9
The 'cosmopolitans' (born elsewhere)	25
University and first job in NW	10
University elsewhere and first job in NW	5
University in NW, first job elsewhere, move to NW	3
University elsewhere, first job elsewhere, move to NW	7
Total	59

Manchester and living in the North West varied amongst them. There were three main routes by which the respondents came to be in the locality.[2] First, a small group of 'locals' had never left the region. They attended a university in the North West, and subsequently found their first job in Manchester and stayed. There were various reasons, of course, why they did not go away to university including a mix of negative and positive factors. As a young actuary explained: 'I think that was more my parents couldn't afford to send me away at the time so I stayed in Manchester for those reasons. Yes, it was financial.' While negative reasons are highlighted by this informant, others noted that there was no need to move away when desired courses at prestigious universities were available locally. For some, attending the local university meant living at home with their parents and maintaining friends from school and the neighbourhood. Others lived in university accommodation but often spent weekends at home so family and community ties were maintained. More often than not, they also met their partners in the locality that subsequently became another tie to the region.

In these circumstances, it is not unsurprising that these informants sought employment in the locality afterwards. As a young accountant suggested: 'I was born here and all my family and friends are here and I didn't particularly have any preference for moving out.' They were able to stay because Manchester offered good opportunities in their professional fields. As a solicitor, who attended Manchester University and still lived in the small town in Cheshire where she grew up, noted:

> It seems to be a good centre for the legal professions. I think it's got nearly all the good firms in the North West. You've got Leeds and Liverpool but Manchester is up there with the best ... I think city centre firms are a lot more professional and they have a lot more going for them, I would want to stay with a city centre firm and I think Manchester is the ideal city to do that.

Other professionals spoke of the opportunities in Manchester and how they compared favourably with other cities in the region, most notably Liverpool. An architect, for example, compared the lack of spirit in Liverpool in comparison with Manchester which is establishing a reputation for young architects with new ideas about the re-use of land and buildings in urban areas.

The importance of family and friends was emphasized by a second group of 'locals', those who came from the North West region, went away to university and then returned to Manchester for their first job. Returning home during vacations, they had maintained contacts with local friends and often returned after graduation to the parental home for financial and other support (Finch 1989; Finch and Mason 1993). They either stayed with their parents for a short period while they established themselves in the world of paid work or remained with their parents for longer periods while studying for professional qualifications. As an accountant disclosed: 'Obviously my mother and father recognized that I was working quite hard on the exams and they weren't too concerned with me helping out with domestic chores etc. So, it was easier, it was comfortable to live there.' It also allowed them to save for a deposit on a house and invariably they bought properties close to family and friends and in commuting distance to Manchester. The familiarity of the locality and knowing a lot of people socially was important. As a young accountant explained: 'I lived in Manchester prior to Sheffield [where she attended university] so it seemed the obvious choice to come back to an area that I knew. Manchester was always the first choice ... This is where I've been brought up. This is where my family is.'

Some informants considered moving to London but there were a variety of reasons why they eventually discounted it. First, they did not like London as a place to live. As an actuary suggested: 'I've always lived near Bolton and when I visited London, I just didn't fancy being there ... I'm used to living in a little village with open spaces and I just felt claustrophobic in London.' Similar reasons were offered by other informants. Elucidating on his decision to practice in Manchester rather than London, a solicitor indicated:

> First, because I have always enjoyed living here. This was my home and it had everything that I wanted and also I think it was a reaction. I didn't want to go to work in London so the natural thing was to come and work in the commercial centre that I knew and that was Manchester. I did not think I was the right sort of person that would fit in London although a lot of my friends were going. It was the perception, right or wrong, that it was a large unfriendly place and it would swallow you up. I suppose I wanted the familiarity of coming back to Manchester. I think it was being allowed to live in an area where I knew I was happy and wanted to live, that being Warrington, where I remained, and the commute into Manchester to work, so you could have the best of both worlds.

London was also rejected as a place to work. A solicitor explained that he was anxious not to follow the stereotypical career path from Cambridge to Law School (in Guildford) to London. His experience of the Cambridge milk round led him to believe that the legal life in London was a very aggressive environment and Manchester, where he had enjoyed some work experience in a large commercial law firm, less so. He suggested:

> You find it now in Manchester that there can be a lot of store set by what time you are working to in the evening. My view of that has

always been that the job has to be done and if the work's there that needs doing that's fine but equally there should be no good reason why to obtain career progression you have to still be here at 7.30 at night every night as its important to have a life outside of the office as much as anything else. It seems the perception I have had of London and the perception of others at other firms in the City is that there is more rigidity in the way you are required to perform than you have here.

The well-documented macho culture of the City (McDowell 1997) was not for them. Moreover, others found that opportunities in London were not as good as they first seemed when job offers were located in satellite offices in the London suburbs with further possibilities of being relocated.

A third group of locals were those who attended university outside the region, then went to work in London and subsequently returned to the North West. The time spent in London was relatively short although it varied from eight months to seven years. All of the respondents, it seems, grew weary of living and working in London and the pull of family and friends was important once again. A solicitor was keen to return to the North West to be closer to family and friends after a spell of four years in London. As she described:

I would never move to London now – ever – even though I think it's a great place to go and visit. The main difference of living in Manchester to London is to actually know your next-door neighbour and people across the street whereas in London you just never did. That wasn't because you were unfriendly or they were unfriendly. It was just you never did. There wasn't any of that local community, certainly where I lived in London, there was never any local community feeling. You worked with people and they lived all over the place compared to where you lived so there was no chance of you going to your local and finding somebody you worked with. There was just none of that.

Being away from family and friends was one aspect of growing weary of living in London.

An important turning point for some informants came when they decided they wanted to buy a property, usually with a partner (and when the novelty of renting with friends had worn off!). High house prices in London precipitated a move out of the capital. An accountant explained the circumstances that led her to move out of London after six years:

My reason to move to Manchester was I had just had enough of London. I was living in a very small flat and I had just met who is now my fiancé in London and we decided to move in together and even with both of us having very good jobs we couldn't afford a house where we wanted a house, so that prompted the move.

Finding a decent place to live in London often required living in the outer suburbs which then meant, in the words of a solicitor: 'getting a tube and getting into the centre of London which wasn't particularly pleasant'. It also meant, as one informant noted above, that people rarely lived close to people they knew. Thus, house prices, commuting difficulties (as well as issues of crime and safety) all pushed people out of London. They could, of course, afford bigger properties in attractive areas on their move north in a way that they could never entertain in London.

Another aspect of growing weary of London was the work environment. Less than a year into her job, an advertiser soon tired of her low-paid demanding job. As she noted:

[In] your first job and you are in a junior position as well, you get to do a lot of the horrendous tasks and you are there very late and I was at a very hard-working agency ... I enjoyed the social side of it because all my friends were there from university but I realized I didn't want to live and work in London.

Another interviewee echoed these sentiments about the different cultures of the two cities. She thought:

the emphasis here [in Manchester] is more on you deal with a portfolio how you feel you should and as long as you manage your time and get the jobs done within the deadlines, it doesn't matter how little or long you stay at your desk. In London it was expected that you would put in longer hours of work and it was also expected at a moment's notice if something was on you would drop everything and stay there. There were horrific stories that people stay there throughout the night.

The appeal of London was often short-lived as the long hours of work, made longer by commuting every day, renting in rundown areas and high house prices all added to the *hassle* of living in London.

For the most part, the interviewees of this study were young people without children although thoughts of having a family often contributed to a move out of London. This was an explicit consideration for some interviewees who had had children after leaving London for the North West. Living in London and raising a family were seen as incompatible. As a solicitor with two children suggested with regard to her move:

This was partly because my husband was very unhappy in his job in London. He's a planning consultant working for private consultancies and he was quite unhappy with his job which was based in the docklands and we'd agree that we were thinking of starting a family and that it would probably be a good idea long term to move north because of family.

Both of them secured jobs in Manchester, they lived relatively close to one set of parents and the interviewee worked part-time while caring for her children. Similarly, a corporate banker explained:

It was a quality of life issue ... I just felt that we would get into a rut of commuting, spending a lot of time away from home, away from each other and particularly if we had a family which we didn't at the time, away from the family and that's not what I wanted. I wanted a decent quality of life.

They opted to move to the North West, were helped by the interviewee's family in finding jobs and a house, and now enjoyed a high quality of life living on the outskirts of south Manchester.

Most of the 'locals' in this research – originally from the North West and now back living and working in the region – had been geographically mobile either by going to university outside the locality and then immediately returning or first pursuing their early career elsewhere – usually in London – before returning 'home'. The close proximity of family (who were also an important source of financial support) and old neighbours and school friends was an important factor in the informants' decisions to return to the North West. These informants, in other words, constituted a local middle class with strong family and community ties.

The 'cosmopolitans'

Almost half (42 per cent) of the sample had no family links to the North West region although, as we shall see, family reasons played a part in their being in the locality. For these 'cosmopolitans', two general routes led to Manchester.[3] First, 13 respondents stayed in or returned to the region having attended either one of Manchester's universities (including Salford and UMIST) or other regional universities (Lancaster or Liverpool). Second, 12 informants relocated from other parts of the country (including London) either for their first job or at a later stage of their career. Those who had attended one of the region's universities described how they had enjoyed living in Manchester and the North West. As students, they had become familiar with the area, and they had established roots, particularly in the form of a circle of close friends from university. A commercial banker described how:

As a student for three years, you do sort of establish some sort of roots and I'd got a lot of friends who stayed around here as well ... so that was it really ... I've got friends here and I was familiar with the territory, I suppose, and I've always liked Manchester.

Another Manchester graduate was anxious to return to her friends in the city. As she suggested: 'I wanted to move back to Manchester because some of my friends were still up here. They had been on four-year courses. I loved being in Manchester.'

As well as friends, family connections were referred to as a significant factor influencing their decision to stay in Manchester. A commercial banker explained that her initial decision to go to university in Manchester and then to stay in the city afterwards was connected to her links to the North (as well as her support for Manchester United!):

That was important, staying in the North West. I wanted to stay in Manchester [after graduation]. It was a positive decision too actually because I came from Yorkshire ... it was an hour away from where my parents live as well. So it was a positive decision to come to Manchester and it was all I ever wanted to do in terms of university choices.

Similarly, an accountant originally from Bradford mentioned that being close to his family was important and this was one of the reasons why he decided not to apply for jobs in London. As he stated: '[It was] the sheer convenience of being in Manchester. The problem of going to London is I'd have to uproot, leave a great deal of my friends who are based in Manchester and also I wouldn't be quite as close to my family.' The proximity of family and friends, and their positive experiences of Manchester and the North West while students, strongly influenced their decision to stay.

Some respondents who had attended universities in the North West moved to London after graduating and then returned to the region. Like the 'locals' who had worked in the capital, these respondents grew tired of long working hours, the general work environment, high rents and commuting. Partners also played an important part in bringing them back to Manchester and the North West. After completing a degree at Liverpool University, an actuary moved to London and commuted back to Liverpool at weekends to see his girlfriend, who wanted to leave the city. He recalled:

She and I discussed what was the best place for her where she should go so that I could also get a job if we decided we were going to take things further. She did not want to live in London but equally then at that stage I'd spent just over three years in London and it was beginning to wear on me and I thought well the attraction was gone.

Through an agency, he got a job in Leeds and after two years was asked by the company to go to Manchester where he and his now wife relocated. Although his move to Manchester had been a company decision, his partner's wishes and her links to the locality meant that a return to the North West was not entirely coincidental.

The second route by which 'cosmopolitans' came to Manchester, followed by respondents who had no direct family links to the North West and had not been to university in the region, was also related to wider family connections. A solicitor commented that part of the reason for her move to Manchester from London was to be closer to her parents, who lived apart. She was also familiar with the city as she had other relatives living there:

My mother now lives in Wales although she used to live in Manchester when she was young, a long time ago. My father is in Shropshire so I am in the middle of the two of them and I have got lots of aunts and uncles who live in Manchester, so I feel a family link with the place rather than having everybody on the doorstep.

An advertising copywriter applied for positions in Manchester because it was conveniently close to his parents' home. As he explained:

The reason why I came to Manchester was there was no advertising agency in Sheffield, which is where I lived with Mum and Dad, and I did not want to go to London where all the big ones are and the only other two places within sort of travelling distance of where I was living at the time were Manchester and Leeds. Having been in Leeds for four years [at university] I did not particularly want to go back and live there.

A partner's career was an important reason why some respondents had relocated to Manchester. A solicitor, who had developed her career in London, moved to Leeds to be closer to her husband who worked in Loughborough. 'So the reason I went to Leeds is that I was brought up in North Yorkshire so I thought, well it's Yorkshire and it's quite close to my parents and I know people in Yorkshire.' She then moved to Manchester when her husband obtained a job in Keele. Other female respondents also moved jobs to accommodate their partners' career moves. Often in dual career households, they were not however powerless 'trailing wives' (Bruegel 1996) but had considerable influence on where to relocate. An accountant who moved from Glasgow to Manchester said of her husband:

> He's an accountant as well but not in practice. This is how we met because we worked together. Then he wanted to move into corporate finance and he just didn't see that the opportunities were the same in Glasgow so we moved down here. Well, I didn't want to go to London. Too many people! It just wasn't for me. So Manchester seemed like the place to come really. He got a number of interviews down here and it all happened very quickly really.

The process of dual mobility was not always one way (as Green 1997 also found) as there were other examples of men who followed their girl-friends or wives to the North West. As an actuary described:

> Manchester sort of fell on us really. My girl-friend at the time was looking for jobs. She's a solicitor. She was looking for jobs in the North and it was very difficulty to get articles and she just had to get what she was given and the only job she came up with was a job in Manchester. It was actually a job in Hyde so she spent two years there. She did a year in Hyde and then I came up a year later.

The director of public relations at an advertising agency explained that he decided to find employment in Manchester to spend more time with his wife, a management consultant whose offices were in the city even though she travelled extensively for business purposes. As he noted: 'I got married 18 months ago. Whereas, previously, my wife and I, before we were married, maintained separate existences during the week ... when we got married, we tried to commit to spending a bit more time together.' That said, he imagined commuting between Manchester and London 'if the right job allowed me to fly up and down twice a week' as he had commuted between the two cities in the past.

Other respondents expressed a general wish to stay in the north of England where they had lived for most or all of their lives. An actuary explained that he chose not to move south as he had always lived in the north:

> I went for several interviews around the country and of the two offers that I got, one being in the south and the other one the [company where he was employed], I decided to take this one, mainly because it was in the north .. The main reason was because I come from Lincolnshire, went to York University, and didn't really want to go to the London area so I wanted to stay north-ish.

A solicitor had intended to move to Leeds, the other main commercial centre in the North but considered moving to Manchester because he was attracted to some of the jobs being advertized there. As he suggested: 'I come from York originally and the intention was always to move to Leeds, that was sort of my grand plan. I started looking for positions in Leeds but also some in Manchester caught my eye'. Manchester was again seen as a city with ample job opportunities and, importantly, as cosmopolitan, lively and young with, in the words of an account manager for an advertising agency, 'a lot of new stuff going on'. It was an attractive place to work and live and fitted the respondents' general criterion of being in the North.

Among the 'cosmopolitans' who had relocated to Manchester after university and first jobs elsewhere were those who had worked in London but had tired of it for the same reasons expressed by others who had worked in London, including 'locals'. Changes in family circumstances were significant in reinforcing their weariness with living and working in the capital and their desire to move north (where they or their partners often came from). Like the 'locals', the impending or recent birth of a first child had precipitated some of the 'cosmopolitans' to relocate to Manchester and proximity to family, especially the child's grandparents, was considered important. Working long hours and expecting his first child, a venture capitalist took the opportunity of a job change that then led to a transfer to Manchester that was

> brilliant because you can live in a real town, you know, which isn't too far out of Manchester. It's a much nicer way of life. It's a much more balanced way of life as well up here. I still work hard but, you know, it's not the same as living in London where you've got an hour, at least an hour at each end of the day to add on just for travelling.

Again, Manchester was perceived as *a smaller version of London* with a big city atmosphere and better quality of life for all the family. It provides the job opportunities these middle-class professionals seek without the disadvantages of working and living in London.

As with the 'locals', the proximity of family and friends was an important factor in the 'cosmopolitans'' decision either to stay in or return to the North West having attended university there or to relocate from other parts of the country for their first or subsequent job. Processes of family formation and changes of household structure were particularly important for those respondents who had relocated from London and were linked to concerns about their family's quality of life. The influence of partners who originally came from and had family in the North also explained why some 'cosmopolitan' respondents had relocated there from the capital. Overall, family and community ties were often central to the migratory practices of the 'cosmopolitans', just as they were for 'locals'.

Conclusion

This chapter has highlighted the importance of family and friends in influencing the migratory practices of young middle-class professionals working and living in Manchester and the North West. They were an important source of help - financial, emotional and social – for 'locals' when making the transition from higher education into high-level employment. Moving closer to family and friends was also an important motivation for the 'locals' who tired of living in London, which often involved working long hours and commuting to suburbs where they had no family and community ties. The relatively close proximity of family and friends was even more important for professionals with young children who wanted the help of kin during a period of family formation. It was not only their assistance in the process of moving that was called upon (Grieco 1987), however, since the ability to socialize more easily with parents, siblings and old school friends also enhanced the quality of the respondents' lives. All of these factors played a part in the migratory practices of the 'cosmopolitans' too, many of whom were attracted to Manchester's universities precisely because their family and friends were reasonably close by in other parts of the North. They were also important to the partners of the respondents which explained why some of them, with no family links of their own to the city or the locality, came to work and live in Manchester and the North West.

While this research has confirmed that geographical mobility remains a prevalent feature of middle-class life-styles (Reid 1998) – since even many of the 'locals' had moved if only to return home later – the effect of migration on family and community ties is not one-way. Rather than having only a detrimental effect on them, geographical mobility can also have the opposite effect. That is to say, migration is not always about moving away from family and friends but can involve moving (back) to be close to them. Of course, the proximity of family and friends may no longer mean living in the same street or even town in that being close may now refer to living in the same region or within an hour's travelling distance as one informant suggested. This might still mark a difference between working-class and middle-class patterns of sociability with the latter somewhat happier with a more 'distant' relationship with their families than the former. With this caveat in mind, this study suggests that family and friends are a crucial component of the middle classes' motivations for mobility, their processes of migration and their life-style practices in an old or new locality. The proximity of family and friends may be as important to the middle classes as the working classes. Patterns of sociability – in which family and longstanding friends play an influential role – may be more similar than different across both classes irrespective of class differences in geographical mobility.

Notes

1. The research discussed in this paper is part of an ESRC project entitled 'The good suburb as an urban asset in enhancing a city's competitiveness' (Reference number L130251046).
2. As there was only one example of a respondent who attended university in the North West, obtained her first job outside the region and returned to the North West later, the discussion focuses on the other three routes of mobility identified in Table 11.1.
3. The discussion in this section distinguishes between those respondents who went to university in the North West (13 informants) and those went elsewhere (12 informants) so the four routes of mobility have been collapsed into two to avoid talking about very small numbers of cases.

12

'If You Had a Whole Year of Weekends It Would be a Very Long Day': Situating and Assessing Time in the Context of Paid and Unpaid Work

Eileen Fairhurst

Introduction

In his seminal paper on 'Cycles, turning points and careers', Hughes (1971, 124) noted that ordering in our society is related to our relationship to the world of work and that work is clearly separated from other social institutions. 'There are a time and place for work; times and places for family life, recreation, religion and politics. The mood and frame of mind of the place of work are supposed to be different from the rest of life.' In the absence of work or a changing participation in work, the pivotal relationship of work, in the Hughesian sense, to the ordering of our lives becomes problematical. Insofar as there is a changing participation in work, retirement may be a turning point upon which further turning points may be predicated. A consequence of this is that there may be more than one retirement career.

The purpose of this paper is twofold. First, to show how retirement is seen as a turning point which sets up the possibility of a number of work-related transitions. Referring to retirement as a transition is not new (Phillipson 1987) but, unlike other studies, I shall show how a number of transitions may be embarked upon. Retirement may not be just one discrete transition from work to non-work but also be one which entails movement from full-time to part-time paid work and/or to unpaid work. Noting how individuals talk about these transitions leads into my second purpose: an explicit focus on how different categories of time are situated in distinctions between paid and unpaid work

The data upon which my analysis is based come from a study undertaken in Greater Manchester as a contribution to Age Concern England's

Millennium Debate of the Age. Chief Officers from Age Concern groups in Greater Manchester sought to gain information from users and potential users of their perceived pattern of need in the year 2000 and beyond. A demographic analysis of the 1991 Census in terms of such variables as age, sex, socio-economic status and ethnic background pointed to the social diversity of Greater Manchester. On the basis of this demographic analysis, specific age groups were studied in particular areas. Ten-year age cohorts within the age ranges 30–79 were targeted. There was a concentration upon groups within the ages of 40–69. Although it was intended to undertake focus groups in each of the ten metropolitan boroughs of Greater Manchester, it was possible to carry out focus groups in only seven of them. A total of eight focus groups took place. Participants of focus groups were identified, on the basis of convenience sampling by age, by Age Concern Chief Officers who acted as facilitators for focus groups. Resulting discussions were tape-recorded, transcribed and analyzed for emergent themes. (See Fairhurst 1999 for further details of the study.)

The data reported here come from only those focus groups held with individuals between the ages of 40 and 69. They included, therefore, individuals who had retired and those who had not. Since focus groups were compiled on the basis of a convenience sample, there is no intention to generalize the findings. Amongst the topics explored were the age at which people did, or thought they might, give up work and what, upon giving up work, people did, or thought they would do. The intention of the study, then, was not to pursue the investigation of temporal matters. It was only on analysis of the transcripts that it became apparent how, when talking about intentions towards and experience of retirement, connections were made initially between its timing and retirement careers. Subsequently, when discussion centred on what it was thought retired people 'did' and what they do 'do', distinctions made between paid and unpaid work were linked back to different categorizations of time. Hence, time was to be 'used', time could be 'on your hands', time could be 'given', time 'needed to be structured' and 'fitting' things into time could be difficult. Given my concern to demonstrate how these temporal matters are evident in talk, I intend to offer extracts from transcripts of focus groups. As these are inferentially rich, I will use the same extracts to make a number of analytic points.

Thinking about retirement

The comment which provides the title for this paper comes from focus group discussions with non-retired men and women who were thinking about their lives prospectively, particularly, the age at which they might finish working.

Extract 1

F1: Well I'm now 45 and I feel you generally look to the responsibilities that your income has on your family life-style. As the children, I hope, become independent I will be looking for part-time work first and probably stay in till the age of 60, in part-time work because I can see there's a value of the social side, as well, to working. I don't see myself going from full-time work to nothing. I would like to be thinking at 50 years old, certainly at the latest, to be looking for part-time work. That's really in the back of my mind, where I've got the advantage of not being a main wage earner; so that's another thing you may have to take into consideration, if things change. So at 50 I would be looking for part-time work and then, hopefully, staying on till 60 in part-time work.

M1: I would say natural progression from paid full-time work into voluntary full-time work; a gradual progression over a number of years.

F2: Well I think perhaps it's a good idea to go to work less hours before you absolutely stop working less hours for paid work, before you actually come to a full stop. That way, perhaps you can get used to a reduction of income because, even though your family dependency on you isn't as great as you get older, you do become a little bit selfish perhaps and want more holidays and different things and you use whatever income you've got. So to come to a full stop I think would be difficult. So perhaps to go into part-time [work] before you decide when you are going to retire would be good. I've got the advantage of five years on the 45 year old and I'm 50 and I can't think that I want to work part-time yet. I'm quite happy still working full-time. Perhaps in another five years I'd look to part-time but not yet.

F1: That's the reality of life, isn't it? I'm 45, thinking five years and you're 50. You're thinking five years. We'll probably never reach those five years. [It] depends.

M1: I think a lot depends also on what pension provisions you've got made, or not, as the case may be.

F1: Or the financial commitments that you've actually got, how long you've actually taken your mortgage up to. It's financial isn't it, yeah I agree with that. That's brought it home to me that I'm thinking five years, you're thinking five years and we'll probably get to 65 and think again, 'I'll just give it another five years.'

F2: I think you want to act just at the moment in time as young as you feel. You don't feel that you're old enough to retire.

These data are inferentially rich about connections made between age, time, turning points, cycles and careers. The first thing to note is that chronological age is used to prospectively identify a time at which the place of work in the ordering of life will be re-assessed. Attainment of a particular age is identified as the time at which decisions may be made about involvement in work. Hence, the age of 50 is a time when full-time employment may change to part-time. Age is used to sequence the turning points from one type of employment to another so that part-time work is sought 'first'. Part-time work prevents the transition from 'full-time to nothing'. In that sense, part-time work is a turning point which both sets up another work career and, thereby, allows for the re-ordering of life. Indeed, part-time work enables and leads into a stage for the consideration of the timing of retirement. 'So perhaps to go into part-time before you decide when you are going to retire will be good' Temporal matters and turning points are implicated in the language used here. Reference is made to 'going into' part-time work and it is during that phase that the timing of retirement, 'when' it will occur, can be decided.

Hughes (1971) refers to work in the ordering of our lives as so taken-for-granted that it is unworthy of comment. This 'naturalness' is clear where reference is made to 'a natural progression from paid to full-time work into voluntary work, a gradual progression over a number of years'. These discussions echo Atkinson's (1980) use of the category 'natural lifetimes'. It is apparent from these extracts that in invoking age in matters of turning from full- to part-time employment, the category of age is linked to other life-stage events. Hence the 'growing independence' of children has implications for financial responsibilities: typically they will reduce in the 40s and 50s. Moreover, those life-stage events may themselves be amplified by gender. A female refers to 'not being a main wage earner' as providing the grounds upon which she may consider part-time rather than full-time employment. Similarly, a man links decision-making to the existence of 'pension provision'.

So far we have seen how connections between age, considering a changing involvement in work and the place of work in the ordering of lives invoked cultural knowledge about life events. Not only life events but also the consequences of work for the individual *qua* person could be invoked. Age as a prospective marker for when work may be re-assessed in the ordering of social life is linked to the realization of 'personal needs' or 'the self'.

Extract 2

> F3: I mean I've given a bit of thought to this now because I'm 43 and I've got this sort of target in my head that at 50 I would like to jump off the roller-coaster. By that I mean the type of job I do now which requires a lot of me. It requires a lot of commitment.

It's very much tidying up all of my values so I've put a lot of energy and a lot of myself into the job. I suppose I've seen 50 as a cut-off point where I want to put more energy into myself, if you like, or to do things for me rather than this relative good or whatever. And something about – I don't want to be in the rat race. You know I don't want to be in traffic jams, in the rush hour, coming and going to work. So I feel I've got that cut-off point at 50. That doesn't mean to say that I don't want to do anything past 50 but I want to do it more focused on my agenda.

F4:   I think the same way as you but I think it's linking with the difference between not being in a stressful environment or having the pressures on. I always said that I wanted to work till 70 but it's getting lower and lower. My ambition is to do voluntary work but it's been very much impeded by financial restraints of having to do the work as opposed to meet your own personal needs.

We can see here how age is identified as a turning point. Age 50 is a 'target' and a 'cut-off point' at which time different work can be undertaken which allows for the re-ordering of time to meet needs of the self. 'Targets', despite conveying connotations of location at a specific point in time, are not necessarily 'fixed'; they may be re-assessed so that they may get 'lower and lower'. There is a kind of flexibility assigned to chronological age. Given this, chronological age, as a turning point for the timing of retirement, is just as capable of moving 'up' as well as 'down'. This is evident in Extract 3.

Extract 3

F5:   Mine [age of retirement] keeps edging up as I get nearer to the recognized retirement age. I should retire next year because I'll be 60 next year. But already I feel anxious about that because I feel work is very important and it's something not only that I find satisfying but it's something I enjoy. At the moment I can't think of anything I'd enjoy doing more so I find it quite hard to think about retirement.

Facilitator: What about anyone else?

F6:   I've already retired and found it didn't suit me and I came back.

Facilitator: How long was it between …?

F6:   About six months I think. Something like that, maybe four months, perhaps a little longer. I just found that I need to be stimulated by work.

Facilitator: What did you do in the six months you were off work?

F6:   Tidied every cupboard, asked neighbours for coffee.

> *Facilitator:*   And when you came to the end of that?
>
> *F6:*   Went for walks, tidied more cupboards, started hobbies that I'd no intention of continuing with, that I'd waited 50 years for. I got a bit fed up. I needed something to do with the adrenaline flow and, you know, I wanted a bit of anger.

Just as in Extract 1, temporality and turning points were implicated in the language used by the participants, so this is the case here. F6 had 'waited 50 years for' the time to start hobbies. In addition, ideas of periodicity and cycles are conveyed in the talk. The interviewer asks F6 what she did in the six-month period when not working. The response is followed by an invitation to indicate what she did when she 'came to the end of that'. F6's reply conveys the cycles of her life at that time. Her second list of activities is punctuated by a repeat of one from her first, 'tidied more cupboards'. This repetition of activities contrasts the 'routine-ness' of unpaid work with the adrenaline-inducing nature of paid work.

The complexities surrounding chronological age as a turning point are apparent in both Extracts 2 and 3. The age of retirement as a turning point is not just contextualized in terms of the termination of work, the contrast between work and no work, but also in terms of the types of consequences of work for the individual. Moreover, the talk shows how individuals orient to work as an emotional arena which, in turn, is implicative of temporality. References are made to the stresses and pressures of work, to the 'rat race' of work, to the satisfactions, enjoyment and stimulation derived from work and to the need for 'anger'. Nor do those matters have intrinsic qualities so that pressures are necessarily 'negative' for individuals. Indeed, the very absence of 'pressures' can be missed and result in a return to work. For F6, then, there was 'too little' to do in 'too much' time.

'Stress' and 'pressures' are linked with the category of work and these emotional activities have temporal dimensions. In such instances 'too much' has to be done in 'too little' time.' As Fine (1996) points out in his study of restaurants, workers have expectations of temporal routines in the day. Stress and pressures arise when 'too much' has to be done in a finite amount of time. The temporal boundaries of the clock as signals of marking the boundary between 'work' and 'non-work time' are pushed out.

Recent critiques of the notion of the life cycle (Bryman *et al.* 1987) have noted that it assumes ideas of inevitability and cannot account for varia-tions. The data here cast these kind of matters into a different light. In par-ticular they raise interesting issues about how matters of age and turning points and cycles are acknowledged as problematic rather than being endowed with predictability and certainty. Such a position requires empha-sis upon members' as opposed to analysts' accounts. The participants' prospective view of their working lives is oriented to in terms of cycles which have clear temporal markers. We have noted in all the extracts so far how chronological age is identified as a turning point for changing type of employment and decision-making but the linking of these different work careers is done in terms of five- or ten-year periods (cf. Fairhurst and Lightup 1982b). Thus, 'I'm now 45', 'at 50 at the latest I'd like part-time work' and 'probably stay in till the age of 60 in part-time work'.

Let me elaborate upon this matter of temporal cycles by returning to Extract 1. The man refers to a 'natural progression' from full-time to part-time work. The way in which orienting to temporal features of life, in terms of five-year cycles, is 'natural' is evident in the interchange that follows. F2 notes that she is 50, the age which F1 identifies as the time to change from full- to part-time employment. She notes that 'perhaps in another five years I'd look to part-time but not yet'. Talking about prospective events can only have salience in the context of putative temporal boundaries but this use of cycles does not imply any inevitability, as is indicated by references to 'we'll probably never reach those five years'. Paradoxically, then, the implied precision in the use of bounded temporal cycles does not have necessarily a consequence for action but rather acknowledges how cycles and turning points are situated in temporal matters.

Temporality and part-time and unpaid work as category-bound activities of retirement

Much of the literature on work and temporality acknowledges a debt to Thompson's (1967) historical analysis. Hence, Richman (1983, 99) refers to capitalism transforming time into a 'scarce and non-renewable resource' which 'cannot be stockpiled like gold in Fort Knox: its use is in its continuous flow'. Such analyzes, though, are grounded in paid and full-time work. The point about my data is that they refer to situations where work may be unpaid and/or part-time. The ways to which time is oriented in such situations may be different. It is to such matters that we now turn. Let me return to another part of the focus group introduced in Extract 1.

Extract 4

F1: We try and imagine a week or a year full of weekends. There's a vast difference when you and I think we're working full-time. Come weekends, there's that much to fit in, isn't there? If you had a whole year of weekends, it could become a very long day.

F2: I think that's when the rest of your family come to the fore, yeah being somebody's babysitter or somebody's extra help. That's the way it's always been in my family.

F1: I mean a lot of retired married people wonder how they ever fitted in working didn't they?

We can see how the contrast between current orientations to the working week and the weekend is used to prospectively picture the place of work in the ordering of life. So predominant is full-time work that unpaid non-work activities are necessarily 'fitted in' at the weekend. That in the absence of full-time employment temporal matters become problematic is suggested by the posing of the proposition 'If you had a whole year of weekends, it could become a very long day.'

Retirement as a temporal category

Not only does this contrast between the working week and the weekend point to the way the ordering of life may be different in retirement but also implies how retirement itself may be oriented to as a temporal category. F2 refers to retirement as the time 'when the rest of your family comes to the fore'. We have seen in Extract 2 also how the age of 50 was not only identified as a 'cut-off point' but also lead in to a time when she could 'do things for me'. In this sense, retirement is a kind of generic temporal category to which a range of activities is attached. These activities should be different to those undertaken before retirement. Their 'differentness' is situated in a contrast with paid work. In the previous extracts the contrasts made were more implicit but here they are explicit.

Extract 5

> M2:   I think it's important to school yourself to believe that it's not the end of something. It's the beginning of something. It's a door opening; it's not a door closing. It doesn't really matter what went before but, if like so many people I knew who lived with the grade or rank that they had and, not being that, was going to make their lives different, I find that sad. Because I think if you need to be known by assistant general manager or whatever you were and not by John Smith then there's something sad with your life. I think you need to do things in retirement but not with the same pressures you needed when you were actually working. I think there's a difference between the kind of things you do in retirement. I think it's necessary to do things that reward you and that you enjoy and not because it's the work ethic that needs fulfilling.

This extract further amplifies the ways talk about work, retirement and temporal matters connects the self and emotional matters. Contrasts are made between the emotional 'pressures' of work and 'enjoyment' of retirement activities which 'reward you'.

The assessment of activities in retirement as having some emotionally satisfying attachments is linked to having the opportunity to spend time as one chooses. Again 'the family' is an important referent.

Extract 6

> M3: I think that this [having grandchildren] is one of the great advantages of getting older; that you have this added joy. I like to spend time with – and, hopefully, that is where we can give some of our knowledge – and children do relate to the older person and we can give that back to the grandchildren.

'Spending time', too, allows the 'giving' of time. The giving of time, through voluntary work is a further way in which the emotional implications of work are apparent.

Extract 7

> M4: There is only so much decorating you can do so I think it's important that there's some preparation, even some help, certainly some information as to what may be possible for you to do so you can get a slowing down period. I work with a voluntary organization two mornings a week. It's not a lot but it is enough to make me feel that I was still wanted and useful. It fulfilled a very useful function for me and I enjoyed it tremendously. There were other things I did, leisure activities. I took up golf which I'd never played before but there again you have got to make some kind of plan. You've got to be able to seize the opportunity to fill your time in other than being at home. You have got to get out of the home. You've got to find yourself in a useful situation. You have got to develop new interests … So you really need to be able to find something that is going to give you an interim period of perhaps a year or two or even longer when you can slow down from being full-time in work, part-time occupation of some kind with an additional interest maybe and build up to get you into the retirement process. And it's all very enjoyable at that point. I never gave my work another thought once I'd left it; which astonished me quite frankly.

Participating in voluntary work not only entailed giving time but also involves the moral assessment of time to be used for meeting emotional needs: 'to feel wanted' (cf. Mellor 2000). That retirement is seen as requiring 'a plan' implicates time as something to be expended: it has a utility.

Structuring life: making time and filling in time

We have seen how the prospective consideration of temporal matters in retirement rests upon ideas of 'fitting in' non-work activities with paid employment so that work structures time. The absence of work may not automatically result in having so much time that satisfying activities may be embarked upon at what ever time is chosen. Indeed 'enjoyment' is situated in the category of work. Those no longer in full-time work structure their lives by 'making time' and 'filling time'.

Extract 8

> M5: I retired three times in all and then found, no, I can't. I get bored. Things that I enjoy when I'm working because I look forward to doing them I make time for them. When I've got all the time in the world, I lie down and read a book and think I'll do it tomorrow but tomorrow never comes so I find that I drift aimlessly. I need something to keep me in and I enjoy working ... I thoroughly enjoy my long weekend because I only work three days in the middle of the week and that's the contrast. I think I enjoy my weekends more because I work than I would otherwise. Then every day would be the same.

When the terms 'week' and 'weekend' are used we conventionally link the activity of work with the temporal period of five days, that is, the week and non-work with the temporal period of two days, that is, the weekend. This distinction allows an assessment to be made of the activities engaged in during those temporal periods. It is important to note that this assessment is not just a consequence of the quantity of time available, the length of time or how much time. The person above works for three days so that for four days he does not. Even though more time is spent not at work than at work, the activity of work is used as the marker. The absence of work gives unfettered time but that very absence obscures the distinction between work and non-work so that paradoxically 'tomorrow never comes' and time becomes timeless. Furthermore, the calendar definition of weekend is extended to become a 'long weekend'.

The inferentially rich connections which are made between work, emotional matters and temporality are pinpointed by the following talk which contrasts a married couple's orientations to retirement and how time is 'filled'.

Extract 9

> F7: I'm the kind of person who puts my head out of the trench and takes up positions in various bodies and I've kept very busy so I've found it interesting and stimulating. On the other hand, my husband who isn't an organization kind of person has found it very boring and unrewarding and in fact has taken up work again in order to fill his time which sounds strange. When he first

retired he got involved in voluntary work and he took too much on. He filled his week as though he was at work and resented it and didn't like it at all and stopped everything that was voluntary.

Though both have filled time in retirement, the emotional satisfaction for each is quite different: for the woman 'being busy' has been 'stimulating' but, for her husband, doing 'too much' has been 'resented'.

Temporal niches, status and retirement

The ways in which work orders our lives has been a recurrent theme throughout this paper. Conventionally work is a source of status but retirement may not necessarily result in its loss.

Extract 10

> M6: In a way, I'm half retired. I am approaching 61 and six months ago I dropped down from working five days a week to two days a week. This was because I wasn't sure whether I'd easily take the break from all work to no work. People say you can fill up your time in no time at all and maybe you can but I wasn't quite sure so I'd thought I'd try it the easy way and fortunately I've got a job where the boss was co-operative. He'd sooner have me back five days a week but it's better than nothing from his point of view. So that is what I'm doing at the moment and I don't know how long it will last. I might hand in my notice next week or it might go on for years. I don't know. I now have that Monday morning feeling on Thursday and I wonder why I'm going to work. I suppose one reason I'm going to work – it still gives me a structure to part of the week. It's a very pleasant working environment, quite sociable with it. There's no hassle there. The boss and I understand each other very well. Everyone works together so, from a work point of view, there's no hassle and it is the sort of job I can do in my sleep.

In addition to matters of 'filling and structuring time', work as an emotional arena and retirement as a potential turning point, all of which have previously been examined, this extract elaborates upon 'temporal niches' and the way the rhythm of work orders our social lives. For Fine (1996), the ability of individuals to carve out 'temporal niches' for themselves in order to have control over their working lives rests upon the possession of status. Hence, both college professors and executive chefs in restaurants, by virtue of their organizational positions, are able to carve out 'temporal niches'. Conventionally, retired people are considered to have little status in a society where it is bestowed by work. Here we have an instance where an individual who, by referring to 'the boss', sees himself in a subordinate organizational position and, thereby, possessing little organizational status. Nevertheless, he is able to carve out for himself a 'temporal niche', away from the organization, in which he is able to assess when he wants to move from one turning point of retirement, full-time to part-time work, to another, part-time to no paid work. Moreover, despite the 'boss's' preference for him to work five days a week the former considers 'it's better than nothing'.

Hughes (1971, 171) refers to the way in which the calendar marks time and he notes how the French revolutionaries 'tried to break the rhythm of life itself by changing the number of days in the week and of months in the year'. The extent to which the calendar affirms such matters is evident here. M6's puzzlement at wondering why he continues to work, despite getting 'that Monday morning feeling on Thursday', not only points to work as an important constituent in the rhythm of life but also provides the justification for that continuation

Concluding remarks

My starting point for this paper was Hughes's (1971) analysis of temporal matters on which rested ideas about cycles and turning points. I have used these to examine talk about retirement by those experiencing it and those thinking prospectively about it. I have demonstrated how chronological age and temporal cycles are oriented to as turning points for assessing continuation in paid employment. I have shown how work in the social ordering of life is implicated in the ways individuals talk about temporal matters. Paradoxically, even in its absence, work is pivotal to the assessment of time. Hence, the puzzlement expressed in the phrase of those retired, 'How did I manage to fit in going to work?'

13

How Brief An Encounter? Time and Relationships, Pure or Otherwise

David H.J. Morgan

Introduction

Much discussion of time seems to concentrate on periods which are in some ways pre-determined whether these be the hidden, but predictable rhythms of everyday life (Zerubavel 1981) or the timetables, dominated by clock time (Thompson 1967). Generally speaking such time periods have clear beginnings, durations and endings whether or not they are regularly repeated (calendars, birthdays and so on) or single events such as particular performances of a concert. These predictable endings – and this chapter is especially concerned with endings – may be of several kinds. They may be formally timetabled in advance, or they may be the subject of some prior negotiation, often accompanied by the mutual consultation of diaries and watches and the use of phrases such as 'I can give you 15 minutes'.

Such regularities are, in modern societies, often associated with the wider rational and organizational structuring of everyday life; in the past, religious calendars might have been of equal importance. They seem to have little to do with interpersonal relationships which may be described, variously, as primary, personal or intimate. Intimate relationships may contain such temporal negotiations and will undoubtedly be influenced on a day-to-day basis by the external timetables of school, employment and transport schedules. Pre-ordered or negotiated endings are frequently part of everyday family living; one only has to think of meal-times, bed-times, time allowed for television or 'quality time' between parents and children. Partners in 'time-hungry' relationships may frequently need to negotiate time spent with each other, balancing a whole range of external and personal commitments and preferences.

However, the intimate relationships themselves would seem to be free from explicit discussions of endings. We cannot easily imagine an adult saying 'I shall be your friend until next November' or 'I shall be your parent for another seven years'. Intimate relationships, as Goffman reminds us in talking of the similar 'anchored relationships', have a

character of non-reversability about them. Once achieved, such a relationship can never revert to a 'non-acquaintance', except perhaps symbolically
(Goffman 1971, 189). Indeed, such prior negotiations would seem to go
against the whole spirit or basis upon which such intimate relations are
supposed to rest. Clearly some sexual encounters – one-night stands or
holiday romances – may have some built-in sense of finality but relationships that include other dimensions of intimacy, emotional sharing and
knowledge of the other, would seem to inhibit the establishment of any
such conclusions.

However, relationships between friends, lovers or within families do
come to an end for reasons other than the death of one of the persons
involved and it is likely that the possibility of such endings will enter into
these relationships in some way or another. The purpose of this paper is to
explore the place of endings within relationships that are not temporally
structured in advance. Time in interpersonal relationships has not been the
subject of a great deal of sociological discussion, perhaps because of a
greater ease or familiarity with the structuring of rational organizations. For
this reason, I shall not be paying a great deal of attention to sociological
literature but will make use of the film *Brief Encounter*, using the published
screenplay (Manvell 1950). It is hoped that such an exploration will open
up the possibilities of further investigations of time in intimate relations
together with, perhaps, other social situations which do not have clear or
readily predictable endings.

This particular exploration will be limited in various ways. For the most
part I shall concentrate on relationships between adults. Such relationships
will have a sexual content although, as in the case of *Brief Encounter*, this
need not be physical sex. The extra-marital affair is perhaps the key
relationship with which I am concerned although, as marriage rates
decline, this may be less important than once it seemed. Given my use of
this particular film I am inevitably focusing on heterosexual relationships
although there is no reason why the issues raised in this chapter should not
be more widely applicable. Clearly this is one of the many issues which
would deserve more extended treatment.

Relationships and late modernity

There has been some considerable discussion in recent years about the
changing character of intimate relationships within late modernity. Chief
among these, of course, has been Giddens's discussion of the 'pure
relationship' (Giddens 1992, 58). These are relationships which are their
own justification; they are not instrumental in the sense of serving any
goal outside the relationship whether that goal be political, economic or,
broadly speaking, functional for the needs of any body or any entity
outside itself. The relationship exists for the mutual satisfaction of the

partners involved. By implication, it is a relationship where considerations of structured inequalities or power are minimized; Giddens, indeed, sees them as examples of democracy applied to intimacies.

In terms of timing, such relationships are clearly not 'till death us do part' since such a claim would be to introduce considerations outside the relationship. Rather, the relationship will continue for as long as each partner derives some satisfaction from it and, by definition, this cannot be determined in advance. As with Simmel's dyad, the relationship ends with the departure of one of the participants (Wolff 1950). Beck and Beck-Gernsheim, who also see love as a 'radical form of democracy for two' (1995, 192), write: 'The meaning of love, of togetherness, is always at risk ... The lovers have two levers to two trap-doors; the end can come very suddenly, on the decision of the other, and there is no appeal' (*ibid.*, 193).

Giddens takes a broadly optimistic view of such relationships, stressing the freedom, the likely equality and the possibilities of mutual growth and development. Other sociologists are less sure. Bauman's 'tourists' and 'vagabonds' imply a somewhat more desparate view of the human condition under late or postmodernity (Bauman 1990). In contrast to the 'pilgrim' where some long-term process of self-knowledge and self-understanding is linked to some wider structured order, the 'tourist' consumes sights and relationships without much in the way of further moral commitment.

However one evaluates such relationships and whatever doubts one might have about their prevalence, it is clear that such relationships constitute a significant feature of modern life and culture. In terms of our considerations of temporality such relationships would seem to raise the following considerations. Given that life-long commitment would seem to be ruled out in advance, how far does the possibility of an ending enter into the relationship itself? Giddens points to a 'structural contradiction' within pure relationships around issues of commitment and open-endedness (Giddens 1992, 137). Some measure of commitment would seem to be required, or might be expected to emerge from the ongoing relationship itself, even while always allowing for the possibility of an ending. Put another way, there is a large and uncertain terrain between the one-night stand and the externally shaped and internally accepted boundaries of traditional marriage. Goffman recognizes this in his discussion of anchored relationships. Such relationships have identifiable names, recognized by both partners (friendship, affair, marriage etc.), have terms which regulate the relationship and have a history: 'Relationships are not born and they do not die; however, like social persons they must have a beginning and must come to an end' (Goffman 1971, 193). The history of the relationship might be spoken of, retrospectively or as part of a process of ongoing monitoring, as having 'stages'.

Further, given that the relationship is in some senses (for example in the intersubjective experiences of the participants) 'out of time' how does it accommodate itself to the other time considerations that structure everyday life? And finally, when the ending is apparent, how is it handled? And, how far do such endings enter into wider understandings of the process of time itself? These are considerable and complex questions and I cannot begin to answer any of them fully. But they would seem to be worth asking.

Time and extra-marital relationships

There are relatively few qualitative studies of affairs and in these studies the temporal theme is more often implied than tackled head-on. Yet time enters extra-marital relationships in all kinds of ways. There are aspects of the affair as a narrative; when did it begin and end? There are questions of the allocation of time, the relative distribution of intersubjectivities, between the lover and the marital partner and home. There are questions about the timing of such matters as to when to tell (if at all) one's marital partner about the lover. There are questions about the extent to which, in affairs as in other areas of life, there are different understandings of time between men and women.

Annette Lawson's study of adultery (Lawson 1989) has a clear understanding of the narrative quality of such affairs: 'Thus I understand adultery as story, a particular drama central to Western culture, but always, because it is a story, available for creative rewriting' (*ibid*, 20) The creative rewriting of the story may vary according to the 'stages' of the relationship, the person to whom the story is being told or the gender and personality of the teller. Thus Lawson writes: 'at the outset, a liaison seems to be a relationship within one's control' (*ibid.*, 264). This sense of being in control clearly has a temporal reference, suggesting the possibility of the relationship being terminated relatively easily before things are seen to be going 'too far'. A relationship which seems more overwhelming or out of control calls into question any sense of an ending or suggests the frightening possibility of a plurality of endings.

Elsewhere, Lawson distinguishes between three types of adulterous relationship: the parallel (which might be condoned by the other partner); the traditional (the secret and more threatening to the marriage) and the recreational. These types may be supportive of the existing marriage, dangerous or transitional, aiding the movement out of one relationship and into another (*ibid.*, 27). Each of these types are temporally structured in different ways. The first could, theoretically, last as long as or longer than the original marriage; the second would seem to more likely require the clear termination of the affair or the break-up of the marriage; the third could be closer to sexual encounters where the temporary and passing character is recognized from the beginning. Clearly there is considerable fluidity within this typology and hence an ever-present degree of ambiguity about their temporal structures.

Gender differences run through Lawson's study. Thus men are more likely than women to talk of 'one-night stands' or 'brief encounters'. These, indeed, tend to be the more traditionally oriented men. But Lawson also found that the more permissive women were also likely to use these terms (*ibid.*, 38). Elsewhere, she contrasts two contemporary myths, the myth of normative marriage and the myth of 'me'. In the former case the temporality is formally clear: 'till death us do part'. In the latter, the temporality is necessarily uncertain since it stresses a narrative ever open and with more affinities to Giddens's later discussion of the 'pure relationship'. Traditionally, it might be suggested, women tended to seek and to find more security and identity in the former but this gender divide is seen as being blurred in Lawson's study as it is in Giddens's more general discussion.

This account of the shift in the gendered character of affairs and heterosexual relationships is very much to the fore in Richardson's study of 'The New Other Woman' (1985), conducted in the United States. This study deals in particular with single women who have affairs with married men. These, she argues, raise questions of some importance and she cites studies which give estimates of between half and two-thirds of husbands having extra-marital liaisons before they are 40 (*ibid.*, 2). To a large extent the imbalance between the married status of the man and the single status of the woman structures the relationship. As with Lawson's study, temporal considerations lie only slightly beneath the surface. Initially, 'brief encounters' (Richardson's usage) are seen as safe, as relatively harmless flings. Few single women actully plan to get involved with a married man and the men rarely hide their marital status. For this single 'other woman': 'Space and time, then, are both controlled by his marital status' (*ibid.*, 60). Thus she has to fit in with his domestic and work schedules and his sense of personal or domestic space. One woman is quoted as saying 'I knew from the beginning that it was going to end' and this is a sentiment echoed by others of her respondents. The ending seems to be less one negotiated directly between the partners themselves but more one the subject of an internal dialogue or understanding within the individual women concerned.

Richardson devotes a whole chapter to endings, distinguishing between the 'shock-out', the 'drag-out' and the 'wind-down'. Clearly these different endings involve different senses of time and change although the description of the kind of ending must necessarily take place after the event at a time when the woman is sure that it is 'all over'. While there might be a realistic assessment that the relationship will end, the kind and pace of ending would seem, again, to be unpredictable.

These two studies clearly show that issues of time are central in the experiences of persons involved in extra-marital affairs and in all kinds of complex ways. Such affairs have a narrative quality and constitute the substance of stories told and re-told to oneself, to analysts or to significant others. A sense of an ending is an ever-present, often uncertain, feature of such relationships. There are often differences in temporal perceptions, partly over the course of the relationship and partly as between the participants themselves. The latter differences are often gendered.

Such studies are almost inevitably based on retrospective accounts. The methodological and ethical issues involved in monitoring changing perceptions of time within the course of a relationship as it is taking place would seem to be insurmountable. It is here that we might wish to turn to fiction for guidance. The purpose of using such a fictional narrative is not to prove anything but to throw a little further light on the way time is understood to structure relationships.

To develop this point a little further it is worth highlighting the overlaps that exist between fictional and 'real' narratives. First, story-telling or narrativity is at the core of interpersonal relationships and everyday conversations. The stories we tell about our own lives are artfully constructed for particular audiences and may well draw upon shared fictional narratives in order to structure the accounts in a persuasive or plausible manner. Thus a witness to a real-life shooting might say: 'It was just like an episode of *Starsky and Hutch.*' In terms of the present discussion it is interesting that the phrase 'brief encounter' occurs in sociological accounts of extra-marital affairs. Reciprocally, authors (including directors, actors and so on) will refer to aspects of 'real life' in order to construct their fictional narratives. Such stories might be seen as being 'truth-full' even where they are not necessarily 'true'. Finally, both real and fictional narrators are concerned with issues of time, about beginnings and endings and how to construct these. Given that sociological accounts are so often relatively static, dealing with the time of this survey or this period of observation, a critical and reflexive use of fictional narratives may be a valuable tool in the understanding of the complex meanings of temporality in everyday life.

Brief Encounter

Brief Encounter was made in 1945, directed by David Lean with a screenplay by Noel Coward. The action of the film takes place, in what is presumably a small town in the South of England, just before the outbreak of the Second World War. The plot is relatively simple. Laura Jesson, a married woman, is in the habit of going to Milford every Thursday in order to change her library books, do some shopping and possibly visit the cinema. While waiting for her train at Milford Junction a piece of grit gets into her eye and a doctor, Alec Harvey, helps her to remove it. On subsequent

Thursdays they meet by accident, have lunch and go to the cinema together, drive out into the country and realize that they have fallen in love. Alec invites her to return to a colleague's flat (where he stays from time to time) but she refuses. At the last moment, however, she rushes from her homeward bound train and returns to the flat. She has hardly had time to remove her wet coat and scarf when Stephen, the owner of the flat, returns and Laura has to make her escape through a back entrance. Later Alec catches up with her at the station and they agree to meet for one last time. Their last few words at Milford Junction are interrupted by her talkative friend, Dolly. She briefly contemplates throwing herself under a passing express train but eventually returns to her husband, Fred.

There are clearly some difficulties with using this particular text. It is a work of fiction, framed by Laura's narrative. Apart from the brief scene between Alec and Stephen in the flat after Laura has fled, the whole film is from Laura's point of view and told in the form of a flashback. We therefore have little chance to understand Alec's perspective on the relationship. However, this fictional quality and the flashback framework might also be seen as being particularly relevant for our purposes. Relationships are constantly the subject of stories. Giddens argues that 'romantic love introduced the idea of a narrative into an individual's life' (Giddens 1992, 39) although it might be more accurate to say that romantic love and other relationships made use of existing narrative conventions and structures for their own purposes. These are the stories we tell to friends, to priests, to analysts and perhaps even our partners. Further, the flashback framework places the questions of endings to the fore; the audience, then and now, would have had a pretty good idea of how this particular story was going to end even if some of the details remain obscure until the end of the film.

Another difficulty for a modern audience is that, in a narrow sense, 'nothing takes place' between Laura and Alec. They kiss and make use of some, although not all, of the kinds of tie-signs associated with anchored relationships (Goffman,1971) but never have a full sexual relationship, a fact supposed to be a source of puzzlement to Trevor Howard, the actor who played Alec and to some of the earlier audiences (Silverman,1998, 64). Clearly, this absence of a sexual relationship, in the narrow physical sense, is a reflection of the conventions and expectations of the time and place in which the film was made. It was almost inevitable that their brief period in the flat should be interrupted. This, however, should not inhibit the present analysis. Issues of secrecy, betrayal and guilt remain very much to the fore. The relationship, although shaped by these external considerations, clearly has some aspect of a 'pure relationship' in that we are invited to consider the relationship itself and its meaning for the participants. Indeed, a consideration of the film highlights the somewhat limited nature of modern discussions of sexuality which tend to revolve around what happens between bodies rather than relationships between people. It is worth remembering what Giddens wrote at the beginning of *The Transformation of Intimacy*: 'I set out to write on sex. I found myself writing just as much about love; and about gender' (1992, 1). Whatever doubts there might be about the appropriateness of this particular film in exploring ideas of relationships there is no doubt that it is highly relevant when exploring issues of time. As Dyer notes: 'Time, its pressure, its fleetingness, is endlessly referenced in the film' (1993, 45). As a point of departure we may see the intersections between clock time and relational time within the film.

Looking first at clock time, Dyer notes that the action of the film takes place over seven Thursdays (*ibid.*). On the first page of the screenplay we read:

> Close shot of Albert as he watches the train go by. The lights from the carriage window flash across his face. From his waistcoat pocket he takes out a watch and chain and checks the time of the train. By the look of satisfaction on his face we know that it is punctual. He puts the watch back and the lights cease flashing on his face ... Insert of Albert's watch, reading 5.35 ...
>
> Manvell 1950, 5–6

Much of the action takes place on the railway station and is shaped by the times of trains. To a modern audience, the action of the film seems to take place in some kind of mythical past where trains are always on time and are plentiful. Virginia Woolf's letters to friends inviting them for country weekends are full of references to train times; trains once seemed part of the natural order of things. And because there is the expectation that trains will be on time, the responsibility is upon the passengers to see that they are on the platform in time. The film has many references to trains nearly missed. The railway timetable also dominates the lives of other participants such as the station master, Albert, and Myrtle, who runs the buffet and who is acutely aware of closing times and licensing hours. It is perhaps significant that Laura buys an expensive 'travelling clock with a barometer, and dates all in one' (*ibid.*, 26) as a birthday present for her husband and this clock plays a minor role in some of the deceptions that follow.

When Stephen returns unexpectedly back to the flat causing Laura to make an undignified exit down the back stairs, Alec says: 'You are back early.' Later in the same exchange, Stephen says: 'I am the one who should apologize for having returned so inopportunely ...' (*ibid.*, 68). This is one of the many examples of the points where personal time, clock time and relational time interact.

Individuals have their own timetables, expectations as to the sequencing and duration of events and with them notions of being late, early or on time. But personal timetables are rarely purely personal; the intersubjectivity of social life ensures that there is frequently a question of the co-ordination or merging of individual time schedules and expectations: 'Whenever two or more people are interacting directly, self-time is partially overlaid with a different type of time frame, namely, "interaction-time"' (Lewis and Weigart 1990, 81). With intimate relationships, further complexities are introduced: 'The pasts and futures of long-time friends or lovers are intersubjectively experienced as so intermeshed that their interaction-time takes on special qualities of shared experience not found in any other interactional context' (*ibid.*, 83). Thus Laura and Alec not only arrange to meet at certain times and share periods of time together. Their talk and their (or at least Laura's) internal reflections deal with the short time of their acquaintance and the uncertainties of the future. The passing of time is not only experienced but is reflexively absorbed into the unfolding relationship.

In several examples we see the intersections between this special kind of relational time and clock time:

> *Alec*: I must go.
> *Laura*: Yes, you must.
> *Alec*: Good-bye.
>
> Manvell 1950, 9

> *Alec*: Well, I must be getting along to the hospital.
> *Laura*: And I must be getting along to the grocer's.
> *Alec* (with a smile):   What exciting lives we lead, don't we? Good-bye.
>
> *Ibid.*, 26

> *Laura*: That's your train.
> *Alec* (looking down):   Yes.
> *Laura*: You mustn't miss it.
> *Alec*: No.
>
> *Ibid.*, 36

It might be tempting to see train timetables as symbols of Fate or possibly as a chorus commenting upon the relationships of Laura and Alec. But this, perhaps, may be an example of bad faith. While the timetable appears to dominate their chances of interaction, their use of the timetable reflects individual and intersubjective decisions. To this extent they willingly participate in their individual and shared temporal fates.

One common question between couples in the progress of a relationship is 'When shall I see you again?' This is a stage when the parties clearly lead independent lives according to distinct timetables but, at the same time, they are negotiating a new set of temporal interdependencies. Within the film there is a scene where Alec asks 'Shall I see you again?' just as his train is about to leave. They have spent most of the day together and Laura realizes her attraction to Alec. Consequently she hesitates. Alec begs her, 'Next Thursday – the same time' and Laura agrees as his train leaves. Their next meeting is after they have failed to meet one Thursday and Alec catches Laura at the station just as she is about to leave for home. He expresses his fear that he might never see her again and the date for next Thursday is set as Alec's train moves off.

These negotiations deal with the continuation of the relationship. More complex negotiations occur when the possibility of an ending is recognized. One longish exchange takes place in a boathouse after Alec has fallen in the lake and is drying his clothes. They recognize that they have fallen in love and their conversation looks backwards as well as forwards:

Alec: (leaning forward and taking her hand): Listen – it's too late now to be as sensible as all that – it's too late to forget what we've said – and anyway, whether we'd said it or not couldn't have mattered – we know – we've both of us known for a long time.

Laura: How can you say that – I've only known you for four weeks – we only talked for the first time last Thursday week.

Alec: Last Thursday week. Hasn't it been a long time since then – for you? Answer me truly.

Laura: Yes.

Alec: How often did you decide that you were never going to see me again?

Laura: Several times a day.

Alec: So did I.

Ibid., 51

Laura goes on to explain that the relationship cannot continue because of the pretence to others this would involve:

That's what's wrong – don't you see? That's what spoils everything. That's why we must stop here and now talking like this. We are neither of us free to love each other, there is too much in the way. There's still time, if we control ourselves and behave like sensible human beings, there's still time to – to ... (bursts into tears)
Alec: There's no time at all.

Ibid., 51

Laura and Alec are presenting a complex picture of interweaving temporal experiences involving the past, the anticipated future or futures and the varying subjective experiences of the passing of time. In Goffman's terms they are exploring the stages of the history of their relationship (Goffman 1971).

The question of the ending, now recognized by both of them, is specifically addressed by Alec at the conclusion of their penultimate meeting:

> I can't look at you now because I know something – I know this is the beginning of the end – not the end of my loving you – but the end of our being together. But not quite yet, darling – please not quite yet.
>
> Manvell 1950, 74

Perhaps there is some notion of a 'proper' ending being explored here. We may speculate that this notion, rather like the notion of a 'good death', involves several related features including a shared recognition of the impending end, an end which is in some sense planned for and which does not take place after, say, a quarrel or a misunderstanding.

While some of the negotiation of the stages and end of the relationship take place directly between Alec and Laura much of it, making use of the flashback technique and the interior monologue, occurs inside Laura's head. Indeed it may be claimed that the whole film, since it is in the first person, revolves around such an internal debate. Towards the early part of the film – but after the relationship has ended – Laura presents an account to herself in these terms:

> This can't last – this misery can't last – I must remember that and try to control myself. Nothing lasts really – neither happiness nor despair – not even life lasts very long – there will come a time in the future when I shan't mind about this any more – when I can look back and say quite peacefully and cheerfully 'How silly I was' – No, No – I don't want that time to come ever – I want to remember every minute–always – always – to the end of my days ...
>
> *Ibid.*, 15

Another example occurs when Laura is walking home from her station: 'By the time we got to Ketchworth, I had made up my mind definitely that I wouldn't see Alec any more.' In the middle of this a neighbour addresses her but she does not hear at first. Here and now are replaced by other temporal considerations.

In some ways, these other temporal considerations may be seen as 'out of time'. These are not the highs and fixes of sexual addiction which Giddens sees as being out of time (Giddens 1992, 72). However, there are several moments in the course of the relationship, at least in the early phases, when normal temporal considerations seem suspended. Here Laura is, in her mind, addressing her husband:

> Oh, Fred, it really was a lovely afternoon. There were some little boys sailing their boats – one of them looked awfully like Bobbie – that

should have given me a pang of conscience I know but it didn't ... I was
enjoying myself – enjoying every single minute.

Manvell 1950, 48

We had such fun, Fred. I felt gay and happy and sort of released – that's
what's so shameful about it all – that's what would hurt you so much if
you knew – that I could feel as intensely as that – away from you – with
a stranger.

Ibid., 49

The complexities of time and relationships are very apparent in these
quotations involving a reconstruction of how she felt then, how she feels
now about how she felt then and imagining a future, involving Fred's
knowledge, that must never come about. This sense of 'time out' takes on a
more tragic turn after her running away from Alec at his colleague's flat: 'I
got to the station fifteen minutes before the last train to Ketchworth, and
then I realized that I had been wandering about for over three hours, but it
didn't seem to be any time at all' (*Ibid.*, 72).

It may be noted, in passing, that Alec and Laura are not the only one's
involved in a specific relational time. There is also the relationship between
Albert and Myrtle conducted across the bar of the station buffet. This takes
on more of the character of a playful flirtation in which the temporal
considerations of work continually intrude: 'I'm afraid I really can't stand
here wasting my time in idle gossip, Mr Godby' (*ibid.*, 7); 'Tim and taide
wait for no man, Mr Godby' (*ibid.*, 8). Yet these playful exchanges are
themselves brief forms of 'time out'.

One question remains. Do the gender differences, noted in the sociological studies, also apply in this fictional account? In one sense the answer
would seem that it is difficult to tell since we only have Laura's perspective,
a theme discussed at some length in Dyer's appreciation of the film
(Dyer,1993). But perhaps that underlines the theme of gender difference. It
would be difficult to imagine the film being made from Alec's perspective
with the concerns about spouse and family which feature so prominantly
in Laura's account. His family life remains much more in the background.
Laura has to get home each Thursday evening; Alec always has the
possibility of staying in Milford for, supposedly, some work-related reason.

There is one occasion when the possibility of different versions is raised.
As Dyer points out, the exchange between Alec and Stephen after Laura has
fled from Stephen's flat, must have been imagined by Laura. When Alec
catches up with Laura after this exchange between the two men, Laura
slightly bitterly suggests that they talked together as 'men of the world',
making light of the evidence of this other woman. It is a brief observation
but enough to raise the possibility of their being multiple versions of this
particular relationship.

The other way in which gender differences are obviously apparent is in the way in which Alec constantly seems to be defining the terms of the relationship. In keeping with the codes of sexual conduct of the day, Alec initiates the action and plays a major part in determining the Thursday's activities such as, for example, hiring a car for a trip out to the country. More importantly, Alec is the one most likely to verbalize the terms of the relationship and its progress over time. He, for example, is the one who says: 'You know what has happened, don't you?' and while he is initially referring to his falling in love with Laura he also frames the discussion in a way to bring out their mutual attraction for each other. Laura's interpretations of the progress and nature of the relationship are more likely to be carried out as part of her interior monologue.

Concluding remarks

It should be stressed that this has not been an exercise in film criticism. For one thing, I have focused almost entirely upon the written text and have said nothing about the direction, the music or the very *look* of the film. Much could be said, for example, of the way in which the performances of Celia Johnson and Trevor Howard express, in their bodily postures and movements and their dress, two different and gendered ways of being in the world.

It has been a sociological exploration, using the film (and stimulated by recent debates about intimacy and about time) to raise and to explore certain themes. I treat the film as being 'good to think with' although doubtless other texts might have been chosen. I believe that relational and interactional time – and the ways in which these may be seen as interacting with clock time – are relatively under-explored themes and I hope to encourage further thought on these issues.

Let us begin with the familiar distinction, in the literature on time, between the idea of time as a resource and time as a set of social meanings (see Hassard 1990, 14). We may suggest that in pure relationships (or relationships that might be assumed to approach this state) that time as a set of social, in the sense of interpersonal, meanings remains very much to the fore. The use of time as a resource might be seen as a sign of a degree of asymmetry within such a supposedly pure relationship or, possibly, that it is about to come to an end. Thus, although Laura and Alec clearly have other sets of temporal constraints and obligations these are mutually recognized (it would seem) and perceived as constraints rather than as bargaining counters. Put another way, the terms of their ongoing relationship would seem to allow for the intrusion of other temporal – and hence relational – constraints. 'That's *your* train,' says Laura (my emphasis) and Alec agrees. The use of the possessive pronoun is not meant to be taken literally but clearly places Alec within other times and other places.

Relational time while it has moments of being 'out of time' should really be seen as woven into the multiplicities of time outlined by Adam (1995, 6) among others: '... time embedded in social interactions, structure, practices and knowledge, in artifacts, in the mindful body, and in the environment'.

These multiple times are given some coherence in the narratives, the overall narrative provided by Laura and the film which is both inside and outside Laura as well as the multiple brief narratives, real or imagined, that take place within the duration of the film. The technique of the voice-over provides an almost perfect way to illustrate the themes of reflexive monitoring, seen as an integral part of modern relationships and biographies.

We need also to consider, briefly, the interrelationships between time and space in this film and in relationships of this kind in general. The interconnections between the two is a truism but striking nevertheless. A sense of place is conveyed with as much detail as the multiple times, the Kardomah café, the cinema and, above all the station with its clock, its buffet, passageways and platforms. The occasional speculations about the restoration of Carnforth (the actual site of Milford Junction) to its former glory bear witness to the abiding impression made by this location.

Yet, if some aspects of the relationship are perceived by the participants as being out of time there is a sense in which the action is taking place out of place. It is a location distant from the family locations of the participants although never entirely free from neighbours and friends who serve to remind Laura of another place. When Laura suggests, earlier in the relationship, that Alec might come over for a meal to meet Fred and the children we are encouraged to see this as a last attempt to place the relationship within a framework of friendship rather than something more threatening. A third of Lawson's women informants (1989, 195) reported having taken their lovers home: 'What makes them thrilling are the transgressions of the known and customary territory – of physical place, bodies and personal space.' As much as Laura might, in a very different sense, wish for the merging of the world of Fred and the children with the interesting and attractive stranger, she knows that this is impossible. Milford and Ketchworth must be kept separate although in practice this too proves impossible. Relational space has the habit of flowing over into physical space.

The point of departure of this chapter was the question about how individuals handle time where the temporal boundaries are uncertain and necessarily so. This uncertainty of temporal boundaries may be seen as an integral feature of many intimate relationships especially, perhaps, those which have some of the elements Giddens defines as characterizing 'pure' relationships. But perhaps the analysis might also be extended to other areas of life where temporal boundaries are imprecise. We may note, for example, the 'greedy' organizations of modern life where the expected temporal commitments of the members are unquestionably open-ended, at least in terms of the informal culture. Or we may take a more comparative perspective, noting, for example, Bourdieu's well-known account of the 'nonchalant indifference to passage of time' among the Kabyle (Bourdieu 1990). Here we find a people who supposedly have mastered the art of passing time with a weak sense of ending.

These are speculations that might be pursued elsewhere. For the time being, perhaps, we may continue to ponder the complexities associated with the seemingly simple question, 'When shall I see you again?'

Bibliography

Adam, B. 1995. *Timewatch: The Social Analysis of Time*. Cambridge: Polity.

Adema, W. 1999. *Net Social Expenditure*. Labour Market and Social Policy Occasional Paper no. 39, Paris: OECD.

Adler, S. and J. Brenner. 1992. Gender and space: lesbians and gay men in the city. *International Journal of Urban and Regional Research* 16, 24–34.

Agulnik, P. and J. Le Grand. 1998. Tax relief and partnership pensions. *Fiscal Studies* 19, 403–28.

Albrow, M., J. Eade, G. Fennell and D. O'Byrne. 1994. *Local/Global Relations in a London Borough: Shifting Boundaries and Localities*. Roehampton Institute of Education: Roehampton Local/Global Studies.

Allan, G. and R. Adams. 1998. Reflections on context. In *Placing Friendship in Context*, eds. R. Adams and G. Allan. London: Cambridge University Press.

Allan, G. and G. Crow. 2001. *Families, Households and Society*. Basingstoke: Palgrave.

Allat, P. 1997. Conceptualizing youth: transitions, risk and the public and the private. In *Youth, Citizenship and Social Change in a European Context*, eds. J. Bynner, L. Chisholm and A. Furlong. Aldershot: Ashgate.

Alldred, P. 1998. Ethnography and discourse analysis: dilemmas in representing the voices of children. In *Feminist Dilemmas In Qualitative Research: Public Knowledge and Private Lives*, eds. J. Ribbens and R. Edwards. London: Sage.

Allen, I. and S. Bourke Dowling. 1998. *Teenage Mothers: Decisions And Outcomes*. London: Policy Studies Institute.

Amato, P.R. 1993. Children's adjustment to divorce: theories, hypotheses, and empirical support. *Journal of Marriage and the Family* 55, 23–38.

Amato, P.R. and A. Booth. 1997. *A Generation at Risk: Growing Up in an Era of Family Upheaval*. Harvard: Harvard University Press.

Anthony, K. 1993. The meaning and use of housing: unconventional arrangements. In *The Meaning And Use of Housing*, ed. E. Arias. Aldershot: Avebury.

Arber, S. and J. Ginn. 1991. *Gender and Later Life: A Sociological Analysis of Resources And Constraints*. London: Sage.

—.1995. *Connecting Gender and Ageing: A Sociological Approach*. Buckingham: Open University Press.

Arendell, T. 1994. *Fathers and Divorce*. London: Sage.

Arendt, H. 1958. *The Human Condition*. Chicago: Chicago University Press.

Ashworth, M. 2000. 'Time and space': carers' views about respite care. *Health and Social Care in the Community*. 8, 50–56.

Atkinson, M. 1980. Some practical uses of a 'natural lifetime'. *Human Studies* 3, 33–46.

Attias-Donfut, C. and S. Arber. 2000. Equity and solidarity across the generations. In *The Myth Of Generational Conflict: The Family and State in Ageing Societies*, eds. S. Arber and C. Attias-Donfut. London: Routledge.

Attias-Donfut, C. and F. Wolff. 2000. The redistributive effects of generational transfers. In *The Myth of Generational Conflict: The Family and State in Ageing Societies*, eds. S. Arber and C. Attias-Donfut. London: Routledge.

Babuscio, J. 1988. *We Speak for Ourselves: The Experiences of Gay Men and Lesbians*. London: SPCK.

Bartlett, S. 1997. Housing as a factor in the socialisation of children: a critical review of the literature. *Merrill-Palmer Quarterly* 43, 169–98.

Bauman, Z. 1990. Modernity and ambivalence. In *Global Culture: Nationalism, Globalization and Modernity*, ed. M. Featherstone. London: Sage.

Beck, U. 1992. *Risk Society: Towards a New Modernity*. London: Sage.

—. 1997. Democratization of the family. *Childhood* 4, 151–68.

Beck, U. and E. Beck-Gernsheim. 1995. *The Normal Chaos of Love*. Cambridge: Polity.

—. 1996. Individualisation and 'precarious freedoms': perspectives and controversies of a subject-oriented sociology. In *Detraditionalisation: Critical Reflection on Authority and Identity*, eds. P. Heelas, S. Lash and P. Morris. Oxford: Blackwell.

Becker, H. 2000. Discontinuous change and generational contracts. In *The Myth of Generational Conflict: The Family and State in Ageing Societies*, eds. S. Arber and C. Attias-Donfut. London: Routledge.

Bell, C. 1968. *Middle-class Families*. London: Routledge & Kegan Paul.

Bellah, R.N., R. Madsen, W.M. Sullivan, A. Swidler and S.M. Tipton. 1985. *Habits of the Heart: Individualism and Commitment in American Life*. Berkeley: University of California Press.

Bennett, R. 1990. Overners: an anthropological survey. In *The Island from Within: An Anthology*, ed. R. Sawyer. Andover: Caric Press.

Bernardes, J. 1986. Multidimensional developmental pathways: a proposal to facilitate the conceptualisation of 'family diversity'. *Sociological Review* 34, 590–610.

Berrington, A. and M. Murphy. 1994. Changes in living arrangements of young adults in Britain during the 1980s. *European Sociological Review* 10, 235–57.

Berthoud, R., S. McKay and K. Rowlingson. 1999. Becoming a single mother. In *Changing Britain: Families and Households in the 1990s*, ed. S. McRae. Oxford: Oxford University Press.

Beynon, H., D. Elson, D. Howell and L. Shaw. 1993. *The Remaking of Economy and Society: Manchester, Salford and Trafford, 1945–1992*. Manchester: Manchester International Centre for Labour Studies, Working Paper 1.

Birdwell-Pheasant, D. and D. Lawrence-Zuniga. 1999. *House Life: Space, Place and Family in Europe*. Oxford: Berg.

Blain, N. and K. Burnett. 1994. Otherness as Englishness: the white settler phenomenon in the Scottish media. Paper presented to the European Film and Television Conference 'Turbulent Europe: Conflict, Identity and Culture'. London: NFT.

Bolton, N. and B. Chalkley 1990. The rural population turnaround: a case study of North Devon. *Journal of Rural Studies* 6, 29–43.

Bourdieu, P. 1990 Time perspective of the Kabyle. In *The Sociology of Time*, ed., J. Hassard, Basingstoke: Palgrave Macmillan.

Bradshaw, J. and J.R. Chen. 1997. Poverty in the UK: a comparison with 19 other countries. *Benefits*, January, 13–15.

Bradshaw, J., C. Stimson, C. Skinner and J.Williams. 1999. *Absent Fathers?*. London: Routledge.

Bruegel, I. 1996. The trailing wife: a declining breed?: Careers, geographical mobility and household conflict in Britain, 1970–89. In *Changing Forms of Employment: Organisations, Skills and Gender*, eds. R. Crompton, D. Gallie and K. Purcell. London: Routledge.

Bruner, J. 1987. Life as narrative. *Social Research* 51, 11–32.

Bryman, A., B. Bytheway, P. Allatt and T. Keil, eds. 1987. *Rethinking the Life Cycle*. London: Macmillan.

Burghes, L. 1994. *Lone Parenthood and Family Disruption: The Outcomes for Children*. London: Family Policy Studies Centre.

Burnett, K.A. 1996. Once an incomer, always an incomer?. In *Women and Access in Rural Areas: What Makes the Difference? What Difference Does It Make?*, eds. P. Chapman and S. Lloyd. Aldershot: Avebury.

—. 1998. Local heroics: Reflecting on incomers and local rural development discourses in Scotland. *Sociologia Ruralis* 38, 204–24.

Burton, R. 1997. Castles in the air, identities and individualism: the Cornish and their 'dimensions of difference'. Paper presented to the BSA Annual Conference. York University.

Butler, R. 2000. A break from the norm: exploring the experiences of queer crips. In *Constructing Gendered Bodies*, eds. C. Brackett-Milburn and L. McKie. London: Macmillan.

Butler, T. 1997. *Gentrification and the Middle Classes*. Aldershot: Ashgate.

Bynner, J., E. Ferri and P. Shepherd.1997. *Twenty Something In The 1990s: Getting On, Getting By, Getting Nowhere*. Aldershot: Ashgate.

Caird, J.B. 1972. Changes in the Highlands and Islands of Scotland, 1951–71. *Geoforum* 12, 5–36.

Castells, M. 1983. *The City and the Grassroots*. London: Edward Arnold.

Champion, A.G., ed. 1989. *Counterurbanization: The Changing Pace and Nature of Population Deconcentration*. London: Arnold.

Chandler, J. 1991. *Women Without Husbands: An Exploration of the Margins of Marriage*. London: Palgrave Macmillan.

Cheal, D. 1991.*Family and the State of Theory*. London: Harvester Wheatsheaf.

Cherlin, A.J., F. Furstenberg, P. Chaselansdale, K. Kiernan, P. Robins, D. Morrison and J. Teitler. 1991. Longitudinal studies of the effects of divorce on children in Great Britain and the United States. *Science* 252, 1386–9.

Cherlin, A., K. Kiernan and P. Chase-Lansdale. 1995. Parental divorce in childhood and demographic outcomes in young adulthood. *Demography* 32, 299–318.

Cheung, S.Y. and A. Buchanan. 1999. High malaise scores in adulthood of children and young people who have been in care. *Journal of Child Psychology and Psychiatry* 38, 575–80.

Clarke, L., P.D. Salvo, H. Joshi and J. Wright. 1997. *Stability and Instability in Children's Lives: Longitudinal Evidence from Great Britain*. London: Centre for Population Studies, London School of Hygiene and Tropical Medicine.

Cockett, M. and J. Tripp. 1994. *The Exeter Family Study*. London: Family Policy Studies Centre.

Cohen, A.P. 1987. *Whalsay: Symbol, Segment, and Boundary in a Shetland Island Community*. Manchester: Manchester University Press.

—. 1989. *The Symbolic Construction of Community*. London: Routledge.

Cohen, P. 1997. *Rethinking the Youth Question*. London: Macmillan.

Cole, J. 1999. *After the Affair*. London: Vermillion.

Coleman, R. 1982. Second homes in North Norfolk. In *Power, Planning and People in Rural East Anglia*, ed. M.J. Moseley. Norwich: Geo Books.

Coles, B. 1995. *Youth and Social Policy: Youth Citizenship and Young Careers*. London: UCL Press.

—. 1997. Vulnerable youth and processes of social exclusion. In *Youth Citizenship and Social Change in a European Context*, eds. J. Bynner, L. Chisholm and A. Furlong. Andover: Ashgate.

Coley, R. and P. Chase-Lansdale.1998. Adolescent pregnancy and parenthood: recent evidence and future directions. *American Psychologist* 53, 152–66.

Crawford, J., S. Kippax, J. Onyx, U. Gault and P. Benton.1992. *Emotion and Gender*. London: Sage.

Crompton, R. and K. Sanderson. 1990. *Gendered Jobs and Social Change*. London: Unwin Hyman.

Crow, G. and G. Allan. 1994. *Community Life*. Hemel Hempstead: Simon & Schuster.

—. 1995a. Community types, community typologies and community time. *Time and Society* 42, 147–66.

—. 1995b. Beyond 'insiders' and 'outsiders' in the sociology of community. Paper presented to the Annual Conference of the British Sociological Association. University of Leicester.

Crow G. and S. Heath. 2002. *Times in the Making: Structure and Process in Work and Everyday* Life. Basingstoke: Palgrave Macmillan.

Damer, S. 2000. Scotland in miniature? Second homes on Arran. *Scottish Affairs* 31, 37–54.

Davis, J. 1992. Tense in ethnography: some practical considerations'. In Anthropology and Autobiography, eds. J. Okely and H. Callaway. London: Routledge.

Day, G. and J. Murdoch. 1993. Locality and community: coming to terms with place. *Sociological Review* 41, 82–111.

Dennis, N., F. Henriques and C. Slaughter. 1956. *Coal Is Our Life*. London: Eyre & Spottiswoode.

Denzin, N. 1989. *Interpretive Biography*. Newbury Park: Sage.

Despotidou, S. and P. Shepherd. 1998. *The 1970 British Cohort Study, Twenty Six Year Follow-Up, Guide to Data Available at The ESRC Data Archive*. Social Statistics Research Unit, London: City University.

Despres, C. 1991. The meaning of home: literature review and direction for future research and theoretical development. *Journal of Architecture and Planning Research* 8, 96–114.

Devine, F. 1992. *Affluent Workers Revisited*. Edinburgh: Edinburgh University Press.

Dex, S. 1987. *Women's Occupational Mobility: A Lifetime Perspective*. Basingstoke: Palgrave Macmillan.

Douglas, N., I. Warwick, S. Kemp and G. Whitty. 1997. Playing it safe: responses of secondary school teachers to lesbian, gay and bisexual pupils, bullying, HIV and AIDS education and Section 28. Health and Education Research Unit, Institute of Education, University of London.

Duncombe, J. and D. Marsden. 1993 Love and intimacy: the gender division of emotion and 'emotion work'. *Sociology* 27, 221–41.

—. 1998. 'Stepford wives' and 'hollow men'? Doing emotion work, doing gender and 'authenticity' in intimate heterosexual relationships. In *Emotions in Social Life*, eds. G. Bendelow and S.J. Williams. London: Routledge.

Dyer, R. 1993. *Brief Encounter*, London: British Film Institute.

Elder, G. 1978. Family history and the life course. In *Transitions: The Family and the Life Course in Historical Perspective*, ed. T. Hareven. New York: Academic Press.

Eldridge, J. 1990. Sociology in Britain: a going concern. In *What Has Sociology Achieved?*, eds. C.G.A. Bryant and H.A. Becker. London: Palgrave Macmillan.

Elias, N. and J.L. Scotson. 1994. *The Established and the Outsiders: A Sociological Enquiry into Community Problems*. Second edition. London, Sage.

Elliott, J. and M. Richards. 1991. Children and divorce: educational performance and behaviour before and after parental separation. *International Journal of Law and the Family* 5, 258–76.

Elwood, S. 2000. Lesbian living spaces: multiple meanings of home. *Journal of Lesbian Studies* 4, 11–27.

Ely, M., M. Richards, M. Wadsworth and B. Elliott. 1999. Secular changes in the asso-ciation of parental divorce and children's educational attainment: evidence from three British birth cohorts. *Journal of Social Policy* 28, 437–55.

Epstein, D. and R. Johnston. 1994. On the straight and narrow: the heterosexual pre-sumption, homophobia and schools. In *Challenging Lesbian and Gay Inequalities in Education*, ed. D. Epstein. Milton Keynes: Open University Press.

European Commission 1997. *Youth in the European Union: From Education to Working Life*. Brussels: Eurostat.

Eurostat. 1995. *Fertility Rates in EU Countries*. Brussels: CEC.

Evandrou, M., ed. 1997. *Baby Boomers: Ageing in the 21st Century*. London: Age Concern.

Fairhurst, E. 1999. *Thinking About Becoming and Being Older: Some Findings from Greater Manchester*. Manchester: Manchester Metropolitan University.

Fairhurst, E. and R. Lightup. 1982. Growing older: issues in the use of qualitative research. In *Current Trends in British Gerontology*, eds. R. Taylor and A. Gilmore. London: Gower.

Ferri, E. 1976. *Growing Up in a One Parent Family*. London: National Foundation for Educational Research.

—. 1984. *Stepchildren: A National Study. A Report from the NCDS*. London: Nfer-Nelson.

Ferri, E. and K.Smith. 1998. *Step-Parenting In the 1990s*. London: Family Policy Studies Centre Joseph Rowntree Foundation.

Finch, J. 1989. *Family Obligations and Social Change*. Cambridge: Polity.

Finch J. and D. Groves, eds. 1983. *A Labour of Love: Women, Work and Caring*. London: Routledge & Kegan Paul.

Finch, J. and J. Mason. 1993. *Negotiating Family Responsibilities*. London: Routledge.

Fine, G. 1996. *Kitchens: The Culture of Restaurant Work*. Berkeley: University of Calfornia Press.

Ford, J. 1999. Young adults and owner occupation: a changing goal?. In *Young People, Housing and Social Policy*, ed. J. Rugg. London: Routledge.

Forsythe, D.E. 1980. Urban incomers and rural change: the impact of migrants from the city on life in an Orkney community. *Sociologia Ruralis* 20, 287–307.

Frankenberg, R. 1957. *Village on the Border*. London: Cohen and West.

Freely, M. 2000. 'Divorce and be damned. *Observer*, 19 November 2000.

Furlong, A. and F. Cartmel. 1997. *Young People and Social Change: Individualisation and Risk in Late Modernity*. Buckingham: Open University Press.

Furstenberg, F. 1987. The new extended family: the experience of parents and chil-dren after remarriage. In *Remarriage and Step-Parenting Today: Current Research and Theory*, eds. K. Pasley and M. Inhinger-Tallman. New York: Guilford Press.

Furstenberg, F. and A. Cherlin. 1991. *Divided Families: What Happens to Children When Parents Part*. Cambridge, MA: Harvard University Press.

Furstenberg, F. and J. Teitler. 1994. Reconsidering the effects of marital disruption: what happens to children of divorce in early adulthood? *Journal of Family Issues* 15, 173–90.

Giddens, A. 1991. *Modernity and Self-Identity. Self and Society in the Late Modern Age*. Oxford: Polity.

—. 1992. *The Transformation of Intimacy: Sexuality, Love And Eroticism In Modern Societies*. Cambridge: Polity.

Gillies, V., J. Ribbens McCarthy and J. Holland. 1999. Young people and family life: analysing and comparing disciplinary discourses. Centre for Family and Household Research, Oxford Brookes University. Occasional Paper no. 3.

—. 2000. *'Pulling Together, Pulling Apart': The Family Lives of Young People*. London: Family Policy Studies Centre/Joseph Rowntree Foundation.

Gilligan, J.H. 1987. Visitors, tourists and outsiders in a Cornish town. In *Who from their Labours Rest? Conflict and Practice in Rural Tourism*, eds. M. Bouquet and M. Winter. Aldershot: Avebury.

Gillis, J. 1997. *A World of their Own Making*. Oxford: Oxford University Press.

Ginn, J. and S. Arber.1993. Pension penalties: the gendered division of occupational welfare. *Work, Employment and Society* 7, 47–70.

—. 1994. Heading for hardship: how the British pension system has failed women. In *Social Security and Social Change: New Challenges to the Beveridge Model*, eds. S. Baldwin and J. Falkingham. Hemel Hempstead: Harvester Wheatsheaf.

—. 1996. Patterns of employment, pensions and gender: the effect of work history on older women's non-state pensions. *Work, Employment and Society* 10, 469–90.

—. 1999. Changing patterns of pension inequality: the shift from state to private sources. *Ageing and Society* 19, 319–42.

—. 2000a. Personal pension take-up in the 1990s in relation to position in the labour market. *Journal of Social Policy* 29, 205–28.

—. 2000b. Gender, the generational contract and pension privatisation. In *The Myth of Generational Conflict: The Family and State in Ageing Societies*, eds. S. Arber and C. Attias-Donfut. London: Routledge.

—. 2000c. Ethnic inequality in later life: variation in financial circumstances by gender and ethnic group. *Education and Ageing* 15, 65–83.

—. 2001. Ethnic inequality in pension acquistion in Britain. *British Journal of Sociology* 52, 519–39.

—. 2002. Degrees of freedom: do graduate women escape the motherhood gap in pensions? *Sociological Research Online* 7, http://www.socresonline.org.uk/7/2/ginn_arber.html

Ginn, J., S. Arber, J. Brannen, A. Dale, S. Dex, P. Elias, P. Moss, J. Pahl, C. Roberts and J. Rubery. 1996. Feminist fallacies: a reply to Hakim on women's employment. *British Journal of Sociology* 47(1), 167–74.

Ginn, J., D. Street and S. Arber, eds. 2001. *Women, Work and Pensions: International Prospects*. Buckingham: Open University Press.

Glover, J. and S. Arber. 1995. Polarisation in mothers' employment. *Gender, Work and Organisation* 2, 165–79.

Goffman, E. 1971. *The Presentation of Self in Everyday Life*. Harmondsworth: Penguin.

Goldscheider, F. and C. Goldscheider. 1993. Whose nest? A 2-generational view of leaving home during the 1980s. *Journal of Marriage and the Family* 55, 851–62.

Goldthorpe, J.H., D. Lockwood, F. Bechhofer and J. Platt. 1969. *The Affluent Worker in the Class Structure*. Cambridge: Cambridge University Press.

Gordon, T. 1994. *Single Women*. London: Macmillan.

Gordon, T., J. Holland and E. Lahelma. 2000. *Making Spaces: Citizenship and Difference in Schools*. London: Palgrave Macmillan.

Grace, M. 1998. The work of caring for young children: priceless or worthless? *Women's Studies International Forum* 21, 401–13.

Gray, D.K. 1993. *Counterurbanisation and the Perception of Quality of Life in Rural Scotland: A Postmodern Framework*. PhD thesis. University of Glasgow.

Green, A.E. 1997. A question of compromise? Case study evidence on the location and mobility strategies of dual career households. *Regional Studies* 31, 641–657.

Grieco, M. 1987. *Keeping It in the Family*. London: Tavistock.

Griffin, C. 1993. *Representations of Youth: The Study of Youth and Adolescence in Britain and America*. Cambridge: Polity.

Grundy, E., M. Murphy and N. Shelton. 1999. Looking beyond the household inter-generational perspective on living kin and contacts with kin in Great Britain. *Population Trends* 97, 33–41.

Gulbrandsen, L. and A. Langsether. 2000. Wealth distribution between generations: a source of conflict or cohesion? In *The Myth of Generational Conflict: The Family and State in Ageing Societies*, eds. S. Arber and C. Attias-Donfut. London: Routledge.

Gurney, C. 1999a. Lowering the drawbridge: a case study of analogy and metaphor in the social construction of home-ownership. *Urban Studies 36*, 1705–22.

—. 1999b. 'We've got friends who live in council houses': Power and resistance in home ownership. In *Consuming Cultures*, eds. J. Hearn and S. Roseneil. Basingstoke: Macmillan

Hakim, C. 1996. *Key Issues in Women's Work: Female Heterogeneity and Polarisaton of Women's Employment*. London: Athlone Press.

Hall, R., P. Ogden and C. Hill. 1999. Living alone: evidence from England and Wales and France for the last two decades. In *Changing Britain: Families and Households in the 1990s*, ed. S. McRae. Oxford: Oxford University Press.

Halpern, C., J. Udry and C. Suchindran. 1997. Testosterone predicts initiation of coitus in adolescent females. *Psychosomatic Medicine 59*, 161–71.

Hanson, T., S. McLanahan and E. Thomson. 1998. Windows on divorce: before and after. *Social Science Research 27*, 329–49.

Hareven, T. 1978. *Transitions: The Family and the Life Course in Historical Perspective*. New York: Academic Press.

—. 1982. *Family Time and Industrial Time*. Cambridge: Cambridge University Press.

Harris, C.C. 1983. *The Family and Industrial Society*. London: Allen & Unwin.

Haskey, J. 1990. Children in families broken by divorce. *Population Trends*. 61, 34–42.

—. 1994. Stepfamilies and step-children in Great Britain. *Population Trends 74*,17–28.

—. 1998. One-parent families and their dependent children. *Population Trends 91*, 5–15.

—. 1999. Cohabitational and marital histories of adults in Great Britain. *Population Trends 96*, 13–23.

Hassard, J. ed. 1990. *The Sociology of Time*, Basingstoke: Palgrave Macmillan.

Haug, F. 1987. *Female Sexualisation: A Collective Work of Memory* translated by Erica Carter. London: Verso.

Haywood, C. and M. Mac an Ghaill. 1995. The sexual politics of the curriculum: contesting values. *International Studies in Sociology of Education 5*, 221–36.

Heath, S. 1999. Young adults and household formation in the 1990s. *British Journal of the Sociology of Education 20*, 545–61.

Hetherington, E.M. 1979. Divorce: a child's perspective. *American Psychologist 34*, 851–8.

Hetherington, E.M. and W. Clingempeel. 1992. *Coping with Marital Transitions: A Family Systems Perspective*. Chicago: University of Chicago Press.

Hetherington, E.M., S. Henderson, T. O'Connor, G. Insabella, L. Taylor, E. Anderson, M. Skaggs, K. Jodl, M. Bridges, J. Kim, A. Mitchell and R. Chan. 1999. Adolescent siblings in stepfamilies: family functioning and adolescent adjustment. *Monographs of the Society for Research in Child Development 64*, V–209.

Hinkinson-Hodnett, A. 1999. *The Pink Paper*, 12 March 1999. Chronos Publishing.

Hobcraft, J. and K. Kiernan. 1999. Childhood poverty, early motherhood and adult social exclusion. *CASE Paper 28*. London: Centre for Analysis of Social Exclusion, London School of Economics.

Holland, J., V. Gillies and J. Ribbens McCarthy. 1999. Living on the edge. Paper presented at the European Sociological Association conference, Amsterdam.

Holland, J., C. Ramazanoglu, S. Sharpe and R. Thomson. 1994. Power and desire: the embodiment of female sexuality. *Feminist Review 46*, 21–38.

Holland, J., R. Thomson, S. Henderson, S. McGrellis and S. Sharpe. 2000. Catching on, wising up and learning from your mistakes: young people's accounts of moral development. *International Journal of Children's Rights* 8, 271–94.

Holloway, S., G. Valentine and N. Bingham 2000. Institutionalising technologies: masculinities, femininities and the heterosexual economy of the IT classroom. *Environment and Planning A* 32, 617–33.

Holloway, W. and T. Jefferson. 1997. Eliciting narrative through the in-depth interview. *Qualitative Inquiry* 3, 53–70.

Hughes, E.C. 1971. Cycles, turning points and careers. In *The Sociological Eye*, E.C. Hughes. Chicago: Aldine-Atherton.

Hunter, J. 1976. *The Making of the Crofting Community*. Edinburgh: John Donald.

—. 1991. *The Claim of Crofting: The Scottish Highlands and Islands 1930–1990*. Edinburgh: Mainstream.

Hutson, S. and R. Jenkins. 1989. *Taking the Strain: Families, Unemployment and the Transition to Adulthood*. Milton Keynes: Open University Press.

Jacobs, S. 1997. Employment changes over childbirth: a retrospective view. *Sociology* 31, 577–90.

James, A. 1993. *Childhood Identities*. Edinburgh: Edinburgh University Press.

James, A. and A. Prout. 1990 Representing childhood: time and transition in the study of childhood. In *Constructing and Reconstructing Childhood*, eds. A. James and A. Prout. Basingstoke: Falmer Press.

James, H. 1980. *What Maisie Knew*. Oxford: Oxford University Press.

Jamieson, L. 1998. *Intimacy: Personal Relationships in Modern Societies*. Cambridge: Polity.

—. 1999. Intimacy transformed? A critical look at the 'pure relationship'. *Sociology* 33, 477–94.

Jamieson, L., G. Jones and C. Martin. 1996. Locality, identity and migration: a study of young people growing up in the Scottish Borders. Paper presented to the British Sociological Association Annual Conference, University of Reading.

Jedrej, M.C. and M. Nuttal. 1995. Incomers and locals: metaphors and reality in the repopulation of rural Scotland. *Scottish Affairs* 10, 112–26.

—. 1996. *White Settlers: The Impact of Rural Repopulation In Scotland*. Luxembourg: Harwood Academic Publishers.

Jenkins, R. 1984. Bringing it all back home: an anthropologist in Belfast. In *Social Researching: Politics, Problems, Practice*, eds. C. Bell and H. Roberts. London: Routledge & Kegan Paul

Johnston, L. and G. Valentine. 1995 Wherever I lay my girlfriend that's my home: the performance and surveillance of lesbian identities in domestic environments. In *Mapping Desire: Geographies of Sexualities*, eds. D. Bell and G. Valentine. London: Routledge.

Jones, G. 1995. *Leaving Home*. Buckingham: Open University Press.

—. 1999. 'The same people in the same places'? Socio-spatial identities and migration in youth. *Sociology* 33, 1–22.

—. 2002. *The Youth Divide*. York: Joseph Rowntree Foundation.

Jones, G. and C. Wallace. 1992. *Youth, Family and Citizenship*. Buckingham: Open University Press.

Joshi, H. 1996. *The Tale of Mrs. Typical*. London: Family Policy Studies Centre.

Kahn, J. and K. Anderson. 1992. Intergenerational patterns of teenage fertility. *Demography* 29, 39–57.

Kent, R.A. 1982. *A History of British Empirical Sociology*. Aldershot: Gower.

Kenyon, E. 1999. A home from home: students' transitional experiences of home. In *Ideal Homes? Social Change and Domestic Life*, eds. T. Chapman and J. Hockey. London: Routledge.

—. 2000. 'Time, temporality and the dynamics of community. *Time and Society* 9, 21–41.

Kiernan, K. 1992. The impact of family disruption in childhood on transitions made in young adult life. *Population Studies* 46, 213–34.

—. 1997a. Becoming a young parent: a longitudinal study of associated factors. *British Journal of Sociology* 48, 406–8.

—. 1997b. *The Legacy of Parental Divorce: Social, Economic and Demographic Experiences in Adulthood.* London: ESRC Centre for Analysis of Social Exclusion, London School of Economics.

—. 1999. Cohabitation in Western Europe. *Population Trends.* 96, 25–32.

Kiernan, K., H. Land and J. Lewis. 1998, *Lone Motherhood in Twentieth Century Britain.* Oxford: Oxford University Press.

Kotlikoff, L. 1992. *Generational Accounting: Knowing Who Pays and When for What We Spend.* New York: Free Press.

Krantz, S.E. 1991. Divorce and children. In *Feminism, Children and the New Families,* eds. S.M. Dornbusch and M.H. Strober. London: The Guilford Press.

Kravdal, O. 1999. Does marriage require a stronger economic underpinning than informal cohabitation? *Population Studies* 53, 63–80.

Kubler-Ross, E. 1970. *On Death and Dying.* London: Routledge.

Laslett, P. 1989. *A Fresh Map of Life.* London: Weidenfield & Nicolson.

Lawson, A. 1989. *Adultery.* Oxford: Basil Blackwell.

Lees, S. 1999. Will boys be left on the shelf? In *Changing Family Values,* eds. G. Jagger and C. Wright. London: Routledge.

Lewis, J.D. and Weigart, A.J. 1990. The structures and meanings of social time. In *The Sociology of Time,* ed., J. Hassard, Basingstoke: Palgrave Macmillan.

Lumb, R. 1980. A community based approach to the analysis of migration in the Highlands and Islands of Scotland. *Sociological Review* 28, 611–27.

Macdonald, S. 1997. *Re-imagining Culture: Histories, Identities and The Gaelic Renaissance.* Oxford: Berg.

Maclean, A. 1984. *Night Falls on Ardnamurchan: The Twilight of a Crofting Family.* London: Victor Gollancz.

Maclean, C. 1997. *Migration and Social Change in Remote Rural Areas: A Scottish Highland Case Study.* PhD thesis. University of Edinburgh.

—. 2000a. 'Making it their home': in-migration, housing and length of residence in a rural Scottish community. Paper presented to the British Sociological Association Annual Conference. University of York.

—. 2000b. Getting out and getting on: Scottish Highland migration in the first half of the 20th century. *Rural History: Economy, Society, Culture* 11, 231–48.

Macleod, A. 1992. *Social Identity, Social Change and the Construction of Symbolic Boundaries in a West Highland Settlement.* PhD thesis. University of Plymouth.

Manlove, J. 1997. Early motherhood in an intergenerational perspective: the experiences of a British cohort. *Journal of Marriage and the Family* 59, 263–79.

Mann, M. 1973. *Workers on the Move.* Cambridge: Cambridge University Press.

Mannheim, K. 1952. The problem of generations. In *Essays on the Sociology of Knowledge* K. Mannheim. London: Routledge & Kegan Paul.

Mansfield, P. and J. Collard. 1988. *The Beginning of the Rest of your Life: A Portrait of Newly-Wed Marriage.* London: Macmillan.

Manvell, R. 1950. *Three British Screenplays: Brief Encounter, Odd Man Out, Scott of the Antarctic,* London: Methuen.

Marsden, D. 1969. *Mothers Alone.* London: Allen Lane.

Marsh, C. and S. Arber, eds. 1992. *Families and Households: Divisions and Change.* London: Macmillan.

Martinson, B. and L. Wu. 1992. Parent histories: patterns of change in early life. *Journal of Family Issues* 13, 351–77.

Maughan, B. and M. Lindelow. 1997. Secular change in psychosocial risks: the case of teenage motherhood. *Psychological Medicine* 27, 1129–44.

McAllister, F. and Clarke, L. 1998. *Choosing Childlessness.* London: Family Policy Study Centre.

McAlpine, J. 1994. Settler watching. *The Scotsman Weekend,* 19 February.

McBee, S.M. and J.R. Rogers. 1997. Identifying risk factors for gay and lesbian suicidal behaviour: implications for mental health counsellors. *Journal of Mental Health Counselling* 19, 143–55.

McCleery, A. 1991. Population and social conditions in remote areas: the changing character of the Scottish Highlands and Islands. In *People in the Countryside: Studies of Social Change in Rural Britain,* eds. T. Champion and C. Watkins. London: Chapman.

McDowell, L. 1997. *Capital Culture.* Oxford: Blackwell.

McLanahan, S. 1988. Family structure and dependency: early transitions to female household headship. *Demography* 25, 1–16.

McLanahan, S. and G. Sandefur. 1994. *Growing Up with a Single Parent: What Hurts, What Helps.* Cambridge, MA: Harvard University Press.

McRae, S. 1999. *Changing Britain: Families and Households in the 1990s.* Oxford: Oxford University Press.

Medick, H. 1976, The proto-industrial family economy. *Social History* 1, 291–315.

Mellor, J. 2000. 'You can't do it for nothing': women's experience of volunteering in two community well women clinics. *Health and Social Care in the Community* 8, 31–9.

Mellor, R. 1992. Changing Manchester'. In *Changes in Work,* ed. H. Beynon. London: Anglo German Foundation.

—. 1997. Cool times in a changing city. In *Transforming Cities, Contested Governance and Spatial Divisions,* eds. N. Jewson and S, MacGregor. London: Routledge.

Mewett, P.G. 1982a. Associational categories and the social location of relationships in a Lewis crofting community. In *Belonging: Identity and Social Organisation in British Rural Cultures,* ed. A.P. Cohen. Manchester: Manchester University Press.

—. 1982b. Exiles, nicknames, social identities and the production of local consciousness in a Lewis crofting community. In *Belonging: Identity and Social Organisation in British Rural Cultures,* ed. A.P. Cohen. Manchester: Manchester University Press.

Millar, J. 1992. Lone-mothers and social policy. In *Social Security and Social Change: New Challenges to the Beveridge Model,* S. Baldwin and J. Falkingham. London: Harvester Wheatsheaf.

Morgan, D. 1996. *Family Connections: An Introduction to Family Studies.* Cambridge: Polity.

Morrow, V. and M. Richards. 1996. *Transitions to Adulthood: A Family Matter?* York: Joseph Rowntree Foundation.

Nadel, J.H. 1986. Burning with the fire of God: Calvinism and community in a Scottish fishing village. *Ethnology* 25, 49–60.

Nardi, P. and R. Bolton. 1998. Gay bashing: violence and aggression against gay men and lesbians. In *Social Perspectives in Lesbian and Gay Studies,* eds. P. Nardi and B. Schneider. Routledge: London.

Neale B. and A. Wade. 2000. *Parent Problems! Children's Views on Life When Parents Split Up.* Surrey: Young Voice.

Neustatter, A. 1998. Living This Life. *Saturday Telegraph Magazine,* 5 September, 106.

Newby, H. 1979. *Green and Pleasant Land? Social Change in Rural England*. London: Hutchinson.

Ní Bhrolcháin, M., R. Chappell and I. Diamond. 1995. *Educational and Socio-Demographic Outcomes among the Children of Disrupted and Intact Marriages*. University of Southampton, Department of Social Statistics, Working Paper no. 95–2.

Ní Bhrochláin, M., R. Chappell, I. Diamond and C. Jameson. 2000. Parental divorce and outcomes for children: evidence and interpretation. *European Sociological Review* 16, 67–91.

Office for National Statistics. 1998. *Birth Statistics 1998*. London: The Stationery Office.

Pahl, J. and R. Pahl. 1971. *Managers and their Wives*. Harmondsworth: Penguin.

Pahl, R. 1968. The rural-urban continuum. In *Readings in Urban Sociology*, ed. R. Pahl. Oxford: Pergamon Press.

—. 1998. Friendship. In *The Politics of Risk Society*, ed. J. Franklin. Cambridge: Polity.

—. 2000. *On Friendship*. Cambridge: Polity.

Pally, R. 1997. Memory: brain systems that link past, present and future. *International Journal of Psycho-Analysis* 78, 1223–34.

Peck, J.A. and M. Emmerich. 1992. Recession, restructuring and the Greater Manchester labour market: an empirical overview. *Spatial Policy Analysis Working Paper 17*, School of Geography, University of Manchester.

Perkins, H. and D. Thorns. 1999. House and home and their interaction with changes in New Zealand's urban system, households and family structures. *Housing, Theory and Society* 16, 124–35.

Perry, C. 1999. A qualitative study of the life experiences of young lesbian, gay and bisexual people in Warrington and Halton: implications for service providers. *Cheshire Public Health Research And Resource Unit*, Chester.

Phillips, S.K. 1986. Natives and incomers: the symbolism of belonging in Muker parish, North Yorkshire. In *Symbolising Boundaries: Identity and Diversity in British Cultures*, ed. A.P. Cohen. Manchester: Manchester University Press.

Phillipson, C. 1987. The transition to retirement. In *Social Change and the Life Course*, ed. G. Cohen. London: Tavistock.

—. 1996. Intergenerational conflict and the welfare state: American and British perspectives. In *The New Generational Contract*, ed. A. Walker. London: UCL Press.

Pilcher, J. 1995. *Age And Generation in Modern Britain*. Oxford: Oxford University Press.

Plummer, K. 1995. *Telling Sexual Stories: Power, Change and Social Worlds*. London: Routledge.

—. 1998. The past, present, and futures of the sociology of same-sex relations. In *Social Perspectives in Lesbian and Gay Studies*, eds. P. Nardi and B. Schneider. Routledge: London.

Ponse, B. 1978. *Identities in the Lesbian World: The Social Construction of Self*. Connecticut: Greenwood.

Power, C. and S. Matthews. 1997. Origins of health inequalities in a national population sample. *The Lancet* 350, 1584–9.

Proctor, C.D. and V.K. Groze. 1994. Risk factors for suicide among gay, lesbian and bisexual youths. *Social Work* 39, 504–13.

Quilley, S. 1995. *Economic Transformations and Local Strategy in Manchester*. Unpublished PhD thesis. University of Manchester.

Rake, K. 2000. *Women's Income over the Lifetime: A Report to the Women's Unit, Cabinet Office*. London: The Stationery Office.

Reibstein, J. and M. Richards. 1992. *Sexual Arrangements: Marriage and Affairs*. London: Heinemann.

Reid, I. 1998. *Class in Britain*. Cambridge: Polity.

Ribbens McCarthy, J., J. Holland and V. Gillies. 2000. Support, guidance, control? Issues of support in the lives of parents and young people. Paper given at Youth Research 2000, ESRC/Joseph Rowntree Foundation. Keele, September.

—. In press. Multiple perspectives on the 'family' lives of young people: methodological and theoretical issues in case study research. *International Journal of Social Research Methodology, Theory and Practice*.

Richards, M. 1997. The interests of children at divorce. In *Families and Justice*, ed. M.T. Meulders-Klein. Brussels: Bruylant.

Richardson, L. 1985. *The New Other Woman: Contemporary Single Women in Affairs with Married Men*, New York: Collier-Macmillan.

Richman, J. 1983. *Traffic Wardens: An Ethnography of Street Administration*. Manchester: Manchester University Press.

Roberts, K. 1993. Career trajectories and the mirage of increased social mobility. In *Youth and Inequality*, eds. I. Bates and F. Riseborough. Buckingham: Open University Press.

—. 1995. *Youth Employment In Modern Britain*. Oxford: Oxford University Press.

Robson-Scott, M. 1999. This Shared Life. *You Magazine: The Mail on Sunday*, 9 May 1999, 45–8.

Rodger, J.J. 1995. Family policy or moral regulation? *Critical Social Policy* 15, 5–25.

Rodgers, B. 1996. Social and psychological wellbeing of children from divorced families. *Australian Research Findings* 31, 174–82.

Rossi, A. 1993. Intergenerational relations: gender, norms and behaviour. In *The Changing Contract Across Generations*, eds. V. Bengtson and A. Achenbaum. New York: Aldine de Gruyter.

Rutter, M. 1981. Stress, coping and development: some issues and some questions. *Journal of Child Psychology and Psychiatry* 22, 323–56.

Ryder, N. 1965. The cohort as a concept in the study of social change. *American Sociological Review* 30, 843–61.

Sandler, J. and P. Fonagy, eds. 1997. *Recovered Memories of Abuse: True or False?* London: Karnac Books.

Saunders, P. 1990. *A Nation of Homeowners*. London: Unwin Hyman.

Savage, M., J. Barlow, P. Dickens and T. Fielding. 1992. *Property, Bureaucracy and Culture*. London: Routledge.

Savin-Williams, R. 1998. *'And Then I Became Gay': Young Men's Stories*. Routledge: London.

Scott, J. 2000. Is it a different world to when you were growing up? Generational effects on social representations and child-rearing values. *British Journal of Sociology* 51, 355–76.

Shaw, C. and J. Haskey. 1999. New estimates and projections of the population cohabiting in England and Wales. *Population Trends* 95, 7–17.

Shepherd, P. 1997. Survey and response. In *Twenty Something in the 1990s: Getting On, Getting By, Getting Nowhere*, eds. J. Bynner, E. Ferri and P. Shepherd. Aldershot: Ashgate.

Shucksmith, M. 1990. A theoretical perspective on rural housing. *Sociologia Ruralis* 30, 210–29.

Silva, E.B. and C. Smart. 1999. *The New Family?* London: Sage.

Silverman, S. M. 1998. *David Lean*, London: Andre Deutsch.

Simon, B.L. 1987. *Never Married Women*. Philadelphia: Temple University Press.

Simpson, B. 1998. *Changing Families: An Ethnographic Approach to Divorce and Separation.* Oxford: Berg.

Sinfield, A. 2000. Tax benefits in non-state pensions. *European Journal of Social Security* 2, 137–67.

Skiffington, K.K. 1991. Noblesse oblige: a strategy for local boundary making. *Ethnology* 30, 265–77.

Smailes, P.J. and Hugo, G.J. 1985. A process view of the population turnaround: an Australia rural case study, In *Journal of Rural Studies* 1, 31–3

Smart, C. 1999. The new parenthood: fathers and mothers after divorce. In *The New Family?*, eds. E.B. Silva and C. Smart. London: Sage.

Smart, C. and B. Neale. 1999. *Family Fragments?* Cambridge: Polity.

Social Exclusion Unit. 1999. *Teenage Pregnancy.* London: The Stationery Office.

Somerville, P. 1992. Homelessness and the meaning of home: rooflessness or rootlessness? *International Journal of Urban and Regional Research* 16, 529–39.

—. 1997. The social construction of home. *Journal of Architectural and Planning Research* 14, 226–45.

Stacey, M. 1960. *Tradition and Change: A Study of Banbury.* Oxford: Oxford University Press.

Stacey, J. 1991. *Brave New Families: Stories of Domestic Upheaval in Late Twentieth-Century America*, New York: Basic Books.

Stanley, L. 1993. On auto/biography in sociology. *Sociology* 27, 41–52.

Stein, P. 1981. *Single Life: Unmarried Adults in Social Context.* New York: St Martin's Press.

Storrie, T. 1997. Citizens or what? In *Youth and Society*, eds. J. Rouche and S. Tucker. London: Sage.

Strathern, M. 1982a. The place of kinship: kin, class and village status in Elmdon, Essex. In *Belonging: Identity and Social Organisation in British Rural Cultures*, A.P. Cohen. Manchester: Manchester University Press.

—. 1982b. The village as an idea: constructs of village-ness in Elmdon, Essex. In *Belonging: Identity and Social Organisation in British Rural Cultures*, A.P. Cohen. Manchester: Manchester University Press.

Target, M. 1998. The recovered memories controversy. *International Journal of Psycho-Analysis* 79, 1015–1028.

Taylor, A. 1998. Lesbian space: more than one imagined territory. In *New Frontiers of Space, Bodies and Gender*, ed. R. Ainley. London: Routledge.

Thompson, E. P. 1967. 'Time, work-discipline, and industrial capitalism', *Past and Present* 38, 56–97

Thomson, R., R. Bell, J. Holland, J. Henderson, S. McGrellis and S. Sharpe 2002. Critical moments: choice, chance and opportunity in young people's narratives of transition. *Sociology* 6, 335–54.

Thornton, A. and D. Camburn. 1987. The influence of the family on premarital sexual attitudes and behavior. *Demography* 24, 323–40.

Titmuss, R. 1958. The social division of welfare: some reflections on the search for equity. In *Essays on the Welfare State*, R. Titmuss. London: Allen & Unwin.

Troiden, R. 1998. A model of homosexual identity formation. In *Social Perspectives in Lesbian and Gay Studies*, eds. P. Nardi and B. Schneider. Routledge, London.

Turner, B. 1999. Towards a theory of the generational habitus: some reflections on the work of Pierre Bourdieu as applied to generational research. Paper given at 'Studying the lifecourse: Theoretical and methodological issues', 7 May, University of Manchester.

Valentine, G. 1993a. Heterosexing space: lesbian perceptions and experiences of everyday spaces. *Environment and Planning D: Society and Space* 11, 395–413.

—. 1993b. Negotiating and managing multiple sexual identities: lesbian time-space strategies. *Transactions of the Institute of British Geographers* 18, 237–48.

—. 1995. Out and about: a geography of lesbian communities. *International Journal of Urban and Regional Research* 19, 96–111 .

—. 1996. An equal place to work? Anti-lesbian discrimination and sexual citizenship in the European Union. In *Women of the European Union: The Politics of Work and Daily Life*, eds. M.D. Garcia-Ramon and J. Monk. London: Routledge.

—. 2000. Exploring children and young people's narratives of identity. *Geoforum* 31, 257–67.

Valentine, G., R. Butler and T. Skelton. In press. The ethical and methodological complexities of doing research with 'vulnerable' young people. *Ethics, Place and Environment*.

VanEvery, J. 1995. *Heterosexual Women Changing the Family: Refusing to Be a 'Wife'*. London: Taylor & Francis.

Walker, R., C. Heaver and S. McKay. 2000. *Building Up Pension Rights*. DSS Report no. 114. London: HMSO.

Wallace, C. and M. Cross. 1990. *Youth in Transition: The Sociology of Youth and Youth Policy*. London: Falmer.

Wallerstein, J.S. and S. Blakeslee. 1989. *Second Chances: Men, Women and Children a Decade after Divorce*. New York: Ticknor & Fields.

Wallerstein, J.S., S.B. Corbin and J.M. Lewis. 1988. Children of divorce: a 10-year study. In *The Impact of Divorce, Single Parenting and Step-parenting on Children*, E. M. Hetherington and J. D. Arasteh. London: Lawrence Erlbaum.

Wallerstein, J.S. and Kelly. J.B. 1990. *Surviving the Break-up: How Children and Parents Cope with Divorce*. London: Grant McIntyre.

Warwick, D. and G. Littlejohn 1992. *Coal, Capital and Culture*. London: Routledge.

Watson, W. 1964. Social mobility and social class in industrialised societies. In *Closed Systems and Open Minds*, eds. M. Glucksmann and E. Devons. Edinburgh: Oliver & Boyd.

Weiskrantz, L. 1997. Memories of abuse, or abuse of memories? In *Recovered Memories of Abuse: True or False?*, eds. J. Sandler and P. Fonagy. London: Karnac Books.

Weiss, R. 1975. *Marital Separation*. New York: Basic Books.

—. 1979. Growing up a little faster: the experience of growing up in a single parent household. *Journal of Social Issues*. 35, 97–111.

Weston, K. 1998. *Long Slow Burn: Sexuality and Social Science*. London: Routledge.

Wight, D. 1993. *Workers Not Wasters: Masculine Respectability, Consumption and Unemployment in Central Scotland: A Community Study*. Edinburgh: Edinburgh University Press.

Williams, N.J. and F.E. Twine. 1991. *A Research Guide to the Register of Sasines and the Land Register in Scotland: A Report to Scottish Homes*. Edinburgh: Scottish Homes.

Williams, W.M. 1956. *The Sociology of an English Village: Gosforth*. London: Routledge & Kegan Paul.

—. 1963. *A West Country Village: Ashworthy*. London: Routledge & Kegan Paul.

Wojtkiewicz, R. 1992. Diversity in experiences of parental structure during childhood and adolescence. *Demography* 29, 59–68.

Wolff, K. 1950. *The Sociology of Georg Simmel*. Glencoe, Illinois Free Press.

Wu, L. and B. Martinson. 1993. Family structure and the risk of a premarital birth. *American Sociological Review* 58, 210–32.

Wynne, D. 1998. *Leisure, Lifestyles and the New Middle Class*. London Routledge.

Zerubavel, E. 1981. *Hidden Rhythms. Schedules and Calendars in Social Life*. Chicago University Press.

Index